A WRITER'S WORKBOOK

A WRITER'S WORKBOOK
STYLE AND GRAMMAR

NORMAN E. STAFFORD

Arkansas State University

Harcourt Brace Jovanovich, Publishers

San Diego New York Chicago Austin Washington, D.C.

London Sydney Tokyo Toronto

Cover: © Emily Mason, *Upon a Jib,* 1989. Oil on Canvas, 54" x 52", Grace Borgenicht Gallery.

ISBN: 0-15-597651-6

Library of Congress Catalog Card Number: 90-83122

Printed in the United States of America

Preface

Although it is designed to accompany James D. Lester's *A Writer's Handbook,* this workbook may be used independently of any other text. *A Writer's Workbook: Style and Grammar* innovatively emphasizes the writing process throughout. It incorporates and interprets traditional terminology and techniques in a contemporary perspective. Points of grammar, usage, mechanics, and punctuation are essential to writing, but they are treated here as conventions that accomplished writers control rather than as rules that control writers' accomplishments.

The workbook's eight parts are keyed to the corresponding chapters and subsections of the parent textbook. Part 1 provides explanations and exercises in prewriting, in creating drafts, and in revising and editing. Subsequent parts move from the broad, complex elements to the narrow, specific elements. Parts 2 and 3 help students master paragraphs and sentences. Part 4 addresses appropriate language throughout an essay, to create cohesion between paragraphs and sentences. The workbook then narrows further to focus on control of conventions. Part 5 reviews basic grammar, and Part 6 shows how to incorporate grammatical conventions into a fluent style. Parts 7 and 8 address the effective use of punctuation and mechanics.

Students will appreciate the four-part format of the individual chapters. Each chapter begins with a brief discussion of the topic and its importance in the writing process. Then it considers the problems that writers may encounter with the topic and provides detailed examples of the topic. When appropriate, illustrations clarify the point. Finally, a series of exercises test the students' grasp of the concepts. (An answer key is published separately for instructors' use.)

Acknowledgments

The encouragement and suggestions of many people have made this book possible. James D. Lester has been both generous and cooperative in helping coordinate my text to his. Bill McLane, executive editor at Harcourt Brace Jovanovich, initiated my interest in the project and offered his support throughout. Stephen Jordan adroitly stepped in as acquisitions editor. No author could have had a better manuscript editor than Sarah Helyar Smith. Her editorial skill as well as her ability to make her suggestions seem my own have firmed the text and hastened its completion. Jennifer Johnson, production editor, processed the proof; Judy Frazier, art editor, handled the illustrations; and Marilyn Whitright, production manager, coordinated the project with the compositor and the printer.

Two colleagues at Arkansas State University were particularly helpful: George Horneker during the early stages of composition and Logan Moon during the final ones. Finally, Ted Rosenthal of the University of Tennessee has been a source of constant encouragement.

Norman E. Stafford

Contents

PART

1

Planning and Writing

CHAPTER 1

Planning an Essay

1a Select a subject.

Successful essays reveal both extensive knowledge of a topic *and* strong feelings about it. These characteristics increase the writer's confidence and make the essay interesting.

Common Problems

Students often choose topics because they believe they are expected to select them—either because they as college students should be interested in such topics or because they think their teachers expect them to be interested. But few students are well informed on, for instance, the desirability of the Stealth bomber, or have strong feelings about it. In this case the Stealth bomber is not suitable for an essay. Equally unsuitable for essays are topics (such as abortion or capital punishment) about which students may have strong feelings but little specific information.

Example

You might know much about current fashions, preparing family meals, and parking regulations at your school. You might also have strong feelings about capital punishment, abortion, and missing classes because you were unable to find a parking spot. Only parking regulations and missing classes for lack of parking engage both your feelings and your knowledge, however, and are therefore potentially successful topics.

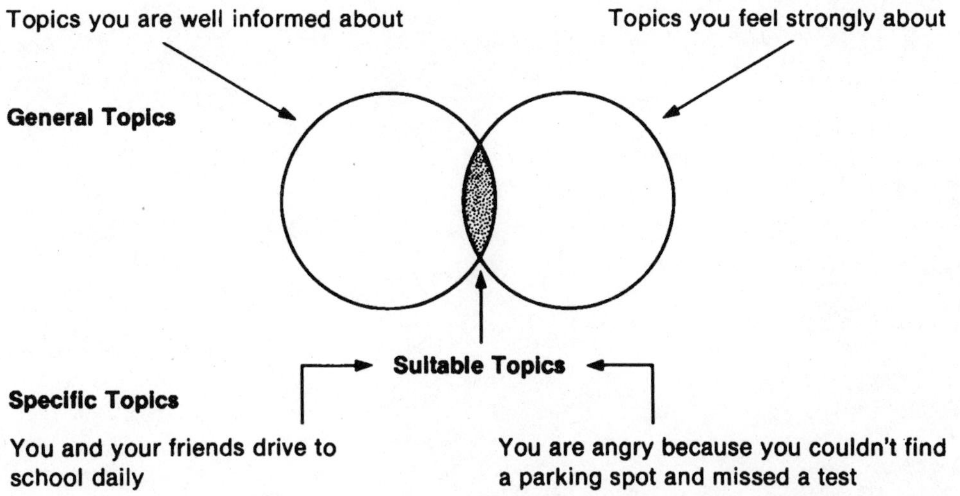

Name ______________________________ Score ______________

Exercise 1a Selecting subject

In column A list ten topics about which you have extensive knowledge. In column B list ten topics about which you have strong feelings. Force yourself to list ten in both columns; that extra effort may result in an effective essay. Then draw a line from column A to B connecting topics that overlap.

A	B
1. ____________	1. ____________
2. ____________	2. ____________
3. ____________	3. ____________
4. ____________	4. ____________
5. ____________	5. ____________
6. ____________	6. ____________
7. ____________	7. ____________
8. ____________	8. ____________
9. ____________	9. ____________
10. ____________	10. ____________

1b Write with a purpose.

The writer's purpose, the reason for writing, determines the information and the focus of the essay.

Common Problems

Any subject may be examined with differing purposes. Essays without a clear purpose lack focus, merely talking *about* a subject rather than making a point. Essays written for composition courses often follow a pattern, such as comparison/contrast, instead of supporting a thesis. As a result, readers do not understand the author's intention.

Examples

One subject can serve different purposes, as in these examples:

SUBJECT: Parking problems at Titanic State University

1. Purpose statement expressing the writer's feeling:
   I want my reader to see that commuters like me are not getting the parking spaces we deserve.
2. Purpose statement explaining facts:
   I want my reader to understand that the parking at Titanic State is inadequate.
3. Purpose statement of persuasion:
   I want the parking regulations at Titanic State changed as soon as possible.

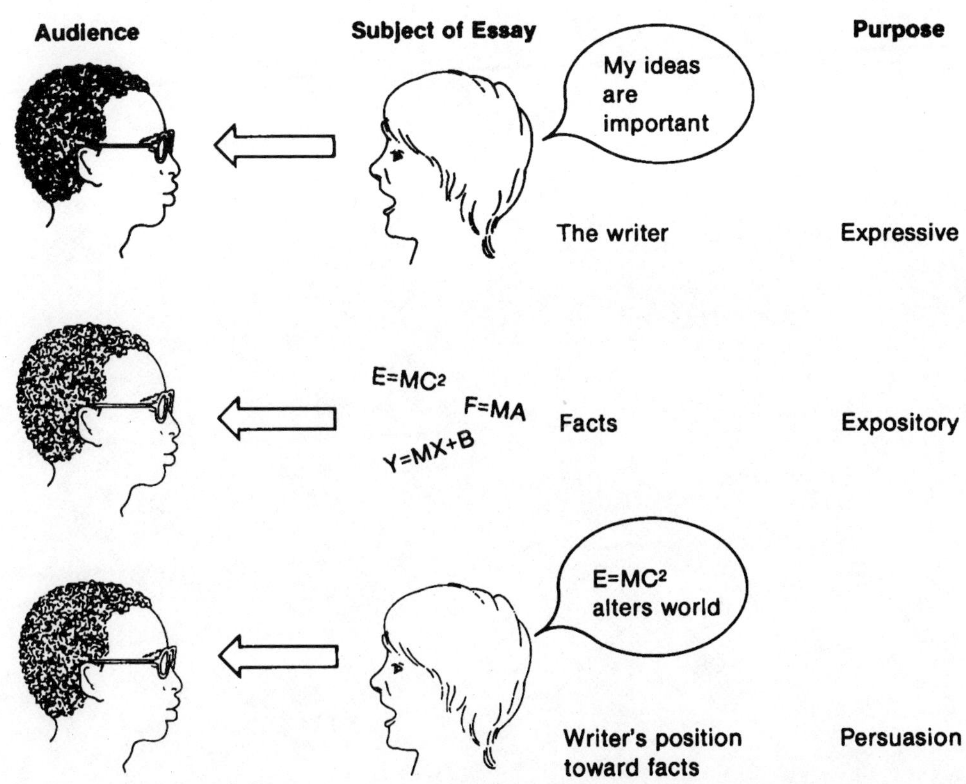

Name ______________________ Score ______________

Exercise 1b Purpose

1. In the spaces provided, identify the following statements of purpose as either expressing feeling (expressive purpose), explaining facts (expository purpose), or changing or confirming a position (persuasive purpose).
   a. I want my readers to help control the spread of acid rain.

   b. I want my readers to understand how difficult it is to find a job teaching the history of art nouveau.

   c. After spending the night on the streets of Philadelphia, I can see much more clearly the plight of the homeless.

   d. I want my readers to understand that my new VCR has ruined my study habits.

   e. I want my readers to join in opposing the requirement that all freshmen live in the dorms.

2. For each of the following subjects, write a sentence that develops an expressive purpose, an expository purpose, and a persuasive purpose.
   a. Corruption in intercollegiate athletics
      Expressive purpose:

      Expository purpose:

      Persuasive purpose:

   b. Living in an apartment while attending college
      Expressive purpose:

      Expository purpose:

      Persuasive purpose:

c. Developing good study habits
Expressive purpose:

Expository purpose:

Persuasive purpose:

d. Working part-time while a full-time student
Expressive purpose:

Expository purpose:

Persuasive purpose:

e. The advantage of commuting to school
Expressive purpose:

Expository purpose:

Persuasive purpose:

1c Consider your audience.

The purpose of writing is to communicate with others, even though the audience and the writer may differ in experience, age, gender, and attitudes.

Common Problems

The demands of a **general** or **specific** audience are different. Blurring these demands results in the omission of necessary information, the inclusion of unnecessary information, the ineffective arrangement of material, or inappropriate language.

Examples

The varying needs of different audiences are demonstrated in the following examples. If you wish to complain about the college's parking regulations, you may choose to write a letter—to the editor of the school newspaper, an administrator or committee, or a friend. The two letters to the editor address a **general audience**—students, teachers, and administrators. The other two letters address **specific audiences:**

1. *General audience,* as in a letter to the editor

    The administration's parking policy is inequitable. Seventy percent of the parking spots are designated solely for the administrators and faculty. The remaining parking, only thirty percent, is available for the students. [natural style]

    In my opinion, it is *imperative* for administrators *to formulate an equitable and fair* policy regarding available parking at *that magnificent seat of knowledge,* Titanic State University. [elevated tone, intended to impress rather than communicate, and redundant style]

2. *Specific audience,* as in a letter to a friend

    None of the *guys* could find a *spot* yesterday. [use of some slang]

    The *jerks* who made the parking rules got no business being at Titanic State. We need an administrator who knows what *he's* doing. [ungrammatical and offensive terms suitable only in a personal letter]

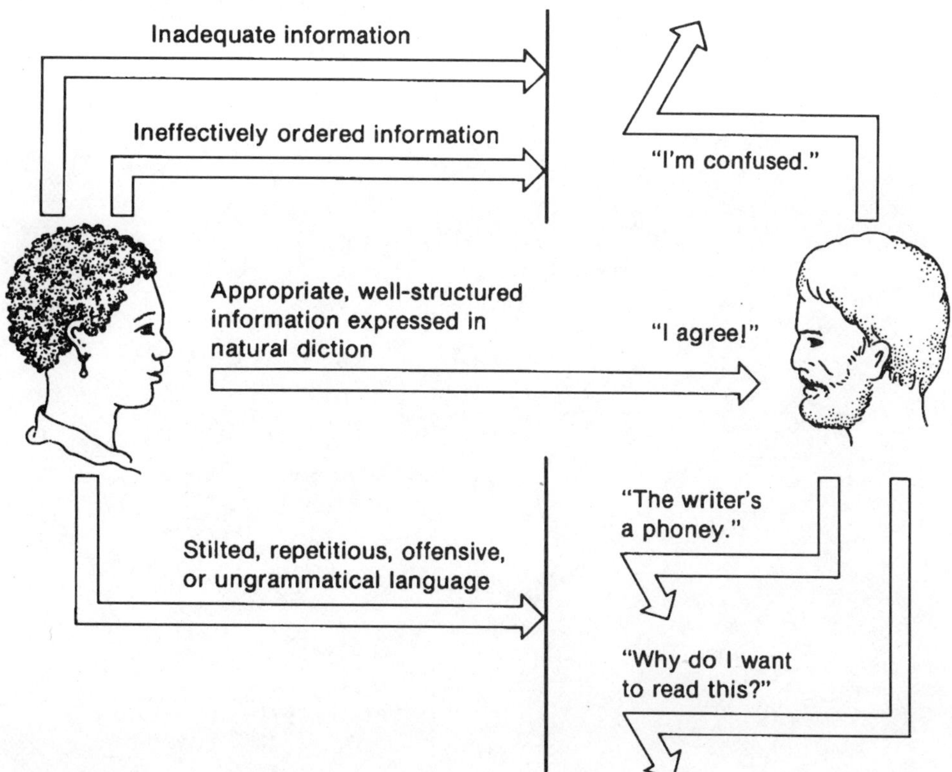

Name ______________________ Score ____________

Exercise 1c Audience

1. Indicate the problems with the following information directed to a *general audience* on the subject of why soap operas are harmful to viewers. Write "correct" for sentences that appeal to a general audience.
   a. Millions watch soap operas daily, including young girls searching for role models. Erica certainly doesn't fulfill this goal.

   b. The content and form of soap operas is superficial. Characters are often mere simulacra of living people, and the plethora of cuts and reaction shots are sophomoric.

   c. While everyone favors the inclusion of a limited degree of sexually explicit material, most soap operas emphasize it too much.

   d. Soap operas appeal to us because they offer a harmless escape from our humdrum lives.

   e. The stories take forever to tell and they say the same stuff over and over until most viewers want to gag.

2. Indicate the problems with the following information directed to a *specific audience* on the same subject. The reader is an avid fan of soap operas.
   a. *Days of Our Lives* and *All My Children,* both of which appear daily, appeal to very different audiences.

   b. Soap operas contain so much sex and violence that only deranged people enjoy them. Certainly no one who has any sense of taste would admit to watching them.

   c. Although soap operas are sociologically biased in favor of the upper classes, that is part of their appeal.

   d. Because many viewers are in their early teens, soap operas should make certain the content is appropriate for those viewers.

   e. Erica is a conniving woman, and that is the source of the show's popularity.

1d Define your writing project.

By establishing early the relationship among three elements of an essay (the subject, purpose, and audience), writers make concrete, in their own minds as well as that of the audience, the direction of the essay and may then begin the writing process confidently.

Common Problems

When writers are not aware of the focus of their essays, they may flounder, waste time, and become discouraged.

Example

A description of the writing project guides the early stages of development. Consider the following:

SUBJECT: Parking at Titanic State University

PURPOSE: To explain why the present situation is inequitable

AUDIENCE: Students, faculty, and administrators at Titanic State University

DESCRIPTION: I want to explain what aspects of the present parking policy are inequitable [the purpose] to students, faculty, and administrators at Titanic State [the audience].

Name ______________________________ Score ______________

Exercise 1d Defining project

Identify two different purposes and audiences for each of the following subjects, and then formulate a complete description of your writing situation.

1. Subject: Intramural volleyball
   Purpose:

   Audience:

   Description:

   Purpose:

   Audience:

   Description:

2. Subject: Riding in taxicabs
   Purpose:

   Audience:

   Description:

   Purpose:

   Audience:

   Description:

3. Subject: College students and their voting habits
   Purpose:

   Audience:

   Description:

   Purpose:

   Audience:

   Description:

4. Subject: A balanced diet in the dorm
   Purpose:

   Audience:

   Description:

   Purpose:

   Audience:

   Description:

Name ______________________________

Exercise 1d (continued)

5. Subject: Annoying habits of college freshmen
   Purpose:

   Audience:

   Description:

   Purpose:

   Audience:

   Description:

1e Generate ideas by doing prewriting exercises.

Because an essay is constructed from information, as much information as possible should be generated through as many techniques as possible.

Common Problems

Before writers can compose a draft of an essay, they must gather facts to make their positions convincing.

Examples

Facts, information, can come from various sources and are more than names, dates, and places. The following are some methods you can use to generate ideas and information, based on the topic of campus parking:

A. *List any ideas you might have on the subject.* Each of the ideas could be the subject of an essay; some specific ideas could support a more general point.
   1. Not enough lots
   2. Spaces poorly arranged
   3. Too many spaces for faculty
   4. Available space at stadium not used
   5. New students blame administration and are resentful
   6. Students may change schools
   7. Students lose respect for school property
   8. Students lose respect for campus police
   9. Rush for parking causes accidents
   10. Long distances from parking spots to classes are frustrating

B. *Ask yourself questions on the subject.* Questions demand answers, and one or a combination of those answers may become the controlling idea of your essay.
   1. Why does the parking problem bother me?
   2. Who is responsible for the lack of spots?
   3. Why do faculty and administrators have so many spots?
   4. Why are their spots close to the buildings?
   5. What can students do to change the situation?
   6. Where can new lots be built?
   7. Why isn't adequate parking part of the plan for new buildings?
   8. How could new parking facilities be paid for?
   9. When would the administration be most willing to meet students about the parking issue?
   10. Why do campus police give parking tickets before students know the rules?

C. *Free-write several sentences on the subject.* The free-writing technique often focuses your ideas. At other times it broadens them. Don't be afraid to change directions, and don't worry about errors. Just let your mind run free.

   I hate the hassle of parking. If I don't get here before 8:00 I never find a spot. I was late for Biology twice last week. Why can't our spots be close to the buildings? Faculty get here early and can get any spot. Why should faculty have special spots? Our fees pay their salaries so we should get preference. I almost got hit last week when some guy cut me off getting to a spot. Parking brings out the worst in students. Maybe I should ride a bike. I need the exercise.

D. *Cluster your ideas.* Clustering helps you visualize possible connections. The technique can lead to an outline, which structures the ideas and expresses them more formally. But to generate ideas, avoid worrying about structure and precision. Begin by writing your subject in the middle of a page. Then create groups of ideas that relate to it and to each other.

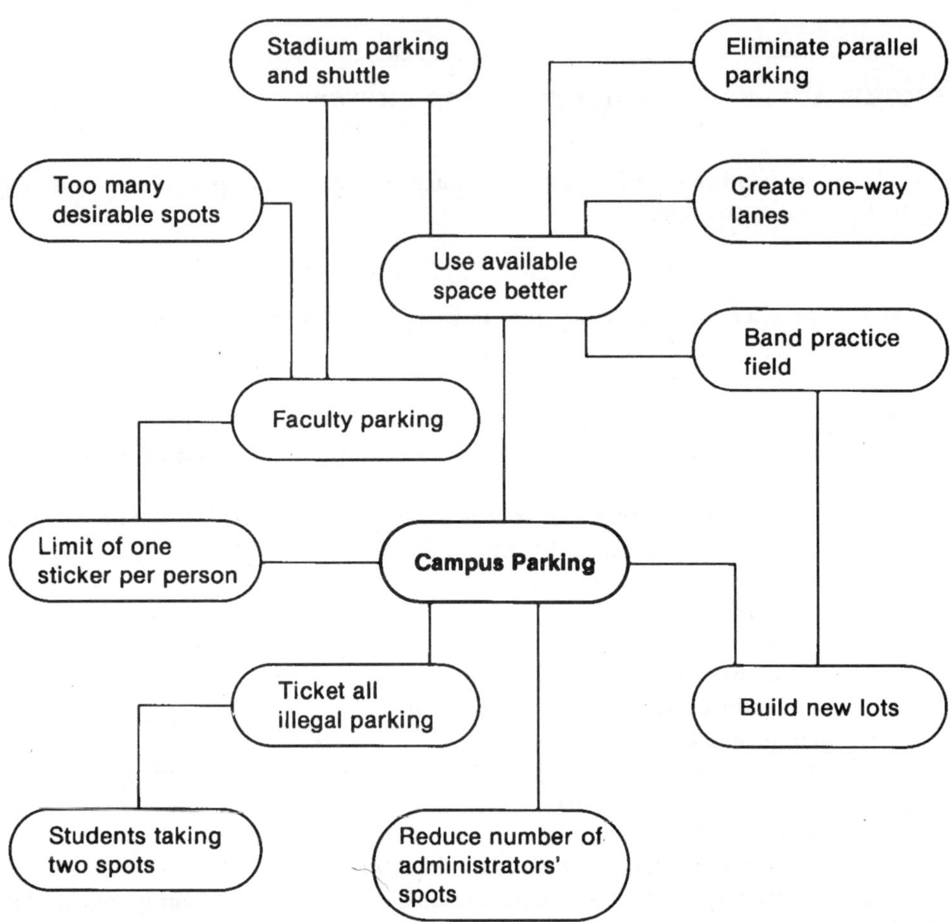

E. *Keep a journal.* Journals are useful for generating many topics you may wish to write about. Write regularly on any subject that interests you for at least ten minutes at a time.

F. *Other methods* are effective techniques for generating ideas. Read about your subject, and watch television documentaries on it. You should also talk to people knowledgeable on the topic. Your teacher may also allow classtime for you to brainstorm a subject.

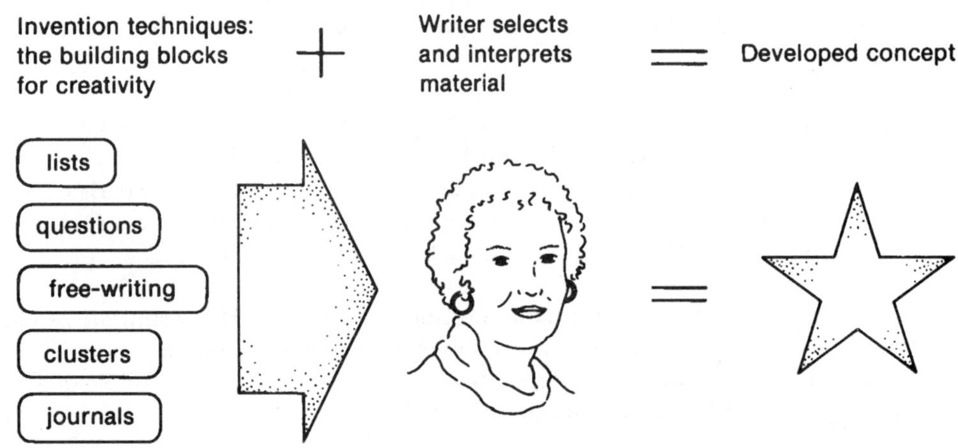

Name ______________________________ Score ______________

Exercise 1e Generating ideas

1. List ten ideas on the subject of drugs.
   a.
   b.
   c.
   d.
   e.
   f.
   g.
   h.
   i.
   j.

2. Ask ten questions on the subject of drugs.
   a.
   b.
   c.
   d.
   e.
   f.

g.

h.

i.

j.

3. Free-write for ten minutes on the subject of drugs.

4. Create a cluster on the subject of drugs.

1f Narrow the subject to a specific topic.

Effective essays are specific. Before forming a thesis, writers should jot down examples from experience or actual incidents they are familiar with. The techniques discussed in section **1e** will help focus general ideas.

Common Problems

A broad topic usually results in a superficial and spotty essay, which doesn't do justice to the subject and loses the reader's attention or interest. The national transportation problem, for instance, is a topic that is too broad for an essay to address adequately. A student's difficulties with inadequate parking facilities at the university is also broad and undefined, but it can be focused.

Example

Narrowing a topic highlights issues that might be overlooked with a broad topic:

GENERAL SUBJECT: The parking problems at Titanic State University

SOME NARROWED TOPICS:

The large number of parking spaces reserved for faculty and administrators

The increasing number of accidents on Titanic State's parking lots

The failure of the appeals process for parking tickets

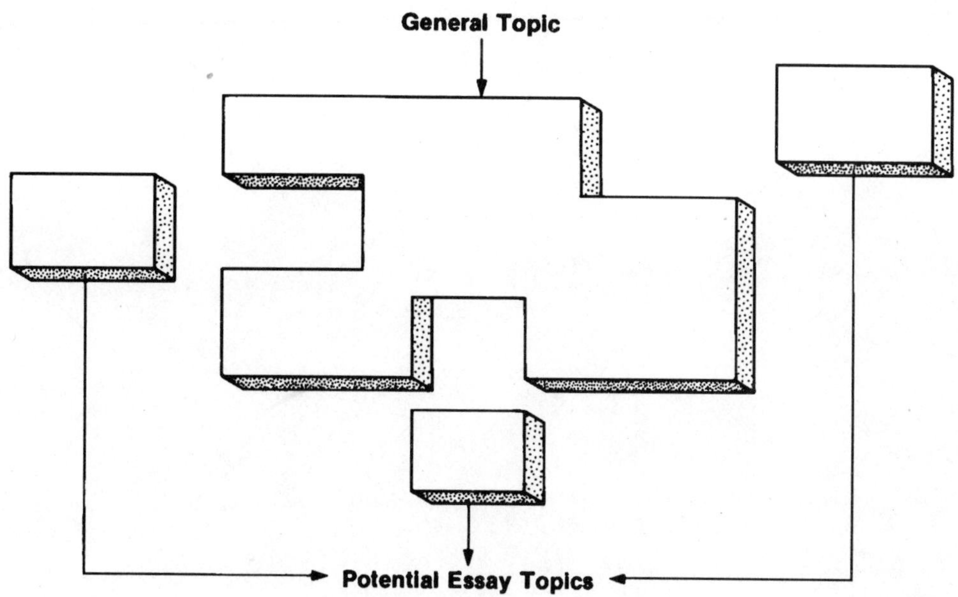

Name ______________________ Score ______________

Exercise 1f Narrowing topic

1. For each broad subject below, write three narrowed topics, each of which deals with one question or issue.
   a. Required courses at your university or college
      1)
      2)
      3)
   b. Intercollegiate football today
      1)
      2)
      3)
   c. The future of cable television
      1)
      2)
      3)
   d. The modern horror movie
      1)

2)

3)

e. Borrowing money from a bank
    1)

    2)

    3)

f. Television and children
    1)

    2)

    3)

g. Censoring rock music lyrics
    1)

    2)

Name ______________________________

Exercise 1f (continued)

3)

2. For the following exercises, create broad subjects and three narrowed topics for each.
   a. Subject:
      1)
      2)
      3)
   b. Subject:
      1)
      2)
      3)
   c. Subject:
      1)
      2)
      3)

1g Focus your topic with a thesis sentence.

A thesis always makes an assertion about a subject. The more precise and specific it is, the better it will guide the writer and the reader.

Common Problems

Some writers do not really understand what a thesis sentence is or what makes a forceful one. Some thesis sentences are not sufficiently narrowed to a position that can be proven in the space available. The assertion is about the subject of the essay and not about the essay itself or the writer; therefore, theses beginning "This paper will explore ..." or "In this paper, I will ..." are generally ineffective. Because the purpose of an essay is to support a thesis, a weak thesis sentence cripples an essay from the start.

Examples

A thesis sentence is (1) a sentence, not a phrase or a dependent clause; (2) the main or controlling idea of an essay; (3) an assertion that must be proven (neither a fact nor a question); (4) a sufficiently narrowed statement that is demonstrable in the available space and time. The following examples illustrate these criteria:

Should required courses be abolished? [Not a thesis sentence. It is a question, not an assertion.]

George Bush is the president of the United States. [Not a thesis sentence. It is a fact, not an assertion that must be proven.]

The need for greater military spending. [Not a thesis sentence. It is not a sentence but a fragment.]

Old age has many difficulties. [Not narrowed. Writers cannot discuss "many" difficulties adequately in the time and space a typical essay allows.]

Barney's Burger Palace is a comfortable place to eat; however, the food costs too much. [Two assertions, not one]

A trip to California in the summer can be interesting. [Not clearly phrased—what precisely does "interesting" mean? How will that term control what the essay says about a trip to California?]

This study will demonstrate the errors in recent attempts at gun control. [An ineffective thesis. It focuses on the essay, not on the subject, which is errors in attempts at gun control.]

The inadequate parking situation at Titanic State University creates a terrible atmosphere for learning. [An effective thesis sentence.]

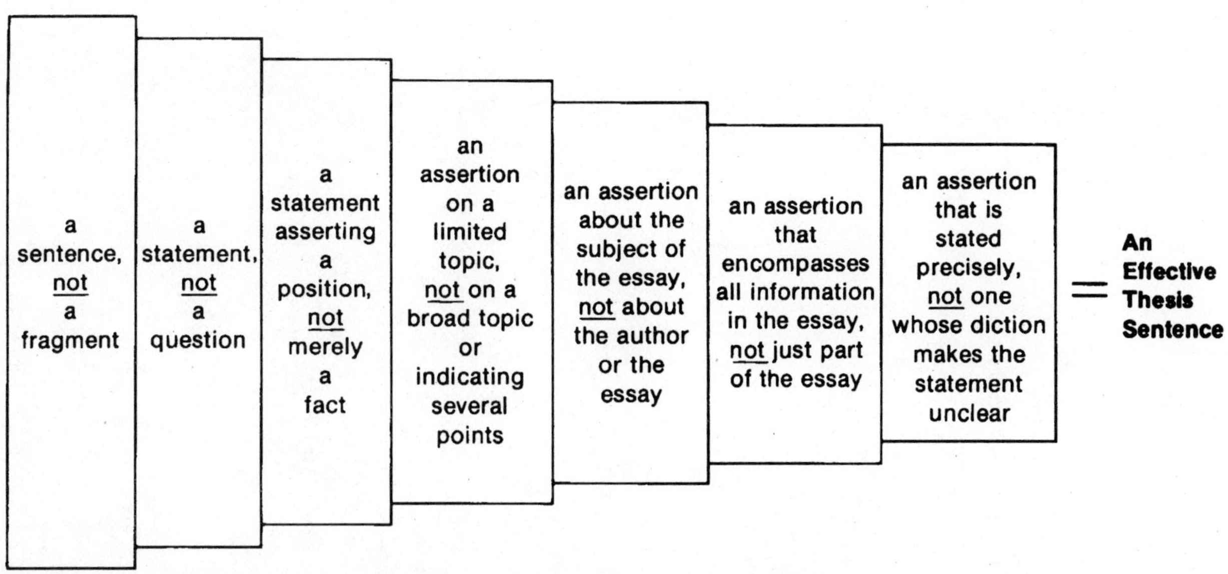

Name ______________________________ Score ______________

Exercise 1g Focusing thesis sentence

1. Place a check mark by the following items that are thesis sentences.
   a. Forest fires: a burning issue today
   b. Will this winter be as cold as many predict?
   c. The United States needs a strong Civil Defense system.
   d. The planet Venus is about the size of the Earth.
   e. Politicians often do not mean what they say.
2. Place a check mark by the following thesis sentences that are sufficiently narrowed, that make only one assertion about their subjects, and that are clearly phrased.
   a. Tennessee needs tougher laws against pornography and prostitution.
   b. Painting a room takes less time than people suppose.
   c. Pollution is a major problem in every country in the world.
   d. The generation gap is a myth.
   e. Our state legislators should show some concern.
   f. Love is a wonderful thing.
   g. The United States should no longer support Israel.
   h. Standardized test scores are not an accurate predictor of success in college.
   i. More women should stand up to men, and they need better paying jobs.
   j. The Stealth bomber is definitely flying high.
3. Construct two effective thesis sentences for each of the following subjects.
   a. The need for a state sales tax increase
      1)

      2)

   b. The value of night classes at your college or university
      1)

      2)

c. The size of American automobiles
   1)

   2)

d. The quality of cafeteria food at your college or university
   1)

   2)

e. Military service as a means of establishing a career
   1)

   2)

1h Use your thesis sentence to suggest a structure for the essay.

A thesis sentence reveals the writer's attitude toward the subject of an essay and can be a guide to both its content and form. Although a thesis sentence makes a single point (see **1g**), the structure of the thesis sentence may also imply the order in which support for the thesis will appear.

Common Problems

Some thesis sentences fail to imply a structure and therefore fail to guide readers. Some writers ignore the structure that the thesis sentence implies, either rearranging the order of ideas in the body of the paper or including ideas that conflict with the thesis. When an essay does not follow the implied structure, readers become distracted and confused and lose interest in the content.

> NOTE: Some teachers and writers prefer a thesis with more than one subject, a divided thesis, which does suggest the order of discussion in the body of the essay (The cafeteria food is terrible because the vegetables are overcooked, because the meat is undercooked, and because the seasoning is bland). Writers must determine whether this explicit guidance is worth the problems which often arise. Such theses suggest that all ideas can be divided into three parts. In addition, when writers refer in the body paragraphs to specific parts of the thesis, they repeat themselves. Divided theses are useful for teaching writers to guide readers, but they are often stylistically ineffective.

Examples

The ways in which a thesis can structure an essay are demonstrated in the examples below:

1. Among students, faculty, and administrators, the administrators definitely have the most convenient parking spaces. [Suggested structure: The essay will discuss the three types of parking in ascending order of convenience. The thesis implies that student parking will be discussed first and that those facilities are least convenient. The more accessible faculty facilities will appear next, and finally the most desirable administrative facilities will be discussed.]

2. Living on campus is better than contending with the problems of commuting and then finding parking spaces. [Suggested structure: The writer will discuss living on campus first and will compare and contrast it to commuting.]

3. The layout of the campus is the main reason Titanic State University has a parking problem. [Suggested structure: The writer will first discuss the layout of the campus (the cause), then the shortage of parking spaces (the effect).]

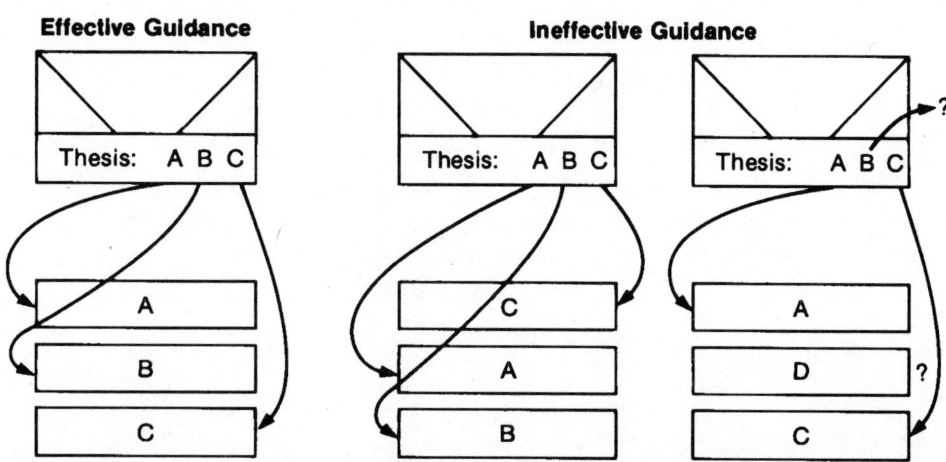

Name ______________________ Score ______________

Exercise 1h Thesis and structure

1. Briefly describe the structure for an essay suggested by the following thesis sentences.
   a. Television is educational as well as entertaining.

   b. The quality of life in a small town outweighs the town's inconveniences.

   c. Despite all our country's accomplishments, the American Dream has a negative side.

   d. Because an increase in the general sales tax will not provide the revenue our state needs, the legislature should pass an additional tax on all luxury items.

   e. Because the snows on Mount Gunnison contain a great deal of water, the county should build the new reservoir in the foothills instead of on the plains west of Johnsonville.

2. Create five thesis sentences, each of which suggests a structure for its essay. Then briefly describe the suggested structure of each.
   a. Thesis sentence:

      Suggested structure:

b. Thesis sentence:

Suggested structure:

c. Thesis sentence:

Suggested structure:

d. Thesis sentence:

Suggested structure:

e. Thesis sentence:

Suggested structure:

1i Create an outline.

An *outline* is a visual representation of an entire topic that is divided into parts to support a thesis. Sometimes imagining that the word "because" follows the thesis helps to formulate the major divisions. The outline usually represents the body of the essay, not the introduction or conclusion, but the introduction, like the thesis sentence, can suggest the arrangement of the outline.

Common Problems

When the outline divides a section, the section must contain at least two subparts. Every "A" must have at least a "B," and every "1" must have at least a "2." A subsection with only one part would be comparable to trying to tear a sheet of paper into one part, a logical impossibility.

Outlines should be grammatically parallel (see section **5b**). All parts are expressed either as sentences or as dependent clauses, or as phrases, or as single words. The same grammatical unit should be used throughout.

Example

The following outlines support one possible thesis on the subject of campus parking:

SENTENCE OUTLINE

Thesis: The inadequate parking situation at Titanic State creates a terrible atmosphere for learning.
[BECAUSE]

I. Inconvenient parking affects class performance.
  A. Students may miss classes entirely.
    1. Students may have to spend an entire hour searching for a spot.
    2. Students may cut classes rather than be late.
  B. Late students may disrupt classes.
    1. Teachers may be distracted.
      a. They may lose a train of thought.
      b. They may take class time to speak to the latecomers.
    2. Students may not be able to follow the teacher's point.
  C. Thinking about their parking problems may cause students to miss class discussion.
II. The parking problem is divisive.
  A. The problem can create a lack of respect.
    1. Students may believe administrators are indifferent to them.
    2. Students may resent teachers who receive preferential treatment.
    3. Teachers will be annoyed by absent or tardy students.
  B. Students may abuse campus property.
    1. They may tear up the grounds by parking illegally.
    2. Some may vandalize school property if they think they are being treated unjustly.

TOPIC OUTLINE

- I. Effect on class performance
  - A. Absenteeism
    - 1. Student inability to attend on time
    - 2. Student unwillingness to enter class late
  - B. Disruption caused by tardiness
    - 1. Distraction of teachers
      - a. Interruption of teachers' concentration
      - b. Time devoted to latecomers
    - 2. Interruption of student concentration
  - C. Inattention to class discussion
- II. Divisiveness in the university community
  - A. Disrespect
    - 1. For administrators
    - 2. For teachers
    - 3. For students by teachers
  - B. Property damage
    - 1. Unintentional destruction of grounds
    - 2. Intentional vandalism of school property

Name ______________________________ Score ______________

Exercise 1i Creating outline

1. Create a sentence outline with at least three major divisions for the following thesis: Eighteen-year-olds should be required to serve in the military or in community service for one year. (Take the opposite position if you wish.)

2. Create a topic outline from the sentence outline generated above.

CHAPTER 2

Drafting the Essay

2a Concentrate on main ideas.

After forming a tentative thesis with several supporting ideas (see chapter 1), writers should complete a draft of the *body* of the essay, with only brief attention, if any, to the introduction and conclusion. At this stage, a thesis can focus the whole essay while the supporting ideas can both focus on and flesh out the parts.

Common Problems

Writers who ignore their thesis sentence in the draft usually produce unfocused essays and undeveloped ideas.

Example

With focus and some development, the following thesis sentence and supporting ideas can provide the frame for a draft.

Thesis Sentence:
  Public education in our state needs additional revenue.

Supporting Ideas:

1. Additional funding is necessary to provide the state's schools with current textbooks and equipment.
2. Additional funding will help reduce overcrowded classrooms.
3. The state is losing effective teachers who seek better paying jobs elsewhere.

The following statements are inadequate as supporting ideas:

1. The state's population decreased by 75,000 last year. [A statement of fact]
2. Our biology class last term did not have enough microscopes to go around. [A specific example to develop a supporting idea]

Name ________________________________ Score ________________

Exercise 2a Main ideas

1. Place a check mark before sentences that could support the sample thesis. Indicate why the others would be inadequate as supporting sentences.

   Thesis Sentence: Students should not work while going to college.

   a. Working takes time away from studying.

   b. Working at Haver's Department Store would be a very good job.

   c. I stayed up until 4 A.M. working and then studied for a math test.

   d. Attending college has many hidden expenses.

   e. A job and school make a student too tired to do either well.

   f. Many students need extra money.

   g. Sometimes students may have to work at the same time their classes meet.

   h. Mr. McCall at Burger Barn likes to hire college students.

   i. Georgia always looks tired in class.

   j. Many students own cars.

2. Select two effective supporting ideas from the exercise above and then create a third main idea for the body of an essay.

   Thesis Sentence: Students should not work while going to college.

   ________________ The number of the main idea for paragraph #1

   ________________ The number of the main idea for paragraph #2

   The third main idea you have created: ____

   ____

3. Compare the first and final drafts of an essay you have written. Indicate in both whether you have an effective thesis and whether you have included major supporting ideas that you develop in separate paragraphs.

2b Write a fully developed introduction.

An effective introduction *prepares* readers in several ways: it introduces the subject, it places the subject in a context, it indicates the writer's attitude toward the subject (that is, it identifies a thesis), and it attracts the reader's attention. To fulfill all these functions, an effective introductory paragraph is rarely brief and is often written after the body of the essay is complete. Because an introduction literally introduces the writer's views, the thesis is often placed at the end of the first paragraph *after* the reader has been thoroughly prepared, although it can be effectively placed elsewhere in the paragraph (see the third example below).

Attention getters can range from an anecdote to a mere reference to the reader ("we" or "you"), or to the merits of the subject itself.

Common Problems

When a writer forgets that an introduction is functionally different from the body and conclusion of an essay, the introduction usually fails to prepare readers for the content of the body of the essay, lacks a thesis sentence, and generally rambles. Such an introduction will confuse rather than guide readers.

Examples

Here are three common types of introductions:

1. Narrowing to the thesis sentence

For a long time the three major networks dominated television in this country. NBC, CBS, and ABC battled each other for the ratings points that meant higher revenues from the sponsors. In recent years, however, a new competitor has appeared on the scene—cable television. *Cable services like HBO and Cinemax and the so-called super stations like WTBS and WGN may soon put the three networks out of business.*

control revealed in beginning broadly and ending narrowly

attention-getter, subject of essay, context

thesis

2. Opening with an anecdote

Last Thursday night I had no homework to do and my roommate Larry was on a date, so I decided to treat myself to an evening of uninterrupted television. From seven to eleven o'clock on several of the twenty channels available on the local cable system, I watched an hour of music videos, a movie, a half hour of news, and a late R-rated movie. As I turned off the set and went to bed, I realized that in the course of the evening I had not tuned in to even one of the programs offered on those staples of my childhood, NBC, CBS, and ABC. I had watched MTV, *Diehard* on HBO, and *Attack of the Martian Catwomen* on Cinemax. I had even watched the news on WGN from Chicago instead of on one of the local network affiliates. If my experience is similar to that of other television viewers in this country, I would say that *cable services like HBO and Cinemax and the so-called super stations like WTBS and WGN may soon put the three networks out of business.*

attention getter, subject of the essay

context

thesis

3. Elaborating on the thesis sentence (thereby suggesting how the essay will be developed in the body of the essay)

Cable services like HBO and Cinemax and the so-called super stations like WTBS and WGN may soon put the three networks out of business. Many of us are aware that the networks have been steadily losing viewers to cable television for the last several years, and the trend is expected to continue. The reasons for cable's popularity are not hard to find. Most cable channels are on all night. Many have few if any advertisements. Cable also has a greater variety of programming than traditional television, and many viewers especially like the adult programming available on a number of cable channels.

thesis and specific subject gets attention; remaining paragraph indicates general subject and content of the body

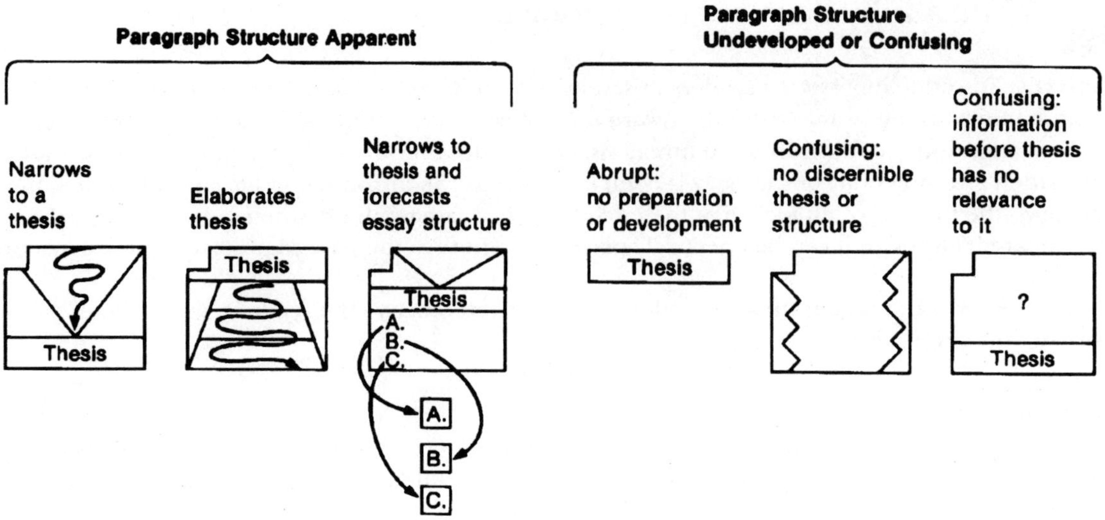

Paragraph Structure Apparent
Narrows to a thesis
Thesis
Elaborates thesis
Thesis
Narrows to thesis and forecasts essay structure
Thesis
A.
B.
C.
A.
B.
C.
Paragraph Structure Undeveloped or Confusing
Abrupt: no preparation or development
Thesis
Confusing: no discernible thesis or structure
Confusing: information before thesis has no relevance to it
?
Thesis

Name ______________________ Score ______________

Exercise 2b Introduction

1. Generate an effective thesis sentence (see **1g**), and develop four different introductory paragraphs.

   Thesis sentence:

   a. Introduction that narrows to the thesis:

   b. Introduction that begins with the thesis and elaborates on it in the paragraph, thus forecasting the structure of the essay:

   c. Introduction that narrows to the thesis and then forecasts the structure of the essay:

d. Introduction that begins with an anecdote:

2. Choose one of the paragraphs you have just written and explain how it attracts reader attention, which sentences or words introduce the subject, which ones define the context, and which identify the writer's position.

2c Write a body that fully explores the issues.

Each major issue should be explored in separate paragraphs (more than one per issue may be necessary). Well-developed paragraphs provide ample facts, examples, comparisons, and so forth to support the main idea of the paragraph (see chapter **6**). To guide readers, sentences or phrases can refer to the thesis or to the purpose of the paragraph.

Common Problems

Supporting ideas for the thesis sentence sometimes are not relevant, not developed appropriately, or not specific enough.

Examples

Developed body paragraphs provide specific facts, examples, comparisons, and other details, as the following examples demonstrate:

THESIS SENTENCE: Cable television may soon put the three major networks out of business.

UNDEVELOPED BODY PARAGRAPH:

A variety of programming is available on cable television. Viewers can see almost any subject they want. They only have to switch channels to see movies, sports, and comedy routines. They may also see religious programming, and some local cable channels offer them some interesting options as well. [This paragraph lacks essential details, such as specific program titles.]

DEVELOPED BODY PARAGRAPH:

A variety of programming is available on cable television. Viewers can see almost any subject they want. They only have to switch channels to see *Predator* and *Lethal Weapon,* college baseball or women's mud wrestling, Roseanne Barr or Robin Williams doing stand-up routines. If they prefer religious programming, they may watch the "700 Club" or the ACTS channel; and some local channels offer off-the-wall options like the "Greater Herdville Duck Calling Contest" or "Bowling for Truck Bed Liners." [This paragraph supports its main idea with specific examples of the kinds of programming available on cable television.]

Developed body paragraphs also provide an evident structure.

THESIS SENTENCE: Despite the inconveniences, living in the dorm is preferable to living in an apartment.

INEFFECTIVELY STRUCTURED BODY PARAGRAPH:

An apartment has no more privacy than a dorm room. Roommates can be as bothersome in an apartment as they are in a dorm. Students have to study, and they may have jobs. Who will stock the refrigerator? One student may buy food for herself, and her roommates will eat it before she can. The neighbors will come by at inconvenient hours. Roommates may use another's soap, and they won't be quiet when others need to study or sleep. When several roommates have friends over at the same time, the apartment will be very crowded. [The paragraph is not clearly developed. It mentions problems with roommates, then inconvenient neighbors, then returns problems with roommates, and concludes by referring to friends.]

CLEARLY STRUCTURED BODY PARAGRAPH:

An apartment has no more privacy than a dorm room. Unless students are better off financially than most, they will have one or more roommates who will not be monks or nuns who have made vows of silence. At least one of them will borrow clothes without asking. Or some will borrow soap if they have forgotten to buy their own. Friends will appear at inconvenient times, and they will usually bring friends of their own who will stay until inconvenient hours in the morning. In addition, neighbors who have no obligations, such as studying for a U.S. History midterm exam, may drop by just to pass time for an hour or so. Yes, life in the dorm is like life as a hermit compared to such an existence. [This paragraph has clear development. It begins by discussing problems with roommates, then shifts to a related subject—problems with friends—and concludes with a different subject—the problems with neighbors.]

Name ______________________________ Score ______________

Exercise 2c Body

1. For each of the major ideas listed below, supply the type of information that would develop a paragraph appropriately.

   EXAMPLE:
   Major idea: Lincoln's background made him a good president.
   Type of information: Provide a brief sketch of Lincoln's career.

   a. Major idea: Homelessness is not a new phenomenon.
      Type of information:

   b. Major idea: Despite what many think, a college education does not guarantee a graduate a good job.
      Type of information:

2. What kind of information is provided in the following paragraphs to develop them fully?

   a. Dorm life is certainly preferable to driving to campus every day. Living in the dorm puts students close to their classes in fairly inexpensive housing. A meal ticket provides food for the semester, and all events on campus are within walking distance. On the other hand, students who commute may live at home for free, but they have a long, expensive drive to make two to five times a week. They must pay for each meal individually at the cafeteria or at restaurants near the campus; and if they wish to attend extracurricular events, they have to either wait around for hours or drive back to the campus. Whatever they do, they always have a long drive back home, often late at night while the dorm resident is safely in bed.

   b. If we do not stop damaging the earth's atmosphere, the future of the planet looks bleak indeed. No one will be sunning at the beach or elsewhere because of the dangerous rays of the sun the atmosphere will now let in. The earth's average temperature will go up. Even a few degrees will cause a rise in sea level, and cities like New Orleans will be flooded within a few years. In addition, world-wide drought will create insurmountable problems for both animal and plant life.

   c. Good friends are not, of course, people who talk behind our backs; but they are also not people who borrow without asking things they know they can borrow. They do not need to be told when we need to talk or when we need to be alone. They never borrow money they do not plan to repay, and they certainly do not need an invitation to show up whenever we are in trouble.

3. Provide one thesis sentence each for essays for which the paragraphs in exercises 2a, 2b, and 2c, respectively, might be part of. Write out the sentences or phrases in each paragraph that guide the reader to the proposed thesis.
   a. Thesis:

      Guidance:

   b. Thesis:

      Guidance:

   c. Thesis:

      Guidance:

4. List five specific facts, examples, comparisons, or other details that would support each of the two major ideas listed below.
   a. Major idea 1: People need to be protected from the dangers of smoking.

   b. Major idea 2: The civil rights of smokers must be protected.

2d Conclude effectively.

A conclusion must relate to the essay's thesis, but it must not merely repeat it. The conclusion extends the thesis by *affirming a theory* or judgement established in the essay, *expressing a concern* about the subject of the essay, *offering a solution* to the problem of the essay, *calling* readers to action, or *raising a question* implied in the essay.

Common Problems

When an essay contains no conclusion, the essay simply stops abruptly. Some conclusions are mechanical and repetitious because they merely repeat the thesis and summarize the argument of the essay. Still other conclusions introduce new ideas or apologize for the content of the essay. Such endings confuse readers, diminish the writer's credibility and the essay's effectiveness, and suggest general lack of skill.

Examples

The need for effective conclusions is clear in the following examples:

THESIS: Although at present they appear to be a blessing, computers will ultimately diminish the quality of human life.

REASON 1: Computers will eliminate jobs for people who are unable to fulfill job requirements.

REASON 2: The speed with which computers calculate will remove the necessity for all but a few people to think and make decisions.

INADEQUATE CONCLUSIONS:

In conclusion, computers will diminish our quality of life because many people will be unable to hold the skilled jobs that will be available to them and because computers will make all the major decisions. Our lives will be either frustrating or boring. [The introductory phrase of the conclusion is unnecessary, and the content of the paragraph repeats what the body has asserted.]

Computers will diminish the quality of our lives by making us more materialistic than we already are. Our leisure time will be devoted to computer games, and we will "keep up with the Joneses" by demonstrating our ability to acquire more computer gadgetry. How could we possibly be happy in such a situation? [This conclusion introduces a third reason, leaving no sense of closure. It also confuses readers because it fails to pull the essay together.]

I know I could have used better examples, but my point is obvious anyway. Computers will make our lives worse even if I can't think of any significant reasons why that will be the case. [This type of conclusion is unacceptable. If authors fail to examine the problem thoroughly or believe their subject is trivial, then readers will not take them seriously.]

EFFECTIVE CONCLUSION:

Computers have an inherent capacity to diminish the quality of our lives, especially if they continue to develop as they have in recent years. But is their conquest inevitable? Not necessarily. They are, after all, just another advance in technology. And technology has given us the potential to produce enough food to feed the billions who inhabit the earth. It has also given us the potential to poison the earth with pesticides. How we use the technology available to us will determine our fate. So it is with computers. At present, they have the potential to perform all of our thinking for us. But if we change our attitudes and use them wisely, they may sustain us in the future. The choice is ours. [This conclusion extends the thesis and proposes a course of action.]

Name ______________________________ Score ________________

Exercise 2d Conclusion

1. Choose one of your own essays (or a sample from your Handbook) and write three separate conclusions using the techniques listed in the first paragraph of this section (page 55).

   a.

   b.

   c.

2. Using the conclusion of a magazine or newspaper article, analyze the author's technique. Then rewrite the original conclusion using one of the techniques indicated in the first paragraph of this section.

CHAPTER 3

Revising, Editing, and Proofreading

3a Revise for coherence.

Revision, or "re-seeing," is re-evaluating the large sections of an essay. The writer determines if the introduction, body, and conclusion fulfill their specific functions and compares the final draft to the outline to make sure the work has a clear structure and a consistent perspective. To revise, review each part separately, deciding (1) if the introduction prepares for the thesis and if the thesis is precise; (2) if the topic sentences of the body paragraphs guide the reader, if the support is developed, and if the order of paragraphs is effective; (3) if the conclusion extends the thesis; and (4) if the title is specific and reflects the purpose of the essay.

Common Problems

The process of revising is impossible if writers edit and proofread the smaller parts of the essay before they review the larger elements. When writers do not examine the essay's functional components, they do not identify the major problems.

Example

The following draft has all the components the writer wants to include in the essay, but it needs considerable revisions. In examining his draft, the writer saw major structural problems, as his editorial comments suggest:

FIRST DRAFT IN REVISION

~~Daily Annoyances~~ *Not my real point*

Dev.

Things that annoy me most would be the distraction that my brother makes as I try to study. When I study I sometimes need peace and quiet. ~~Any distraction of noise around me keeps my mind wandering to other things beside what I am doing. During the spring months, insects is~~ *irrelevant* another distraction toward me. The annoyance of our pet cats is also a distraction. The noise of my brother, pets and insects annoys me very much. expand thesis

topic sent.? My brother always wants me to play with him, especially when I have alot of work to do. He gets home from school and wants to talk to me. He likes to tell me everything he has been doing at school. Sometimes he asks my opinion about what he should do. Other times he just wants to hear what I have been doing. I just can't get anything done when he wants to talk. Dev Dev

~~He also wants me to play some kind of sports with him.~~ We have a basketball hoop in our back yard, and he asks me to play with him. Even when I say no, I can hear the ball bouncing outside. That is annoying at times. But more often than not, it is tempting. I like to play basketball, and despite the problems I have with my brother, I like him and like to play ball with him. I know that I will probably not have that many more years to be with him either. He will have new friends and not want to play with me. And I will have other things to do too. Next year I may live in an apartment and then we won't have much time together. red. this idea in concl.

weak topic sent. He also gets phone calls all the time. We share a room so I have to listen to him. He doesn't want to go to the phone in the kitchen because he doesn't want Mom to hear what he's talking about. He doesn't mind if I'm there because we share so much anyway. But I can't study when he is on the phone. I can't go into the other room for two reasons. First Mom is there, and she can be almost as irritating as my brother. And I have my desk and everything else in my room. I am comfortable there, and when my brother is studying or even listening to his walkman, I enjoy having him in the room.

add ¶ on solution

Even though my brother can be a pain in the neck, I do like his company. He is one annoyance I can put up with.

To revise the structure, the writer narrowed the focus of his essay and revised the content. What began as structural revision required adding an entire paragraph as well as developing existing paragraphs.

REVISED VERSION

Brother, I Can Spare the Time

I am probably like most college freshmen; I take my schoolwork seriously and must adjust to more difficult courses than I ever faced in high school. At the same time, I like to think that I am fairly "laid back," that I can overlook the minor problems that bother most of my friends. But recently I have come up against a problem that has really frustrated me. My brother, Marcus, who is now a senior in high school, still wants me to be the same as I was a year ago and do the same things. Even though I live at home, the demands on my life are different from what they were, and Marcus doesn't realize that. He has become a real annoyance to me. The problem is that I want to change some of his actions without destroying the closeness that we had and I hope will continue to have.

When he gets home from school, Marcus wants to talk to me just as he used to, but that is no longer possible. I try to get most of my studying done early in the afternoon, so I can finish for the night by 9:00. But Marcus likes to tell me everything that happened to him during the day or to ask my opinion about something he plans to do. Other times he just wants to hear what I have been doing. Once we start I just can't get back to studying.

Unfortunately, my problem doesn't end when I finish talking to Marcus. When he's not talking to me, Marcus "lives" on the phone. We share a room, so I have to listen to his conversations. He doesn't want to use the phone in the kitchen because Mom would overhear him. He doesn't mind my hearing him because we share so much anyway. But I can't study when he is on the phone. Going to the kitchen or living room is no better for me than it is for Marcus. First Mom is there, and she interrupts my studying almost as much as my brother. I also have my desk and books in my room, so I don't think I should have to leave to find peace and quiet.

An even greater problem than just talking or listening to Marcus is that he also wants me to work out with him, especially, it seems, when I have a test coming up. We have a basketball hoop in our back yard, and he likes to play a game of one-on-one before dinner. Even when I say no, I can hear the ball bouncing outside. The noise is annoying, but an even greater problem is that I am very tempted whenever I hear Marcus playing. I like basketball, and despite the problems I have with my brother, I like the exercise and the challenge of playing ball against him.

When I think about my problem, I see the easy solution but immediately <u>reject</u> it. I could simply not talk to Marcus when he gets home after school, and my parents would side with me and make him use the kitchen phone. Those actions would also solve the basketball problem, too; he wouldn't want to play with me any more. A better solution would be for both of us to change. I can plan a break when he gets home, but I can set a time limit on it. I might also talk Marcus into studying with me, which would prepare him for next year when he enters college. We could also play basketball before dinner, just not as often as either of us would like. But Marcus has to give in a little too. He needs to change his phone habits, or at least use the kitchen phone more often. Or maybe we could get an extension cord for both of the phones. He could have privacy in the hall, and I could have a quiet place to study.

Clearly, working my problem out with Marcus is the best solution. In fact, it could bring us even closer together. The problem that I face with him is typical of the kinds I will be facing in the future: most will have no simple solution. <u>How</u> I work out this problem is far more important than eliminating the problem itself. Successfully working it out can help me, and Marcus, mature and will contribute to our remaining psychological as well as biological brothers.

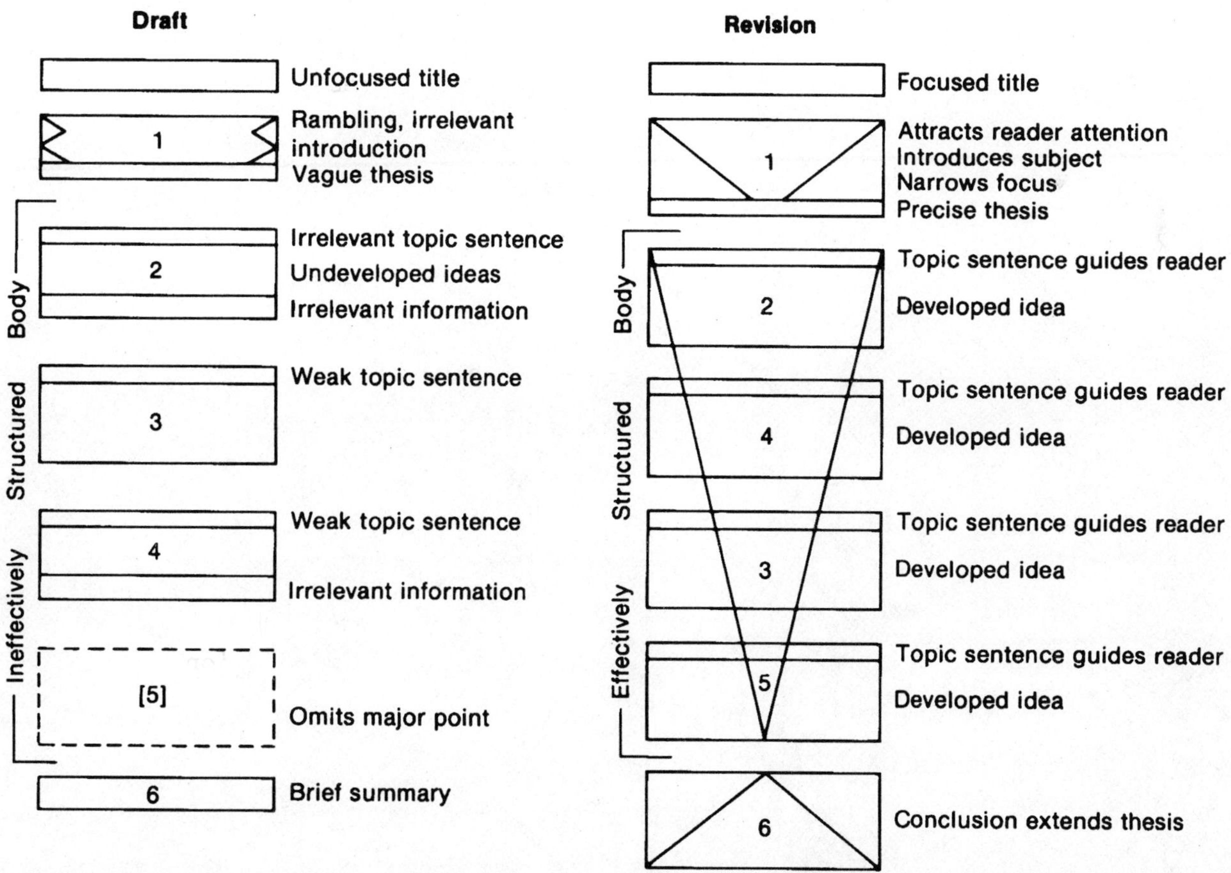

Name ______________________ Score ______________

Exercise 3a Revising for coherence

1. Revise the introduction, body, conclusion, and structure of the following essay as suggested by the above example. The assignment for the essay below is to describe something that terrifies the writer.

Things That Terrify Me

Police sirens and icy roads always terrify me. When I hear a siren, I know that someone is in trouble or hurt. And that worries me. When I got older and drove, I was always afraid when I heard a siren because I was afraid I might have done something wrong and the siren was the policeman pulling me over. Icy roads scared me even when I was a child, but they are worse now that I drive. I always enjoyed snowy weather when I was in elementary school because I enjoyed playing in the snow and because if it snowed a lot, school would be dismissed and I could play outside with my friends. But these things frighten me now.

When I was a child, we lived in a neighborhood where we always heard police sirens. I remember once the police stopped next door to our apartment. Fire trucks were there too. All of my friends and I heard the siren and went to the house to see what was happening. A neighbor had a heart attack, and an ambulance took her away. That night I couldn't sleep. I just could hear the sirens in my dreams all night long. Ever since that time I have been afraid of sirens.

Once when my father was taking us to visit my aunt and uncle, he got a speeding ticket. We went to visit them every Fourth of July. We still do, but now not everyone can go like we used to. My sister and I were playing in the back seat when all of a sudden I heard my father say, "Oh, no!" My sister and I sat up straight as quick as we could. That's when I heard the siren. My father got a ticket and had to pay fifty-five dollars later. When we pulled over to the side of the road, I was scared. I didn't know why the policeman was stopping us. When we started driving again, my father was mad at both Michelle and me and shouted at us for no reason at all. My mother didn't say anything, she just sat there with her arms folded and said nothing.

When I first got my driver's license, I took the car to school and when I got out it was snowing. I started to drive home and found that the streets were as slick as ice. I saw a lot of accidents when I was driving home. I heard police sirens too. All going to accidents. Everything was alright as long as I was going straight and didn't have to turn. But I had to make a left hand turn. As I did, my rear end kept going and I went in a complete circle. I didn't hit anything, but when the car stopped, I just sat there with my heart pounding. Wouldn't you know it, I heard a police siren. I looked up and saw a police car coming straight toward me. I just sat there and thought I was going to cry. But the policeman just drove past. I started up and drove straight home. But that siren scared me almost as much as the icy road. If I had got a ticket, my parents would have grounded me until graduation. And I wouldn't have driven again until I owned my own car.

It's funny how things frighten you. Police and fire trucks usually help people, but their sirens have always scared me. Icy roads probably scare most people. But to me both are terrifying, more than they should be. Maybe some day I will outgrow my fears. I hope so.

2. Revise a draft of one of your own essays following the procedure indicated in the above illustration.

3b Edit for tone, point of view, and general mechanics.

Editing, which is easier after revising, focuses on the smaller units of an essay—sentences, clauses, phrases, and words. Writers edit their work to achieve a consistent tone and point of view and a strong control of grammar, usage, mechanics, and punctuation. Isolating sentences, rather than examining them in the larger context of a paragraph or an essay, highlights their problems.

Common problems

The content of a paragraph can be so absorbing that the writer neglects the essay's finer points, not because of carelessness as much as lack of practice. Tone is sometimes inconsistent because the tone in writing and speaking usually differs. An inconsistent point of view often results when writers think second person (*you, your*) will attract readers or when, in trying to avoid sexist language, they create agreement errors. Wordiness is the result of imprecisions, repetition, or redundancy.

Examples

The primary tasks in effective editing are described below.

1. Problems of consistency

   a. Tone

   INCONSISTENT: A father who wants a good relationship with his son should reinforce his positive behavior and not *get on his case* every time he makes a mistake. [The emphasized phrase is too informal.]

   CONSISTENT: A father who wants a good relationship with his son should reinforce his positive behavior and not criticize him every time he makes a mistake.

   b. Point of view

   First person (*I, we*) focuses on the *writer* or, in the plural, on the writer as part of a group. Third person (*he, she, it, they, one*) focuses on the *subject* the writer is discussing. Second person (*you*) focuses on the *reader*. In most college assignments, second person is inappropriate except as an attention getter or in writing instructions. *One* often sounds stilted.

   INCONSISTENT: Being a lifeguard is a great summer job. Everyone looks up to you, and you get a great tan. [People look up to the lifeguard, not to the reader; the lifeguard, not the reader, gets a tan.]

   CONSISTENT: Being a lifeguard is a great summer job. Everyone looks up to her, and she gets a great tan.

   INCONSISTENT: *Everyone* should turn in *their* homework on time. ["Everyone" is singular; "their" is plural. The writer is trying to avoid the sexism implied in the traditional handling of pronoun/antecedent agreement: "Everyone should turn in *his* homework."]

   CONSISTENT: *Students* should turn in *their* homework on time. [Using the plural avoids the problem.]

   c. Tense

   Inconsistent tense is often the result of nonstandard dialect, of not pronouncing the indicator of tense, or, often, of a failure to pay attention to detail.

   INCONSISTENT: John *walk* to school even in the coldest weather.
   Karla *use* to own a 1958 Ford Thunderbird.

   CONSISTENT: John walked to school even in the coldest weather.
   Karla used to own a 1958 Ford Thunderbird.

2. Problems of wordiness

WORDY: *There are* five boys *who* will be cut from the basketball team.
The car *was* driven *by* Heather.
We *have a* need to write precisely.
It is a *true fact* that war is a *terrible tragedy.*
It is a *basic and fundamental* law of nature.
Due to the fact that John has no car, I will drive him home.

CONCISE: Five boys will be cut from the basketball team. [Expletive phrases (*there is, it is*) are usually wordy.]
Heather drove the car. [The passive voice is often wordy.]
We need to write precisely. [Strong verbs often reduce wordiness.]
It is a *fact* that war is a *tragedy.* [Redundant: all facts are true, and tragedies are terrible.]
It is a *basic* law of nature. [Redundant: "basic" and "fundamental" have the same meaning.]
Because John has no car, I will drive him home. [Use a specific word rather than an equivalent phrase.]

3. Problems of conventions: Edit to follow grammatical conventions.
UNCONVENTIONAL: The United States should support Eastern *European countrys. Because it is in our national interest.* [misspellings, fragment]
Collecting comic books is not just a hobby for children, many adults now collect comic books too. [comma splice]
Hawaii appears to be a paradis*e t*hat is the opinion of many who have vacationed there. [fused sentence]
Watching the television, the cat was curled on my lap. [dangling modifier]

CONVENTIONAL: The United States should support Eastern *European countries because it is in our national interest.*
Collecting comic books is not just a hobby for children. Many adults now collect comic books, too.
OR
Collecting comic books is not just a hobby for children; many adults now collect comic books, too.
Hawaii appears to be a paradise. That is the opinion of many who have vacationed there.
While I was watching the television, the cat was curled on my lap.

Name ______________________ Score ______________

Exercise 3b Editing

Edit the following sentences. (Sentences may contain more than one error.)

1. In light of the fact that George is my friend, I visited him often when he was in the hospital.
2. Japanese technology use to be inferior to that of the United States.
3. I think blue is my favorite color.
4. The seven-game championship series was won by the Detroit Pistons in four games. Because two starters for the Los Angles Lakers were injure.
5. There is a need for diplomacy between the Unlited States and Central America.
6. According to recent discoveries, dinosaurs may not be extinct, in fact, birds may be living dinosaurs.
7. Although seismologists are unable to predict that earthquakes will occur within decades they are sure to occur within centuries.
8. Modern physics has become so technical that it is beyond the ability of the average guy to understand it.
9. Every member of the debate team must put forth their best effort if they expect to win the tournament.
10. If one wants to be a lawyer, he should major in English as an undergraduate. Because English gives you a broad background.
11. The new Chinese restrant was by far the best one we eat in.
12. The final aims and goals of a government should be clear to all its citizens.
13. Felix's first position upon graduation was as a seller of preowned automobiles.
14. Opal told Derrick that she love him for eternity he learn quickly how short eternity is.
15. Modern biologists are studying jeans and making remarkable discoveries that will greatly effect humanity in the 1990s.
16. Over ten years after dying, people still believe Elvis is alive.
17. There are many people who have seen every episode of *Star Trek*.

18. The novel *The Bluest Eye* was written by Toni Morrison, it will soon be a major motion picture.

19. President Bush likes country music because the lyrics relax you.

20. *The Phil Donahue Show* doesn't grab the audience *The Oprah Winfrey Show* does.

3c Proofread with care.

Proofreeding demands close attention to detail, writers are often judged by their spelling, punctuation, and neetness. Reading each sentence, for errors rather than for content focuses the writer on these necesary details.

Common Problems

A writer is often more concerned with the content of their essays than with the minor details so they overlook them. Homophones, words that sound the same but are spelled differently, often create problems to.

Example

Compare the effects of proofreading in the examples below:

SENTENCE NEEDING PROOFREADING:

The affect of a students' paper is often determine by the close attention to detail's that so many find tedious, many people don't know how to judge the worth of a essay; so they comment on that which they do konw—grammer, usage, mechanics and punctuation.

SENTENCES AFTER PROOFREADING:

The effect ["impression" is the intended meaning] of a student's [the apostrophe belongs after the singular form of "student"] paper is often determined [the "d" was omitted] by the close attention to details [no apostrophe is necessary for the plural] that so many find tedious. [comma splice] Many people don't know how to judge the worth of an [use "an" before a word that begins with a vowel sound] essay, [a comma, not a semicolon, joins two sentences joined by a coordinating conjunction] so they comment on that which they do know [misspelled]— grammar [misspelled], usage, mechanics, [the series comma is necessary here] and punctuation.

Name ______________________ Score ______________

Exercise 3c Proofreading

1. Correct all the errors in grammar, usage, mechanics, and punctuation that occur in the introductory sections on page 71.
2. Underline all the typographic errors on an early draft of one of your essays. (Errors that occur in early drafts are corrected in later drafts.)

PART

2

Paragraphs

CHAPTER 4

Paragraph Unity

4a Develop one key idea and focus it with a topic sentence.

A paragraph should deliberately develop one key point and identify it in a topic sentence. Effective **topic sentences** guide the information in the remainder of the paragraph. In body paragraphs, topic sentences also relate those paragraphs to each other and to the thesis sentence in the introductory paragraph.

Common Problems

Without a topic sentence that identifies one key idea, a paragraph merely discusses the essay's subject and cannot provide unity and fluency.

Examples

The following paragraphs indicate the function of an adequate topic sentence.

> Many students drop out of college after the first year or two. College administrations go to considerable trouble and expense to recruit new students. Something needs to be done. Students fail academically, and they do not have friends at school. It is better to retain students already enrolled. Fraternities and sororities could really help out with this aspect of student retention.

Because this paragraph has no topic sentence, its ideas do not clearly relate to each other, provide no direction, and do not unify it. The next version begins to focus the issue with a topic sentence.

> *Fraternities and sororities should be key elements in any university's plans for student retention.* Universities need to retain students they already have enrolled if they are to survive. It costs a great deal to recruit new students, so it is better to keep those already on campus. They should join fraternities or sororities. Students enjoy the extracurricular activities of these organizations, but the fraternities and sororities also stress academics. In addition, they do worthwhile community service, and having been affiliated with such an organization can aid students in later life. Belonging to a fraternity or sorority is well worth the cost. The Greek organizations and the school administration need to work together.

Although the first sentence in this paragraph is a topic sentence, the paragraph does not explicitly develop it. The paragraph generalizes about retention and about fraternities and sororities, but it does not explain directly why or how these organizations could be key elements in a school's retention plans. The following paragraph develops the topic sentence.

> *Fraternities and sororities should be central elements in any university's plans for student retention.* Studies reveal that membership in extracurricular organizations makes it more likely that students will return the following year because such organizations create a sense of belonging for

> students and provide social incentives for them to stay in school. Fraternities and sororities probably have this effect on students better than any other organizations on campus. In addition, despite their reputations for excessive partying and for taking up their members' time with other extracurricular activities, most Greek organizations emphasize maintaining a good grade point average, sometimes one above what is required by the university as a whole. The focus on succeeding academically is especially emphasized with freshmen, the group most likely to have difficulty adjusting to the rigors of academic life and the group most likely to have a high drop-out rate. Thus, universities would do well to consider fraternities and sororities in any plans they make for maintaining the levels of their student enrollments.

The key idea of this paragraph is the first sentence, which unifies developing that idea; that is, how fraternities and sororities keep students enrolled.

Some ways in which topic sentences refer to the thesis of an entire essay and provide direction for the whole are illustrated below:

Subject: Capital punishment

Thesis sentence of the essay: Capital punishment should be abolished in the United States.

Topic sentence 1: *One reason capital punishment should be abolished* is that it is unevenly administered, both from state to state and even within states.

Topic sentence 2: *Another reason capital punishment should be abolished* is that if an executed person is later discovered to be innocent, the state has no way of correcting the injustice.

Topic sentence 3: *The most important reason that the death penalty should be abolished,* however, is that it is really not justice but revenge.

The phrases "One reason," "Another reason," and "The most important reason" indicate how the three body paragraphs of the essay relate to one another. They each discuss *reasons* that capital punishment should be abolished. The repetition of the phrase "capital punishment should be abolished" and the use of the alternate "the death penalty should be abolished" remind the reader of the thesis sentence.

Name ______________________________ Score ________________

Exercise 4a Topic sentence

1. Place a *Y* before each sentence that develops the topic sentence. Place an *N* before each sentence that is merely related to the subject or that fails to develop the topic sentence.

   Subject: Body building
   Topic sentence: Men and women can benefit from body building.

   a. Body building improves the muscle tone of the entire body.
   b. More body building facilities are available than ever before.
   c. The size and shape of muscles can be determined by the amount of weight used, the type of exercise, and the number times the exercise is repeated.
   d. Numerous magazines for both men and women are devoted to body building.
   e. Recent studies reveal that body building provides more cardiovascular exercise than had previously been thought.
   f. Even light workouts with weights on a regular basis improve the posture.
   g. Men and women can engage in body building by using free weights, machines such as the Nautilus, resistance devices employing springs or heavy rubber bands, or even calisthenics.
   h. Body building equipment is much more attractive than it used to be.
   i. Americans are not exercising as much as they should.
   j. Body building introduces people to others with similar interests.

2. Underline the topic sentences in each of the following paragraphs. Strike through any sentence that does not expand and develop its topic sentence.

   a. The weather in the Mid-South is often dangerous. Tornados can occur at any time of year, of course, and within a fairly wide temperature range. But the threat from fog can also be deadly, and at times in the late afternoon in winter a slight drizzle can suddenly turn the roads icy with no warning at all. A sudden rain storm can also soak anyone who is unprepared. Snow, which most people in the region are poorly prepared for, can also cause hazards on highways as well as the kinds of overexertion that lead to heart attacks.

   b. The telephone is as much an annoyance as a convenience. Of course, it is indispensable for acquiring information quickly about how long the drug store will be open, what a new steel-belted radial will cost, or when we can get in to see the dentist. The telephone is necessary as well for emergency calls, and it is admittedly convenient for overdue conversations with friends who live at a distance. A number of different long-distance services are now available. On the other hand, during the course of the day we may receive any number of calls from acquaintances we would rather not talk to (or would rather not talk to for long); or calls that we would welcome if they had not come in the middle of work or during supper; or calls from siding companies, people selling raffle tickets, or those taking surveys on how we feel about the administration's stand on allowing Canadian comedians into the United States without a rigorous security check. The telephone is most annoying of all, however, when it rings at two in the morning and we find ourselves making statements to disbelieving callers, such as, "No, Bruce is not here, never has been here, and probably will not be back any time soon."

3. Place a check mark before the topic sentences that both (a) clearly connect to each other and (b) clearly relate to the stated thesis sentence.

   a. Thesis sentence: The cat is man's best friend.

      ____ Those who think the dog is man's best friend are wrong.

      ____ Cats are not very friendly at times.

      ____ Generally, one does not have to clean up after a cat.

____ Dogs are used for protection.

____ Most cats will leave their owners alone when the owners have other things to do.

____ Cats come in a variety of species.

____ Dogs can be very loyal.

____ Hair balls can be a problem.

____ Cats can be very loyal.

____ Cats and dogs have little in common.

b. Thesis sentence: Even a fried hamburger can taste good if it is prepared correctly.

____ Next, the burger must be removed from the grill thirty seconds before it is well done.

____ Broiled hamburgers are better than fried hamburgers.

____ Besides, fast food is generally not good for us.

____ In addition, Burger Boy has the best hamburgers in town.

____ First, the burger must be correctly seasoned.

____ Basically, fried chicken is as bad for us as fried hamburgers.

____ Hamburgers are still America's favorite fast food.

____ Unfortunately, most Americans do not like fried liver.

____ Second, hamburger usually has a lot of fat in it.

____ Most important of all, the burger must have just the right condiments put on it.

4b Place the topic sentence for best effect.

The topic sentence (main point) is often the first sentence of a paragraph. In special cases, the topic sentence may be placed elsewhere. For example, introductory paragraphs may conclude with the topic sentence, which is the essay's thesis. Or a paragraph might begin with a transitional sentence followed by the topic sentence.

Common Problems

When the topic sentence is buried in the middle of a paragraph, rereading may be the only way to determine the main point.

Examples

The following paragraphs are examples of effective placement of topic sentences.

> *The fog created a danger for every living creature on the road that morning.* Bill not only slowed down to fifteen miles an hour, but also kept checking his rear view mirror to look for cars that might run into the back of his truck. He saw an Oldsmobile and a Trans Am in the ditch within a quarter mile stretch; and he was sure he saw a cow wander into the middle of the road and look about for something to graze on.

The placement of the topic sentence is a guide to the point of the paragraph.

> However, the cost is not the only feature to consider in buying a Bentex 4000 computer. *Should buyers have trouble with the hardware, they will not find service easy to come by.* Bentex Incorporated has only two service centers in the United States: one is in Boston; the other, in San Francisco. Buyers must pay shipping costs, as well as parts and labor; and the average time that elapses between shipping a unit to the service center and its return is seven months.

The first sentence is transitional and relates the paragraph to the one preceding it. The second sentence, the topic sentence, is still a clear guide.

> When traveling in the western United States, we often encounter boarded up abandoned mines, their earthly riches long ago hauled away. But why can these supposedly useless man-made caverns not be put to some good use? Some might store industrial waste. Others could store essential supplies a community might need in a natural disaster or nuclear war. Some might even be made livable and reduce in some small way the problem of the homeless. *Yes, a mine is a terrible thing to waste.*

Because the topic sentence of the paragraph is really a punch line, it is the last sentence of the paragraph.

Name ______________________________ Score ______________

Exercise 4b Topic sentence placement

1. Underline the topic sentences in one section of both a textbook and a magazine article. Be prepared to discuss these questions orally or in writing, as your instructor decides:
   a. What paragraphs have clear topic sentences? How often do they appear in the middle or at the end of paragraphs?
   b. How do the topic sentences in textbooks differ from those in magazine articles?
   c. How can you use the topic sentences in your textbooks as an outline or guide to the content of a chapter?

2. Underline the topic sentences of the following paragraphs. Which seem to you to be effectively placed? Place a *Y* in the blank for those you think are properly placed and an *N* in the blank for those you think are not.

_______ a. I was so surprised when Rick took me to the Wall of China. It was the most beautiful restaurant I had ever been to, both in its appearance and in its atmosphere. When we entered, I just stood there. The walls were a brilliant shade of red, and the furnishings were red, black, and gold. A wonderful smell filled the air, and soft oriental music floated through it. The book-size menus were in their own way just as beautiful as the setting. They were filled with great-sounding dishes, and our waiter even described them in detail for us. The parchment paper menus felt crisp and smooth under my fingertips as I looked for just the right dish to select. Petite Chinese women scurried past our table adding to the atmosphere.

_______ b. When my boyfriend and I had entered the Italian Villa restaurant, I was shocked by the old, weathered picnic tables covered in tattered red and white checkered table cloths. The atmosphere was very laid-back but comfortable, not formal. The place was nothing like what I had expected. Our waiter looked as if he could care less that we were there, but he was very helpful in suggesting the special for the day: butterfly shrimp, corn bread, and cole slaw. Cornbread and cole slaw in an Italian restaurant! We couldn't believe it.

_______ c. As we placed our order, the waitress smiled and was very friendly. She told us her name was Margaret and she talked to us almost the whole time we waited, so the time passed quickly. As we watched the young man cooking our waffles, he talked to us, too. His name was Scott and he showed us all the tricks to make waffles quickly, yet taste and look great. Mine looked so good, but it tasted even better. The syrup was homemade, and with the pure butter, the waffles seemed to melt in my mouth. I ate so much I felt like a pig, but the waffles were too good for me to stop. We all ate until our plates were empty. Few restaurants live up to their advertising, but this one did. Now I know what the ideal breakfast at a restaurant should be.

4c Eliminate irrelevant details.

Information should be related to the topic sentence (the main point), not simply to the essay's subject.

Common Problems

Even an effective topic sentence may not prevent occasional wandering to irrelevant details that the subject suggests.

Example

Some sentences in the paragraph below are irrelevant to the effective development of the paragraph.

> Having grown up in America and being accustomed to its freedom, I have often wondered about experiencing foreign cultures. *My father had traveled to Europe right after graduating from college, and I would like the same opportunity.* The news coverage would probably be far different than I have experienced. *I have always enjoyed reading of sensational crimes in the daily papers.* But even England with its tradition for freedom doesn't allow newspapers to print facts about crime, facts which we Americans could read in our papers. I don't think I would have any problems living in foreign countries in good times, *except that I don't like unusual foods.* But if I had any legal problems, I would be afraid that I wouldn't receive the justice I have come to expect in the United States.

The italicized portions should be deleted because, although related to the subject, they are not related to the specific topic.

Eliminate irrelevant details

Name ______________________________ Score ______________

Exercise 4c Irrelevant details

1. Underline the sentences in the following paragraphs that are irrelevant to the development of the topic sentences.

   a. My prom night wasn't at all what I had expected it to be. I had thought that Rod and I would look great together. But he showed up at my house wearing a red tuxedo jacket, and my gown was emerald green. It was beautiful and the most expensive dress I had ever owned. But when we stood next to each other, we looked like a Christmas tree. I had also hoped that we would go to the prom in a nice car. I'm not snobby, but when I saw his parents' van instead of their BMW, I could have cried. His father had to take the BMW on a business trip, and Rod's Toyota was in the shop, as usual. When we arrived at the prom, the music was so loud we could hardly talk. I liked the music, and the group was really great, especially the guitarist. It was just too loud. But my prom night did teach me an important lesson: in the future, when I go to a special event, I won't get my expectations up, and then if I do have a wonderful time, it will be a total surprise.

   b. I enjoy working on my 1967 Mustang, even on the tedious task of replacing and setting the points. The Mustang is a classic now, and all my friends like driving in it on weekends. I was lucky to get it. My father's boss likes me and sold it to me cheap. The points and related parts are small and in such a confined area that it makes working on them rough. Still I enjoy doing it, probably because it was the first major job my father let me do on his car. He taught me everything I know about cars, and I'll always be grateful for that. After I remove the old points and am ready to install the new ones, I turn the engine over slowly until a lobe on the distributor cam is in contact with the points. I then can begin the actual setting. I pry the points either to or from the cam lobe, thus changing the gap. Once I adjust the gap by eye, I check the gap with a feller gauge set at .021. Because my eyes are good, I am usually close to the mark. I am even better than my father at doing this part, but I know my sight won't always be that good. So I shouldn't brag. If I find the setting off, I repeat the process until the gap is correct. Once I have the gap properly set, I tighten the points down in the distributor. This part is fairly difficult because if I am not careful the screw will slightly move the points. The first time I replaced the points, I made this mistake, even though my dad had warned me about it. He even laughed when we were resetting them. So now I always remember to recheck the points. As the final touch, I apply a small amount of grease where the cam lobes come in contact with the points in order to cut down on wear.

2. Identify the portions you would eliminate from the two paragraphs in exercise 1 above, and explain the authors' purpose for including the information.

CHAPTER 5

Writing Coherent Paragraphs

5a Choose an organizing principle.

When a paragraph displays a clear organizing principle, its content is coherent and it serves a direct purpose within the essay as a whole. Paragraphs developed according to common methods of organization can achieve coherence easily.

Common Problems

Content alone will not communicate meaning or provide a clear structure. A writer whose thought processes are more important than the subject is usually confusing.

Example

The conventional principles of organizing or structuring a paragraph are as follows:

1. *Chronological order* proceeds from the first to the last, from the earliest to the most recent.

    In the Congress, a House bill is first referred to the appropriate committee, which investigates the merits of the bill. If the committee approves, the bill goes before the entire House where it is debated and voted upon. If it passes, the bill goes to the Senate where it undergoes a similar procedure. If it passes Senate scrutiny, the bill is sent to the president who either signs it or vetoes it. As a result of this process, few laws are enacted without careful consideration.

    The steps a House bill must follow structure the paragraph.

2. *Spatial order* examines a subject from a particular perspective in the physical world—from the inside out, from the outside in, from top to bottom, or from bottom to top.

    The fork stabbed into the center of the yolk. As the dome of the yolk collapsed, the yellow liquid flowed onto the white, some of it dripping onto the plate.

    The movement from the center outward structures the process.

3. *Climactic order* moves from the least important to the most important (the structure can also be effective when reversed).

    Obviously, good friends must have compatible personalities. They also need to have some common interests. If they are not honest and trustworthy with one another, the relationship will fail. But no friendship can last without mutual respect. In fact, respect encompasses all the other qualities.

    The paragraph moves from the least to the most essential quality of friendship.

4. *General-to-specific order* begins with a hypothesis and follows with support.

   In recent years, political candidates have shown little respect for the American voter. They think either that the voters don't care what happens to the country or that they are too stupid or lazy to notice that the candidates differ very little on substantive issues. How else can we explain the campaigns that focus on the candidate's personality rather than on major issues, such as inflation, the environment, or the homeless? Campaign ads have often attacked the candidate's patriotism or failure to support the rights of the victims of crime, as if all serious candidates aren't patriotic or favor crime.

   The writer has taken a stand and then offered evidence as support.

5. *Specific-to-general order* begins with examples and builds to a hypothesis or general conclusion.

   Political campaigns in recent years have focused on the personalities of the candidates rather than on major issues, such as inflation, the environment, or the homeless. Campaign ads have often attacked the candidate's patriotism or failure to support the rights of the victims of crime. This tactic suggests that the candidates differ little on crucial issues or that they believe that the public is not interested in serious political debate. In either case, the candidates insult the American voter.

The writer hopes that the examples will make the conclusion acceptable. Specific-to-general, or *inductive,* reasoning is often less confrontational than general-to-specific, or *deductive* reasoning.

6. *General-to-specific-to-general* begins with a hypothesis and follows with support that leads to a generalization. For example, the sample paragraph 4 above could end with a new generalization:

   In recent years, political candidates have shown little respect for the American voter. . . . If we the American voters stop voting for those who insult our intelligence, politicians will have to take stands on the truly important issues of the time, and we can have a government that serves our needs and solves problems rather than avoids them.

The new generalization assumes greater validity than it would normally have because it logically follows from what has preceded it.

7. *Question-and-answer order* creates a back-and-forth structure that moves readers quickly through the points of the argument.

   Are the animal rights activists correct that we don't need to use animals for testing products? The answer depends on what products we are talking about. Many would argue that we do need to use animals for some medical testing but that we don't need to use animals as extensively as we have done. And we certainly don't need to abuse animals in cosmetic tests, which have resulted in rabbits being blinded and suffering needlessly. But if we don't test cosmetics, might not people be blinded or burned? No one is suggesting that cosmetics not be tested; they can be tested without using animals. But why change what we are presently doing if the animals have been bred for testing and if they are drugged so they don't experience pain? If we have any respect for life, we should not intentionally harm or kill living creatures without a very good reason. Many people say that two cells—a human ova and a sperm—need to be protected. It should be obvious that a fully developed animal with a brain and nervous system merits as much consideration.

The drama of the question-and-answer method gives weight to the answers, as if the writer were answering questions of a real antagonist rather than created questions.

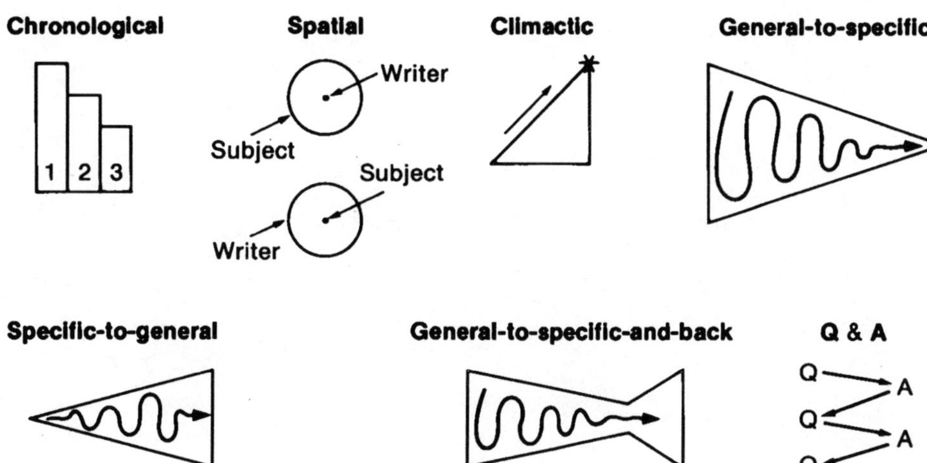
Chronological
1
2
3
Spatial
Writer
Subject
Subject
Writer
Climactic
General-to-specific
Specific-to-general
General-to-specific-and-back
Q & A
Q
A
Q
A
Q
A

Name ________________________________ Score ________________

Exercise 5a Organizing principle

1. List at least five steps that you follow in a *procedure* that you do well (preparing a particular recipe, shooting a jump shot, writing a successful essay exam). Then write a paragraph in which you explain why the order of the steps is important to your success.

2. Write two paragraphs in which you *describe* the same event from two different physical perspectives (watching a sporting event from a front row seat and then from a back row, or if you have been involved in the event, from the playing field itself; or looking at a city from the window of a tall building and then from ground level).

   a.

   b.

3. Choose a quality, such as love, patriotism, sportsmanship, and list five characteristics of that quality. Then write a paragraph in which you discuss these characteristics in either *ascending or descending order* of importance.

4. Take a position on an issue, and write three paragraphs in which you support your position: one moving from the *general to the specific,* one moving from the *specific to the general,* and one moving from the *general to the specific and back to general.*

a.

b.

c.

Name ____

Exercise 5a (continued)

5. Write a paragraph on a controversial issue and support your position by using the *question-and-answer* structure.

6. Examine essays you have written and choose two paragraphs that illustrate two of the conventional methods of structuring paragraphs. Be prepared to submit them or discuss them in class.

5b Use parallel structures to enhance paragraph cohesion.

Repeated structures create familiarity. To reinforce reader confidence, experienced writers use parallelism in sentences, in paragraphs, and in chapters (each chapter in this workbook follows the same format).

Common Problems

Complex sentences or paragraphs can be confusing unless readers are guided by both content and repeated structures which are carefully placed.

Examples

The following sentence is effective because it displays parallel structures.

> *Patiently circling* the sky in wide arcs, *suddenly spotting* a telltale movement in the brush, *instantly plummeting* to the earth in a flash of golden brown, *finally impaling* its prey on razor-sharp talons—the red-tailed hawk completes her daily ritual for survival.

The adverbs ("patiently," "suddenly," "instantly," "finally") and participles ("circling," "spotting," "plummeting," "impaling") create a parallelism of paired single words, which introduce and reinforce four parallel phrases. The momentum of the phrases builds to the central point, the hawk's ritual.

The next sentences illustrate a more complex use of parallelism:

> Battles in the war against drugs will be won *when the federal government effectively prevents* drugs from entering the United States and *when dealers know* they will be severely punished. But the war itself will continue *until addicts receive* appropriate treatment and *until average citizens—both young and old—stop believing* that illicit drugs are *both glamorous and harmless.*

The sentences are clear and cohesive because they contain parallel structures. Each sentence comprises an independent clause and two dependent clauses that are made parallel by subordinate conjunctions—"when" and "until." A further parallel structure contrasts the two sentences by the coordinating conjunction "but."

The diagrams illustrate the parallelism in the two examples above.

Example 1

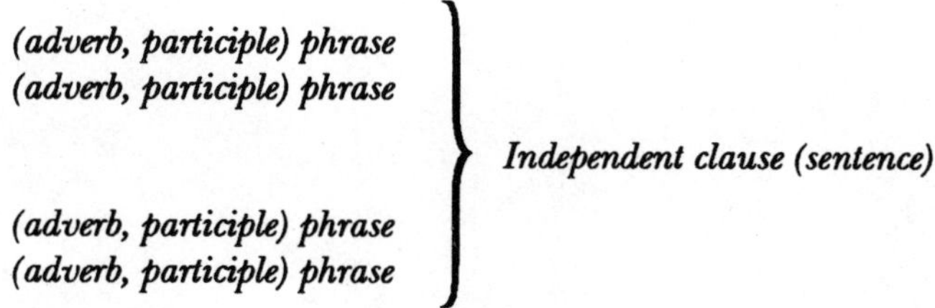

Example 2

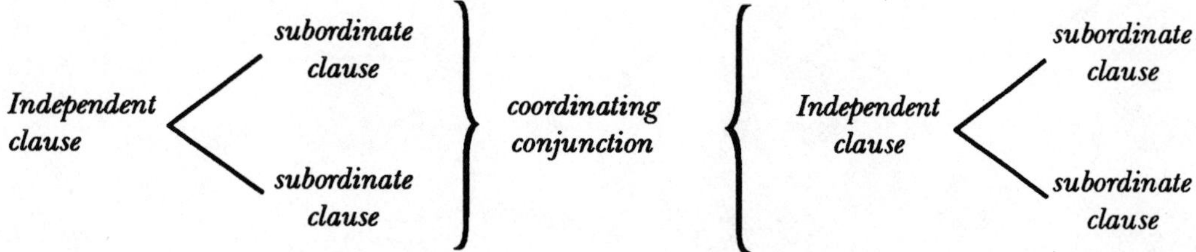

Name ______________________ Score ______________

Exercise 5b Parallel structures

1. Fill in the blank with a parallel word, phrase, or dependent clause.

   a. To eat well every day, to have a roof over our heads, and to ______________ is the goal of most people.

   b. John always wanted to hang glide because he loved to be in the great outdoors, he wanted to fly like a bird, and he ______________ .

   c. The drummer shook his head as he kept the beat; the lead guitarist leapt across the stage as he picked; and the vocalist ________ as she ________ .

   d. The snake slithered into the tent, coiled within inches of the sleeping camper, and ______________ .

   e. The soldiers knew that the enemy was hiding in the woods, that ______________, and that they would eventually be victorious.

2. Combine the following short sentences to form one or two sentences with parallel words, phrases, or dependent clauses.

   a. Elephants have legs like tree trunks.
   Elephants have ears like huge leaves.
   Elephants have trunks like boa constrictors.
   Elephants have skin like dried clay.

   b. The Chicago Bulls have the top scorer in the NBA.
   The Bulls had the best draft in 1989.
   Scottie Pippen is one of the better small forwards in the league.
   The Bulls should win the Central Division title.

c. Many people prefer the early *Cheers* shows to the more recent ones.
Other people liked *I Love Lucy* better than Lucille Ball's later series.
Still others enjoyed Bob Newhart more as a psychologist than as the owner of a New England inn.

d. Science frightens many people.
To some it seems a threat to religious beliefs.
Some people think it is impossible to understand science without extensive training.
Scientists have not popularized their subjects.

e. Computers benefit students.
Most business could no longer be competitive without computers.
Police departments across the country are much more efficient now that they are equipped with computers.

5c Use clear transitions.

Transitional words and phrases point out the relationship between parts of sentences, between complete sentences, and between paragraphs.

Common Problems

Omitting necessary transitions or using inappropriate transitions can disrupt an essay's coherence and confuse the reader.

Example

The following is a partial list of words and phrases that enhance coherence:

To add information:
first, second, next, and, also, furthermore, additionally, in addition, besides, moreover

To show contrast:
however, notwithstanding, nevertheless, but, yet, although, still, on the contrary, even though, on the one hand/on the other hand, conversely

To compare:
also, likewise, similarly, in like manner, in the same way, in comparison

To show cause and/or effect :
consequently, therefore, so, thus, in effect, for this reason, as a consequence, as a result

To conclude:
therefore, accordingly, in closing, in conclusion, in short, to sum up

To introduce an example:
specifically, for example, to illustrate, one kind of, for instance, to name a few

To show chronology:
meanwhile, soon, after, before, when, immediately, shortly, thereafter, finally, after a short time, the next day, at the end of the day, one year later, then

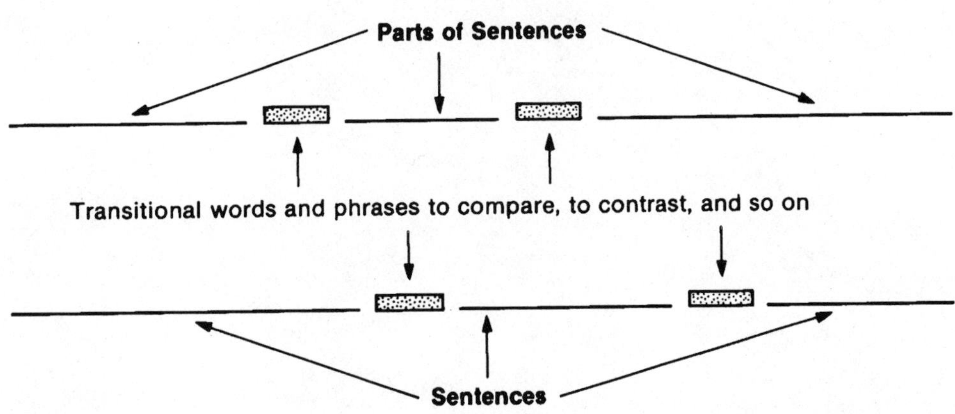

Name ______________________ Score ____________

Exercise 5c Transitions

1. Circle all the transitional words and phrases you have used in an essay you have written. Be prepared to justify your choices in class.
2. Using the transitional words and phrases in the list on page 101, write two sentences for each type of transition, a total of fourteen sentences.
   a. To add information:
      1)
      2)
   b. To show contrast:
      1)
      2)
   c. To compare:
      1)
      2)
   d. To show cause and/or effect:
      1)
      2)

e. To conclude:
1)

2)

f. To introduce an example:
1)

2)

g. To show chronology:
1)

2)

3. Explain what is inappropriate in the use of the transitional words and phrases in the following sentences, and replace them with appropriate alternatives.
a. Fred was the shortest player on the basketball team, *but* he couldn't jump very well.

b. In the 1990s far fewer people are expected to move to the Sun Belt. *For example,* the tax base for the schools in that area will probably not increase.

c. *Although* she had known her for ten years, Marcia knew that Anita liked pizza with everything but anchovies.

Name ___________________________________

Exercise 5c (continued)

d. J. R. had received several tickets for speeding; *therefore,* his father let him drive to the prom.

e. *In short,* the best way to succeed in life is to follow the guidelines that friends, relatives, and teachers offer and to read the major works of philosophy and religion that have guided humanity over the past two thousand years.

5d Repeat key words and phrases.

Like the repetition of grammatical structures (see section **5c**), repetition of the same word or synonyms in a paragraph or essay creates coherence. Reading a passage aloud and judging how the wording sounds permits writers to determine whether to repeat the key word or to use a synonym.

Common Problems

A term that is repeated too often or the use of inapplicable synonyms (which sound as if they were from a thesaurus) creates a monotonous and unnatural style.

Example

The following paragraph repeats a key term:

> *Birding* is one of the fastest growing pastimes. But in earlier times, *birding* got a bad rap. Birdwatching, the earlier term for "*birding*," was a hobby limited to absent-minded eccentrics. Perhaps the change to *birding* was an attempt to shed the negative image. Hiking, hunting, fishing, even nature walking were acceptable activities. But *birding* was not. Times have changed. *Birding* can now claim devotees from all walks of life—young and old, male and female, rural and city dweller, the Wall Street broker and the busy parent of four children. Truly, *birding* is "in"!

Repetition of the key term both helps the paragraph cohere and reflects the writer's pride in the term and the hobby.

Name ____________________ Score ____________

Exercise 5d Repetition

1. The following paragraph lacks cohesion because the key term, *apartheid,* occurs only once. However, the paragraph would be ineffective if the key term replaced each pronoun, term, and phrase that substitutes for *apartheid.* The paragraph needs balance, both repetition of the key term and its equivalents. First underline any word or phrase that substitutes for *apartheid.* Then revise the paragraph by substituting equivalent terms for the key term *in appropriate situations.* (Remember that mere substitution of *apartheid* for every equivalent will create an ineffective repetition.)

   Most Americans had never heard of *apartheid* before the 1970s. But the term has been in use for decades. Literally, the word means "separateness." It is an Afrikaans word that now has a very special meaning. It has narrowed to refer only to the racial segregation policy of South Africa. Perhaps when the dehumanizing policy has been abandoned, the term will return to its broader meaning. When that time comes, the world will be a better place.

2. Revise the paragraph on birding on page 107 to reduce the number of times the key term appears. If you repeat the key term, be prepared to justify the repetition.

CHAPTER 6

Developing Paragraphs

6a–6i Write fully developed paragraphs.

To develop paragraphs, accomplished writers often unconsciously use conventional methods (i.e., narration, description, illustration). Not only do these conventions add information, but they also guide readers and structure paragraphs. Novice writers, then, should develop skimpy paragraphs by consciously applying these techniques.

Common Problems

Paragraphs that do not rely on the conventional methods of development often include minimal information, are structured ineffectively, and fail to maintain reader interest.

Example

Samples of nine methods of developing paragraphs are provided below:

1. *Narration* illustrates a point by telling a relevant story.

> When I was growing up, I knew everyone who lived on my block, and they knew me—more importantly, they knew my parents. As far as I knew, they were also friends of my parents, who expected me to show respect to all adults, especially their friends. What was true for me was also true for the other children on the block. That fact, to a large extent, determined our behavior. Some parent was always "looking out for us," that is, was waiting to tell our parents if we misbehaved. But in our hearts, we knew they were also there to protect us. Even though we rarely admitted it, we took pleasure in both the guidance and the protection. Middle-class children today often lack both those experiences. They are suffering from the same problems that have always plagued children from the lower end of the socio-economic strata. The difference now is that the average American is becoming aware of the problems.

The writer has introduced a general subject by relating a personal childhood incident.

2. *Description* illustrates a point by appealing to the five senses (sight, hearing, taste, smell, touch).

> Her face was filled with grooves so deep that it was difficult to determine the exact position of her eyes. Her mouth was merely another line, longer and straighter than others. Her nose was flat against her face, protruding no more than her cheek bones and less than her chin. She was not yet fifty. To say that her life had been hard would be an understatement.

The appeal to the reader's sense of sight illustrates the concluding general statement.

3. *Example* illustrates a point by offering a single, specific instance to represent a general situation.

> "Why, I could drive all day and never reach the end of my property," the large man said as he stared down at his listener. Tilting his head to one side, the smaller man replied, "I know just what you mean. I once had a car like that myself!" When my English teacher told that story, I finally understood the difference between *exaggeration* and *understatement.*

The specific example makes clear to both the writer and reader the difference in the terms.

4. *Definition* is a form of classification that illustrates a point by separating a term from other members of its class.

> To the average person, the word *bug* includes all insects, and *insects* includes spiders and centipedes. To laypeople, all are bugs. But that classification is backward. Centipedes, spiders, insects, and bugs all belong to a single group, the phylum *arthropods.* And centipedes and spiders, in fact, are not even insects. Insects have only six legs. Spiders have eight—two too many to qualify. Centipedes have far too many, although not one hundred as their name implies. Where then do bugs belong? All bugs are insects, but not all insects are bugs. Bugs are insects of the order *Hemiptera,* whose heads have structures for piercing and sucking. It is this quality that often makes them so irritating to humans and that causes us to use the word *bug* as a verb when someone bothers us. For example, as a biology major, it *bugs* me when people don't care about precise terminology.

The writer helps readers understand why a particular term transferred its meaning by attributing qualities to it that are not shared by terms many think are similar to it.

5. *Process* illustrates a point by tracing or discussing the steps of an action or a procedure.

> Dental hygiene is much more complex than it used to be. Dentists used to tell us to brush after every meal, but they knew that most of us brush only in the morning or before we go to bed. But now we must floss daily, actually brush after we eat—not just after meals. And to make matters worse, we must brush in a particular way—along the gum line, using short strokes and a soft-bristled brush. We are also told to use a fluoride rinse if our drinking water is untreated.

Tracing the steps in this process illustrates the opening topic sentence.

6. *Cause and effect* illustrates a point by demonstrating the consequences or effects of an act.

> For years Americans have thought of aerosol containers as a sign of our high standard of living. We have sprayed our hair to keep it neat and our bodies to keep them clean. We have simplified the task of painting by spraying rather than by brushing. And we have complicated the process of applying a few drops of oil with aerosol sprays. Ironically, this sign of civilization might result in depletion of the ozone layer and a subsequent increase in skin cancer and a warming of the earth's atmosphere. In the long run, the picture is even more bleak. If the ozone layer continues to disintegrate, civilization itself is in jeopardy. What once was seen as a luxury must now be seen for the hazard it is.

The cause and effect relationship reveals the danger that the writer wishes to present.

7. *Classification* illustrates a point by dividing a subject into components according to specific criteria designed to *distinguish* the components from one another. Classification emphasizes the *difference* of the parts.

> A successful football team must have strong offensive and defensive units. The so-called skilled positions on the offense usually receive the most attention—the quarterback, the running backs, and the receivers. But they won't look very good if the team doesn't have a strong offensive line. The defensive linemen generally get more credit than offensive linemen, prob-

ably because their skills are often highlighted by individual plays. With the emphasis today on the passing game, the defensive backfield often gets credit for stopping the opponents or blame for letting them score.

Although a single entity, a team is composed of separable parts. The classification into the offensive and defensive units and subclassification into the backs and linemen make the whole understandable. When classifying, writers must be certain not to have overlapping categories. An invalid classification of a football team would be to say it is composed of an offense, a defense, and talented players. Both the offense and defense of a successful team have talented players.

8. *Analysis* illustrates a point by dividing a subject into components in order to understand the *relationship* of the parts to each other. Whereas classification emphasizes the distinctiveness of parts, analysis focuses on their relatedness.

> *Lethal Weapon* was one of the best paired cop movies to appear in many years. Unlike so many movies of this kind, both partners were likeable, fully developed characters. Danny Glover, the actor playing the older detective, was a family man and a caring human being. Mel Gibson, the younger cop, was not just a matinee idol: the character he portrayed had genuine problems with which the audience could identify; his wife had died, and he couldn't accept the loss. The plot was also very involving and didn't rely solely on chase scenes, violence, or sex to keep the viewer interested.

The writer explains how the parts of the film contribute to its total effect.

9. *Comparison and contrast* illustrate a point by examining the similarities and the differences between two or more subjects.

> I hate it when a guy refers to me as a chick. Think about it! A chick is a baby chicken. Chickens are noted for being stupid. But that's not the main problem. Chicks are totally dependent and helpless. They are also soft and cuddly. They offer physical pleasure, not intelligence and good conversation. Who respects a chick? But even if I accept the term as a compliment, as many guys intend, it falls short. A chick is cute, not beautiful, just cute. Some compliment. And what must it say about a guy who wants a girl to be like a chick? Does he have any self-confidence? Does he care for her as a person? Any guy who calls a girl a chick is a real turkey!

The comparison reveals what the writer finds to be an offensive or, at best, unthinking attitude by some males.

Name ______________________ Score ______________

Exercise 6a–6i Full development

1. Write an introductory paragraph in which you introduce the thesis by *narrating* a story, an anecdote, from your experience.

2. Write a *descriptive* paragraph in which you appeal to at least three of the five senses. Do not identify by name the object or the experience you are describing. Instead, let the details of your description make it evident to your reader.

3. Write a paragraph in which you relate one actual *example* of why you like or dislike a particular restaurant that you frequently eat at or a store that you often shop in.

4. Write a paragraph in which you *define* a term that you are familiar with but that can be confused with similar terms (e.g., New Wave music as opposed to rock music, a nerd as opposed to a conscientious student, a jock as opposed to a student athlete).

5. Write a paragraph in which you relate a *process*, the steps you regularly follow in doing a specific action well—for example, parallel parking, preparing a meal, or studying for an exam.

6. Write a paragraph in which you discuss an action (a *cause*) and its *effects*, such as staying up all night when you must work the next day, exercising regularly, or listening to a style of music.

Name ______________________________

Exercise 6a–6i (continued)

7. Write a paragraph in which you *classify* the members of a group that you are familiar with. Make clear how the categories are distinct, and be careful that they don't overlap.

8. *Analyze* why you prefer a specific television series, such as *Cheers, All My Children, Designing Women,* or *The Cosby Show.*

9. Write a paragraph in which you *compare* and/or *contrast* your preference of one musical group over another, one brand of clothing or cosmetics over another, or college over high school (or vice versa).

10. Write a paragraph in which you help your reader understand something that you know well but the reader is not familiar with by *comparing* it to something familiar to the reader. For example, explain how a job you have had as a life guard was like a paid vacation (if you enjoyed it) or like being a zoo keeper (if you did not enjoy it).

6j Combine paragraph patterns.

Skimpy paragraphs can be expanded and developed through a combination of the conventional patterns. Make sure that the combination illustrates a point rather than merely fills space.

Common Problems

Conventional patterns that seem more important than the point they are intended to illustrate sometimes pad the paragraph and suggest the writer's insincerity.

Example

The following paragraphs combine several conventional patterns.

> When I was seven or eight, my mother often took my next door neighbors and me to the Museum of Science and Industry. One of the rules was that we had to stay with her until we reached the entrance, but once inside, she let us run ahead. She had no fear for our safety or that we would get lost. She always knew where we would be—at the train exhibit, playing in the cabin of an actual full-sized engine and looking over at the electric model trains as they roared through the miniature countryside. I loved the feel of the cold metal controls. And I remember smelling the coal (there was no coal, and I knew it even then, but I smelled it nonetheless) and listening to the whistle, or at least to the sound of the whistle that I made or that came from the Lionel models. That was how we began many pleasant trips to the museum. As I got older, though, the museum lost its appeal, I think because I associated it with "kid stuff."
>
> But when I went back last summer with two friends, not with my mother this time, I realized how much I had missed by staying away so long. The trains still held their fascination, but for different reasons. I realized how much technology had advanced and regretted that trains seem to be on the decline in the United States. I still enjoyed the model trains, but I was more aware of the workmanship than I had been. And I still used my imagination, but not to be the engineer. I imagined how it must have been for people to travel across the country in those old trains, how excited they must have been. And, yes, I still smelled the coal.

narration

description

analysis

comparison and contrast

cause and effect (effect of the visits)

Name ______________________________ Score ______________

Exercise 6j Combination of patterns

1. Examine a feature story in a magazine, such as *Atlantic*, *Ms.*, or *Harper's*, and list the different patterns of development you find.

2. Examine an early draft of one of your own essays and list the patterns of development that you used in your paragraphs.

3. Write two paragraphs on the same subject. In the first, develop the paragraph using at least three conventional patterns. In the second, rewrite the first paragraph using three different conventional patterns as a means of development.

CHAPTER 7

Improving Paragraph Style

7a Write in a clear style.

Natural diction (the choice of words and how they are put together), neither too formal nor too informal, creates the most effective style. Such diction reflects the writer's age and educational level and varies according to the purpose, the subject, and the audience. Using the active voice and strong verbs helps achieve a clear, natural voice.

Common problems

Unnatural diction usually leads to an inconsistent and imprecise style and an insincere tone. Elevated diction seems artificial, and extreme informality implies lack of seriousness.

Examples

Methods of maintaining natural diction are as follows:

1. Keep the diction appropriate for the subject, audience, and purpose.

> John, the concert was excellent.

Appropriate to all general readers, the name is specific, and the adjective is neither informal nor stilted.

> Hey, man! The concert was a blast.

This diction is appropriate only for an informal letter to a close friend of a similar age.

> Computers with two-disk drive provide greater flexibility and capacity than those with single-disk drive. If one drive is a hard disk, the computer is even faster and with a far greater capacity.

This is diction for an audience familiar with computers. The third person is also appropriate for academic writing.

2. Prefer the active voice.

PASSIVE: The mayor *was elected* by the people of New York.
ACTIVE: The people of New York *elected* the mayor.

PASSIVE: Information *was given* to the students about successfully taking essay exams.
ACTIVE: The guidance counselor *gave* the students information about successfully taking essay exams.
OR
ACTIVE: The guidance counselor *informed* the students about successfully taking essay exams.

The first passive sentence de-emphasizes the actor, the people of New York, and is lengthier than the sentence in active voice. The second passive sentence omits the actor completely, making the sentence abstract, a more serious stylistic problem than in the first sentence. The revised versions eliminate a nominalization ("information"), reduce the wordiness, and use more vivid verbs.

3. Eliminate wordy or redundant phrases.

   WORDY: *In my opinion,* students benefit from a summer break.
   CONCISE: Students benefit from a summer break.

   WORDY: The off-year elections will be a *horrible* catastrophe for the incumbent party.
   CONCISE: The off-year elections will be a catastrophe for the incumbent party.

Readers recognize that the ideas writers express are their opinions and thoughts. Such phrases are necessary only in contexts where the writer's position is distinct from another position in the essay. A catastrophe is, by its nature, horrible, and the term is not needed to emphasize that quality.

Name ______________________ Score ______________

Exercise 7a Combination of patterns

1. In the following sentences, indicate whether the diction is appropriate for the subject and the probable audience:
   a. Whether evolution and natural selection are both theories or whether evolution is a fact and natural selection a theory are questions which shall be debated well into the twenty-first century.

   b. Because the San Francisco 49ers have won more games than any other team in the last decade and because their coach has been an exemplary figure in the sport, many have said it merits the title "America's team."

   c. It seems to me the deficit is a big problem. We'll be paying it off until all those of my generation are over the hill. And that will cause the whole country a lot of problems.

   d. One of my greatest moments in high school occurred when I was a senior and was voted class president. I didn't think that I would win because my opponent belonged to the "in" crowd, and I wasn't a part of any single group. Maybe that was why I won; some people in each group voted for me.

   e. A discovery had been made that there was a need for seating enhancement in the stadium due to pre-game booster ticket request information.

2. Change the following sentences into active voice. Supply an actor when necessary.
   a. Susan was called on by her teacher to answer five questions.

   b. No explanation of why she broke up with Ken was given by Barbie.

   c. Don't worry; the research project will be done by the end of the semester.

   d. When Joe's father arrived home, the car had been washed and polished.

   e. Social Security benefits have been cut.

f. Mistakes were made.

g. The course was designed to challenge even the most skilled golfer.

h. To evaluate the recent movies about Viet Nam, the history of the war must be examined.

i. The senator said that the road project was canceled.

j. This set of exercises is done.

3. Cross out the unnecessary phrases in the following sentences. If you think a sentence is correct, explain why.
   a. In my opinion, the administration needs to make more parking spots readily available to students.

   b. Many commentators think Gorbachev has gone to the far extreme, but I think he is the best hope for the Soviet Union.

   c. If we want coffee, downstairs is a cafeteria where we can buy it.

   d. To me the sun is the basic source of energy in most plants.

   e. *Bicameral* means that a legislative body has two separate chambers, in the United States, a House and a Senate.

Name ______________________________

Exercise 7a (continued)

4. Using a natural style, revise the following sentences by combining sentences and editing to create a coherent paragraph that builds to the most emphatic point, a point which you create. Be sure your audience understands your purpose.
   a. Three scoops of ice cream were in the bowl.
   b. A banana was sliced lengthwise.
   c. Vanilla wafers lined the edge of the dish.
   d. The dish was long and shallow.
   e. One scoop of ice cream was strawberry.
   f. A cherry was on top of each scoop of ice cream.
   g. Chocolate syrup oozed over one scoop of ice cream.
   h. Whipped cream was on top of the ice cream.
   i. One scoop of ice cream was vanilla.
   j. Butterscotch syrup flowed over one scoop of ice cream.
   k. One scoop of ice cream was chocolate.
   l. A tiny paper umbrella was sticking in one scoop of ice cream.
   m. Chocolate shavings were on the whipped cream.
   n. The umbrella was red, yellow, and blue.

7b The purpose determines style.

Because diction and other conventions vary depending on the goal, writers must determine whether they wish to focus on their own thoughts, explain a subject, or persuade readers of a particular position.

Common Problems

An unclear purpose, as reflected in inappropriate diction, point of view, and other conventions, often confuses readers.

Examples

Expressive writing focuses on the writer's thoughts and feelings, is usually written in the first person, and uses personal anecdotes:

> I usually enjoy our local museum, but I had an eerie feeling on my last visit. While browsing around, I discovered an exhibit I had not seen before, a model of a nineteenth-century doctor's office. It was in a dark corner of a large room and was easy to pass over. As I looked at the doctor examining his patient on a wooden bench, my attention turned to the wall behind him. There I saw hammers, chisels, saws, and one instrument resembling a prying bar. Then I realized why I had that eerie feeling. The office seemed far more like an amateur carpenter's shop than a place where people went to be healed.

While the paragraph describes a particular place, it emphasizes the writer's response to that place.

Explanatory writing focuses on a subject other than the writer to clarify that subject for the reader. Third person, rather than first, predominates.

> Dinosaurs are still alive. Traditional paleoanthropology holds that these giant creatures became extinct 65 million years ago and that human beings did not arrive on the scene until well after the last of the dinosaurs had long vanished from the earth. That theory has now been challenged, and the new theory will probably win out. Robert Bakker, a paleontologist at the University of Colorado, is one of the leading proponents of a controversial theory which asserts that dinosaurs were not the slow, cold-blooded beasts we have all been taught about. Rather, they were fast-moving, warm-blooded animals having little in common with today's reptiles, the animals that researchers have used in the past as their models for understanding dinosaurs.
>
> If Bakker is correct, not only will scientists have to re-evaluate the conclusions they have drawn over the past hundred years, they will also have to accept that dinosaurs are alive today. Where are these dinosaurs? Everywhere. They are birds!

These paragraphs focus entirely on the subject, and while the ideas are controversial, the writer tries strictly to inform, not persuade.

Persuasive writing seeks to change the reader's position or opinion. It makes and defends assertions. Third person dominates although first person occurs as well:

> If movie and television violence makes children more aggressive, it stands to reason that violence has the same effect on adults. One example illustrates my point. Last Friday, a friend, Tim, asked me to see a video, *Tango and Cash.* Tim told me it would be fun—a good escapist movie with clever dialogue. In the opening scene, though, I saw two men go through the windshield of their truck and fall at the feet of their captor, Ray Tango, played by Sylvester Stallone. In real life, both men would have been killed instantly by such trauma. But these two were only mildly shaken up, still able to hurl expletives at Stallone.
>
> From that point on the movie went downhill. Numerous people were shot to death, others were hurled from balconies, and one nasty villain was killed by a grenade dropped in his trousers by Cash, played by Kurt Russell. Our heroes received enough beatings to kill them ten times over; they were lowered into a tank of water while a cretin touched it with a live wire—not even electrocution phased them.

> What made these actions especially frightening was my friends' (three others joined us at Tim's) response to them. They laughed like children at a cartoon show. Later, they even talked about the more gruesome scenes. It made me wonder what might have happened if I had seen the movie at a theater where the audience was more unbalanced than my friends. It's scary to think about: even a slight kick in the face hurts me.

These paragraphs offer specific details, but they have been chosen to move the audience to a particular position.

Name ______________________________ Score ______________

Exercise 7b Purpose

1. Write an *expressive* paragraph in which you explore your feelings about a particular activity you frequently engage in (getting up early, driving to school, visiting a particular place). Focus on feelings rather than just describing the activity. Your goal is simply to provide insight into your personality and beliefs.

2. Write an *explanatory* paragraph describing a particular school policy (required courses, parking, grading). Provide the necessary details, but exclude your position on the policy.

3. Write a paragraph in which you *persuade* readers that the policy in exercise 2 is beneficial or needs changing.

4. Write a paragraph in which you describe the tasks you must do or have done at a job you hold or have held. To help the reader visualize what you had to do, decide whether you are simply explaining your job or trying to persuade your reader of something.

5. Write an expressive paragraph in which you explore your feelings about the duties you discussed in exercise 4.

7c The audience determines style.

Whether discussing themselves, informing, or persuading, writers must adapt techniques to a particular audience.

Common Problems

Ignoring the audience usually means that the writer omits necessary details, includes unnecessary information, or uses an inappropriate tone.

Examples

The following paragraph, which discusses attitudes toward the poor, assumes the reader has traditional American values and a shared ethical belief. The use of *we* assumes that the audience probably shares the negative attitudes.

> Are we our brother's keeper? Do we want to be? Most of us think we are supposed to be, but we don't behave that way. Some of our reasons for not helping others are pretty good. We don't want to give handouts to people who really aren't in need because we don't like being cheated. And we know we can't help all those in need, so we help no one. But the problem is deeper than that. We seem to believe that helping people is not really in their own best interest. Helping people will make them lazy and unable to help themselves. We also admire people who make it without anyone's help. That's the American Dream—hard work, wealth, and happiness. But if we admire those who make it on their own, we seem to have disdain for those who fail, especially for those who have failed so often that they no longer try. When we see such people on the street, we turn away. Do we turn because we think they are different from us? Or is it the more frightening possibility that we realize how similar to us they are? Are we our brother's keeper? Do we want to be?

If the point of view changes to second person and some phrasing is revised, the writer loses audience sympathy:

> Are you really your brother's keeper? Do you want to be? I am certain most of you *say* you are, but you sure don't behave that way. Some of your reasons for not helping others almost sound logical. You don't want to give handouts to people who really aren't in need because you don't like being cheated. And you can't help all those in need, so no one gets any. Sounds reasonable. But the problem is deeper than that. You act as if helping people is not really in their own best interests. Helping people, you seem to say, will make them lazy and unable to help themselves. And isn't part of the problem that you also admire people who make it without anyone's help? That's the American Dream—hard work, wealth, and happiness. To give to those people would be un-American. And if you admire those who make it on their own, how can you help not having outright disdain for those who fail, especially for those who have failed so often that they no longer try? When you see such people on the street, you probably turn away. Do you turn because you think they are different from you? Or is it the more frightening possibility that you realize how similar to you they are? Are you your brother's keeper? Do you want to be?

The second-person point of view, the writer's assumed superiority to the audience, and sarcastic phrases are all offensive. The information in the two paragraphs is the same, but the effect on an audience differs greatly.

Name ______________________ Score ______________

Exercise 7c Audience

1. Compose two paragraphs explaining how you managed to drive a car into a telephone pole when it was the only car on the street, the weather was excellent, and the car was in perfect mechanical condition. The audience for your first paragraph is a close friend with a history of automobile accidents; the audience for your second paragraph is the parent (or spouse or significant other) who owns the car.

   a.

   b.

2. Revise a letter to the editor or one of your essays so that the audience differs significantly from the one to whom the piece is presently addressed.
3. On separate pages, write two letters explaining your decision to change your major from business to environmental studies. The first letter is to your parents who have always wanted you to enter the family business, a small department store. The second letter is to your brother (or sister) whom your parents had similar plans for but who went into social work instead.

7d Use rhetorical schemes to enhance paragraph style.

Rhetorical devices, which are listed below, help capture and maintain the reader's interest.

Common Problems

Avoiding rhetorical devices makes writing bland and uninteresting.

Examples

The following devices strengthen style:

1. ***Alliteration*** (repeated consonant sounds)

> Walking on a *w*indy day a*w*aken*s* the *b*ody and the mind. A *b*ri*s*k *b*ree*z*e quite literally in*s*pire*s* u*s*. Our *b*lood cour*s*e*s* through our *b*odie*s* and give*s* a rush of energy. *F*ew *f*ears can *s*urvive the on*s*laught of a fall breeze.

The repetition of the *w, s, b, z,* and *f* sounds moves the reader along quickly and reinforces the idea of walking in the wind.

2. ***Rhythm and cadence***

> I have been bitten and stung more times in the last two days than I have in the previous eighteen years of my life. I have eaten half raw chicken. I have eaten a baked potato with a center which hadn't even begun to cook. I have worn wet socks for an entire day. I have worn clothes that were so dirty I would hesitate to take them to a laundromat. I have not washed my face or combed my hair in two days. I have not seen a bathroom in three days. And you have the nerve to ask if I enjoyed my first camping trip!

The repetition of key phrases establishes a rhythm that mounts to the climactic last sentence. Variation in the use of stylistic devices is usually the most effective means of maintaining a pleasing rhythm. Continuous short, choppy sentences or long, wordy ones generally disrupt sentence rhythm.

3. ***Repetition***

> Do we have the right to hurt others? No. We can protect ourselves, and that may involve hurting others. But we are merely preventing someone from hurting others—us. Do we have the right to hurt ourselves? Still no. All people have rights, and we can't take away those rights even from ourselves. Should we have the right to smoke? Most emphatically no! The evidence is overwhelming that smoking hurts both smoker and nonsmoker alike. It should therefore be made illegal.

The repeated questions and answers establish a rhythm that builds to the writer's conclusion. Note that the answers to the questions are essential, not just for the rhythm but because not all readers would answer them as the writer would. Were the writer to include others' opinions as well, the effect of the paragraph would be destroyed.

4. ***The structured series***

> The people in Eastern Europe want freedom. They do not want repression. The people in the United States want the same. The people of Eastern Europe want affordable housing. They do not want to spend most of their earnings for subsidized housing or to live in boxes. Those of us in the United States want that too. The people of Eastern Europe want access to meaningful jobs which pay a decent wage. They do not want to live on welfare or to do busy work for sustenance wages. We want that too. The people of Eastern Europe want food to be available at a reasonable price. They don't want to wait in lines for handouts or have quality food available only to the privileged. The people of Eastern Europe want free access to quality consumer

goods. They don't want poorly made goods for themselves and quality goods only for the wealthy. We want that too. Because we understand that the desires and dreams of those in Eastern Europe are the same as our own, and because we are willing to give our tax dollars to them, we should be equally willing to give our tax dollars to the homeless in the United States.

The repeated positive and negative sentences comparing two groups create an expectation, which contrasts with the concluding sentence and thus emphasizes it.

5. ***Dialogue***

"Don't you ever go out on that ice. I don't care how cold it is or how long it's been frozen. Lake Michigan never freezes completely, and if you fall through, you'll be dead in a minute!" When I was growing up in Chicago, I heard that statement, or variations of it, every winter. Any time my friends and I were dressed for playing outside, one of our mothers would deliver that threat. If we weren't thinking or if we wanted to assert our manhood (if boys not old enough to be Boy Scouts can assert manhood), we would make a mistake in the way we answered. Then we were in danger of being grounded unless we backed down sufficiently:

"Yesss, Mom."

"Don't use that tone with me, young man."

"I didn't say anything."

"You don't have to, and don't you raise your voice. In one minute, you're not going anywhere."

Pause.

"I'm sorry, Mom. I know its dangerous. I only said it that way because I know I'm not supposed to play on the lake. But I'd never do that—honest."

"That's more like it. Now run along, and be home in time to change clothes before dinner."

Then I'd run down to the lake and play cops and robbers on the ice. The curls of the frozen waves were great places to hide. And if I were careful, I could sneak up on one of my "enemies" and shoot him with my BB gun before he had a chance to return fire.

"Young man, don't you ever point that gun at a living thing, not even at a sparrow."

But that's another story.

Including the exact words of a speaker other than the writer varies the discourse from direct to indirect and maintains reader interest.

6. ***Special word forms***

"Fffffftt. Fffffftt. Kuuwang. Thwock." No, I didn't misplace my fingers on the keyboard. Those are the sounds of Robin Williams telling what a cowboy hears as two arrows zoom past him followed by the sound of his own bullet missing the Indian and ricocheting off a rock before the third arrow hits the cowboy in the shoulder.

The *onomatopoetic* words attract the reader's attention.

He was a legend in his own mind.

The saying "legend in his own time" reveals the person's arrogance and creates a bond with readers who recognize the *play on words.*

Because they disagreed with his ruling, the *stupidents* threw bottles at the referee.

A similar bond is created through the *blend* of "stupid" and "student" to indicate disapproval of the students' action. (Varying syntax is not always successful and should be used only sparingly.)

Name ______________________ Score ______________

Exercise 7d Rhetorical schemes

1. Write a paragraph in which you create a particular mood—a restful day at the beach, a noisy party—and reinforce that mood through *alliteration.*

2. Using the words to a song that you are familiar with, paraphrase the action creating *rhythm and cadence* in your prose. You may wish to use some lines of the song in your paragraph.

3. Create a paragraph in which you *repeat* a word or phrase to emphasize a point. You may wish to describe aspects of a problem and at intervals repeat a question to guide readers. Or you may wish to repeat a word or phrase that assumes a different meaning as the paragraph progresses.

4. Develop a paragraph that includes both sides of an argument in a *structured series* in order to build to a statement of your position. Choose a controversial issue in which no one answer has been universally accepted, such as smoking in public, registering hand guns, or legalizing drugs.

5. Using the ideas in the paragraph below, compose a paragraph that varies the language through *direct discourse* (quotations). Include dialogue that might occur if you were talking to your child about the career to which he or she might aspire:

   When we hear stories on television about people growing up in the 1930s through the 1950s, people like the Waltons or the Cunninghams of *Happy Days,* we often hear what little boys and girls wanted to be when they grew up. Little boys wanted to be firemen or policemen, or if they had ambition they wanted to be doctors. Little girls wanted to be secretaries or nurses; the ambitious ones, dancers or teachers.

6. Develop a paragraph describing an event you witnessed—a concert, a basketball game, a birthday party—and create *new words* to convey your emotional or sensory experience. Avoid common terms, such as "Wow," "Bang," or "Zap."

Name ______________________________

Exercise 7d (continued)

7. By altering an existing saying, by using standard terms in different ways, or by combining standard words to create new words, generate five sentences that attract reader attention.

   a.

   b.

   c.

   d.

   e.

PART

3

Sentences

CHAPTER 8

Sentence Coordination

8a Use coordination to form compound sentences.

A compound sentence joins two or more independent clauses (see chapter **23**). The clauses are grammatically equal, but to indicate different relationships between the clauses, they may be joined in four ways: by a comma and a coordinating conjunction, by a semicolon alone, by a semicolon and a conjunctive adverb, or by a colon.

Common Problems

Overpunctuation or underpunctuation of coordinate sentences can confuse readers. Overpunctuation occurs when one of the four conventional methods joins a sentence and a *dependent* element or joins parts of a phrase or clause. Also sometimes overpunctuated are sentences joined by a semicolon or a colon (instead of just a comma) and a coordinating conjunction. Underpunctuation occurs when a coordinating conjunction alone joins sentences (surprising readers with a second clause), a comma alone, or a comma and a conjunctive adverb (creating a *comma splice* in both cases, chapter **25**,) or when sentences are connected with no punctuation (resulting in a *fused sentence,* see chapter **25**).

Examples

The four conventional methods of punctuating compound sentences are provided below:

1. Join dependent clauses with a comma and a coordinating conjunction (*and, but, or, nor, for, so, yet*).

   Gene shot the ball in a high arc, **and** it swished through the hoop.

   Outside, the house was unkempt, **yet** the inside was beautiful.

2. Indicate a close relationship between independent clauses with a semicolon alone.

   Politicians like wielding power; they also like notoriety. [a similarity]

   We like cats for their independence; we like dogs for their dependence. [a contrast]

3. Use a semicolon and a conjunctive adverb (see section **20e**) to join sentences and indicate a particular relationship.

   Punctuating effectively is a complex skill; **however,** the individual rules are not. [contrast]

   OR

   Punctuating effectively is a complex skill; the individual rules, **however,** are not. [contrast]

Buffy wishes to be a brain surgeon; **consequently,** she took science courses in high school. [cause and effect]

OR

Buffy wishes to be a brain surgeon; she, **consequently,** took science courses in high school. [cause and effect]

4. Use a colon between independent clauses when the second clause amplifies or explains the first clause.

Steffi Graf is a great tennis player: her mental toughness, devastating serve, and incredible speed make her a formidable opponent.

Name ______________________________ Score ______________

Exercise 8a Compound sentences

1. In the following sentences, place a comma and a coordinating conjunction when necessary. If a sentence is correct as shown, place a *C* before the sentence. If a sentence requires a comma, include the comma and circle it. If a comma should be omitted, draw an *X* through the comma, and circle it.

   a. Little Bo Peep has lost her sheep, and doesn't know where to find them.

   b. Everyone likes Charlie for he is a jolly good fellow.

   c. James will not go to Memphis with us, nor will he go as far as St. Louis.

   d. I really liked *Tom Sawyer,* but not *Huck Finn.*

   e. Horace ordered pizza for the second night in a row but that's all right with me.

   f. Harold gave his copy of *Hamlet* to Raymond, and Arnold.

   g. Vincent can go to college, or he can join the Marines.

   h. Open the apartment door and get out of my way!

   i. Wendy borrowed Jill's hair dryer, for her own was broken.

   j. After I finish studying, and after I finish cleaning my room, we can go to the movie.

2. Rewrite sentences *e* and *h* in exercise 1 and join them with a semicolon and a conjunctive adverb. Then rewrite those two sentences embedding the conjunctive adverb in the second sentence.

   a.

   b.

   c.

   d.

3. Rewrite sentences *c* and *d* in exercise 1 so that a semicolon joins them effectively.

   a.

   b.

4. Which of the three sentences in exercise 1 could be joined with a colon? In each case, explain why.
   a.

   b.

   c.

5. Rewrite the following sentence using a comma and the appropriate coordinating conjunction:

   Julie liked the novel *The Color Purple*; she did not, however, like the movie version.

8b–8c Use parallel constructions and repetitions to strengthen and clarify coordinate ideas.

As sentences increase in length, repeating words and grammatical structures makes the sentences easier to understand and more fluent.

Common Problems

An essay may seem rambling or confused if the relationship among the parts is not reinforced through the repetition of key words or grammatical structures.

Examples

The role of symmetrical structures is indicated in the examples below:

Hazel rode the bus *to* Minneapolis, *to* St. Paul, and *to* Duluth.

Repeating the word *to* makes clear that Hazel rode the bus to three rather than to two places.

Frank is a friend *whom* Ed depended upon for support *but who* deserted him when it benefited him.

Without the *who,* readers might erroneously think Ed deserted Frank.

Note that *and/but, who/whom,* and *and/but which* are only idiomatic if a *who/whom* or *what* clause appears earlier in the sentence. Otherwise, use only *who/whom* or *which* without *and.*

For it to serve the needs of its citizens, *for it to merit* the respect of other nations, and *for it to continue* to exist, a democracy must ensure that its citizens have free access to information.

Repeating the phrase form makes each element equally important.

Because he had a pleasant personality, because he was a good sport, and because he owned the only bat and ball, our team will miss Jim very much.

The dependent clauses mount to an anticlimax.

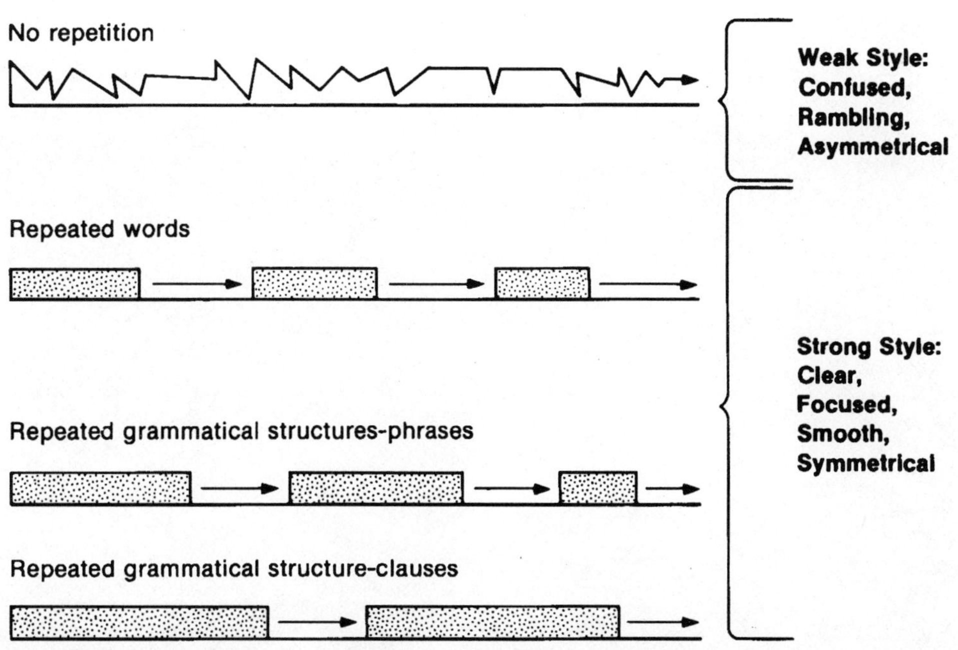

Name ______________________________ Score ______________

Exercise 8b–8c Parallel constructions, repetition

1. Revise the following sentences by repeating a word, phrase, clause, or grammatical structure to create the meaning or emphasis indicated in parentheses.
   a. History regards Margaret Sanger as a leader of a major movement and women's rights activist. (Make clear that history regards Sanger as a leader and activist.)

   b. Mark Twain advocated both the fair treatment and respect of African Americans and use of dialect to reveal character in fiction. (Make clear that Twain is supporting two rather than three qualities in fiction.)

   c. U2 is a group which has become very popular but explicitly supports a specific social agenda. (Make clear the contrasting clauses.)

   d. A racing bike should be lightweight. It should not be too big for the rider to control. It should not be fragile. It should be as large as possible. It need not cost the buyer a fortune. It should use quality parts. (Balance the contrasting sentences.)

   e. Americans should buy American cars. Buying them increases the jobs in the United States. Buying them reduces the United States' dependence on foreign countries. Buying them instills pride in American citizens. (Combine the four sentences into one with parallel grammatical structures which explain why Americans should buy American cars.)

2. Create five sentences using the parallel structures suggested to strengthen coordinate ideas.
   a. Repeat a single word:

   b. Use either the *who/and who(m)*, *which/and which*, or *who/but who(m)* structure:

   c. Use a series of phrases:

   d. Use a series of dependent clauses:

   e. Use a series of independent clauses (short sentences):

CHAPTER 9

Sentence Subordination

9a Subordinate less important ideas.

Complex sentences emphasize independent clauses by making other clauses dependent. Subordinating ideas makes the author's position clear.

Common Problems

Simple and compound sentences equalize ideas. Their frequent use fails to communicate the proper emphasis and becomes boring.

Examples

The following sentences express two ideas of equal importance:

The hurricane destroyed whole sections of Charleston. Very few people died.

Because the *first* clause is dependent, the following sentence emphasizes the *second,* the independent clause:

Although the hurricane destroyed whole sections of Charleston, very few people died.

Because the *second* clause is dependent, the following sentence emphasizes the *first* clause, which is independent:

The hurricane destroyed whole sections of Charleston, although very few people died.

A dependent clause can begin a sentence, end it, or even be embedded within the independent clause.

The hurricane, in which very few people died, destroyed whole sections of Charleston.

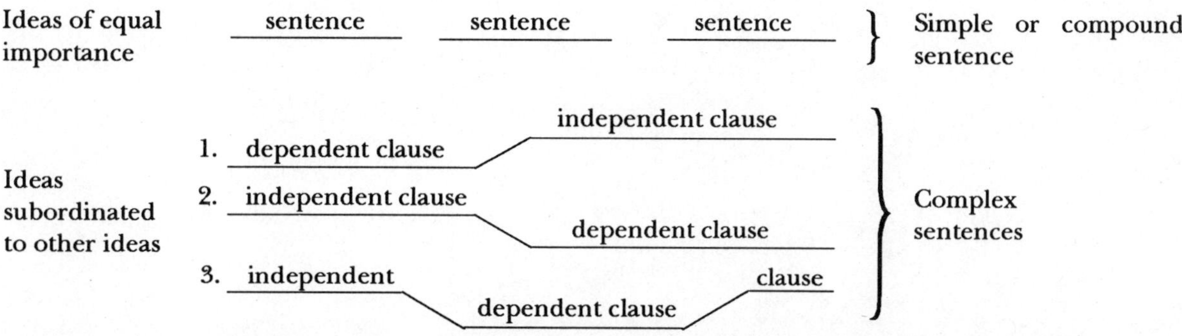

Name ______________________________ Score ______________

Exercise 9a Subordination

Subordinate one of the following pairs of sentences to emphasize a particular point. Explain the emphasis you have created. Then reverse the procedure and create another sentence that emphasizes the other clause. Explain the emphasis you have created.

1. President Bush was extremely popular after his first year in office. The American people approved of the invasion of Panama.

   Version 1:

   Explanation:

   Version 2:

   Explanation:

2. The population of the Sun Belt is growing. Industries are failing in many Northern cities.

   Version 1:

   Explanation:

   Version 2:

   Explanation:

3. Mike Tyson was more successful in the ring than in his personal life. The heavyweight division lacked serious challengers for the title.

   Version 1:

   Explanation:

Version 2:

Explanation:

4. The Superbowl rarely lives up to the pregame hype. The playoff system does not produce the two best teams in the NFL.
   Version 1:

   Explanation:

   Version 2:

   Explanation:

5. The ACLU protects First Amendment rights. Many Americans object to the ACLU.
   Version 1:

   Explanation:

   Version 2:

   Explanation:

9b Use the subordinating conjunctions.

Subordinating conjunctions connect a dependent clause (the lesser idea) to an independent clause (the greater idea).

The subordinating conjunction can introduce an *adverb* clause, which modifies a verb, noun, an adjective, or another adverb. Or it can introduce an *adjective* clause, which modifies a noun or a pronoun, in the form of a *relative pronoun.*

Common Problems

If writers are unfamiliar with subordination, they may fail to make relationships clear and the writing style fluent.

Examples

The subordinating conjunctions listed below can be used to indicate important transitions and relationships.

Subordinating Conjunctions (Adverbial)	Relative Pronouns (Adjectival)
after	that
although	which
as	who
as if	whom
because	whoever
before	whomever
if	whose
since	
so that	
unless	
until	
when	
whenever	
where	
whether	

More Precise	More Casual or Ambiguous
because (causation)	since, after, as (time and causation)
although (contrast)	while (time and contrast)
as (a conjunction)	like (a preposition)
who (to refer to living creatures)	that
whom (for the object of a verb)	who (for the object of the verb—many consider this usage of *who* unacceptable.)

Since the sun has set, the temperature *has dropped* twenty degrees.

The adverbial clause tells *when* the temperature dropped and thus modifies the verb phrase *has dropped.* If the writer intends, instead, to tell *why* the temperature dropped the more appropriate phrasing is *Because the sun has set.*

The *people who live down the road* own a new Cadillac.

The adjectival clause describes the noun *people,* the subject of the sentence. If the noun had named an inanimate object instead of a living creature, the relative pronoun *which* would replace *who:* "The house *which* is located at the end of the road belongs to the Sosnowskis."

The use of *who* or *whom* depends on whether the word is used as a subject or object (see **28g**):

The man *who* shot the rabbit was very happy.

(*Who* substitutes for the implied *subject [the man]* in the clause "who shot the rabbit.")

The man *whom* I saw shoot the rabbit was very happy.

(*Whom* substitutes for the implied *object* in the clause "I saw [him] shoot the rabbit.")

Note: Although informally many subordinating conjunctions are synonymous, writers should choose conjunctions carefully to convey precise meaning.

Name ______________________ Score ______________

Exercise 9b Subordinating conjunctions, relative pronouns

1. Join the following sentences with subordinating conjunctions.
   Revise the sentences to remove any repetition.
   a. Indicate a contrast.
      Annie had dated Fred for three years. She disliked his table manners.
   b. Indicate a time relationship.
      The students attended the dance. The football game was over.
   c. Indicate causation.
      Led Zepplin performed at the hotel. The hotel had standing room only.
   d. Indicate a condition.
      Francie could go to the pizza parlor. Bill went to the pizza parlor.
   e. Indicate a time relationship.
      Buffy's mother was waiting at the door. Buffy came home at 4:30 a.m.
2. Join the following sentences with relative pronouns.
   a. The village was very scenic. The village had cobblestone streets.
   b. The cat loved to catch mice. The cat's name was Rhett.
   c. The mayor welcomed the marine home. The marine's wife sat beside him.
   d. Clark asked Lana for a date. The dates were in Lana's purse.

e. The woman's basketball team was undefeated. The administration gave an award to the team.

3. Revise the following sentences to make them more precise. If the sentence is precise as written, place a check before the sentence.

a. The families that survived the plane crash took refuge in a local school.

b. Melissa wrote the firefighter a thank-you note as he had rescued her.

c. The man who embezzled from the savings and loan company was acquitted.

d. After he had written his essay, Jon submitted it to his teacher.

e. John is strong like a bull.

f. While Jorge seemed faithful, Norma often had reason to doubt him.

g. After he had been cut from the basketball team, Wilt wept.

h. While he was swimming, Jeff focused on his breathing and his stroke.

i. Since Elvis has died, many people have claimed to have seen him alive.

j. The people who the bill was intended to help attended a banquet for its sponsor.

9c Use subordination to revise short, choppy sentences.

Subordination can reinforce the relationship of short sentences to others in a paragraph, can convey precise meaning, and can create variety.

Common Problems

A series of sentences implies that each idea in these sentences is of equal importance in developing the topic sentence, but in fact they are rarely equal. A style that relies on short, choppy sentences is ineffective in conveying meaning because it is unable to show the relationships among the separate ideas.

Examples

The following sentences fail to emphasize a single point:

> Martha walked through the woods. She saw a squirrel. The squirrel leapt to a tree. Martha laughed.

The revised sentences focus on a particular point and reveal a relationship among the ideas:

> As she walked through the woods, *Martha saw a squirrel,* which made her laugh when it leapt to a tree.

> As she walked through the woods, *Martha laughed* when she saw a squirrel leap to a tree.

> *The squirrel leapt to a tree,* causing Martha, who was walking through the woods, to laugh.

Name ______________________________ Score ______________

Exercise 9c Subordination of short sentences

In the following sentences, use subordination (both adverbial and adjectival conjunctions) to emphasize a single point. Revise the wording to eliminate repetition.

1. The drummer tapped his foot. He nodded his head. He played the drums.

2. The earth split apart. The bridge fell. People screamed. An earthquake hit the city.

3. Jake typed the story. Brett watched Jake. Brett smiled. Jake smoked a cigarette.

4. The praying mantis was motionless. The praying mantis was on the branch. A butterfly landed on the branch. The butterfly moved slowly. The mantis moved quickly. The mantis caught the butterfly.

5. The superbowl was boring. Jim had awaited the superbowl. Jim was sad.

6. The sentence was long. The judge convicted the shoplifter. The shoplifter laughed at the judge.

7. The party was over. The music stopped. The people went home. The people were very happy.

8. The star exploded. The astronomer looked through the telescope. The astronomer was amazed. Light shot from the star. The astronomer saw the star.

9. Tom walked softly. Gerry ate the cheese. Gerry didn't see Tom. Tom said hello to Gerry. They made sandwiches.

10. A red wagon was in the driveway. Mr. Rogers sang. He was thinking about driving. The wagon was close to the car. Mr. Rogers ran over the wagon.

9d Subordinate one or more clauses of long compound sentences.

Because subordinating one clause in a compound sentence emphasizes the independent clause, subordination usually relates ideas more precisely than does coordination.

Common Problems

Although coordinating conjunctions indicate the close relationship of two independent clauses, they may be overused and thus obscure the important relationships among the paragraph's idea.

Examples

A compound sentence comprises two or more independent clauses.

independent clause **independent clause**

Philip had trained for months, and he won the race with ease.

An independent clause can be subordinated in different ways:

1. A subordinating conjunction makes one clause dependent.

   Because Philip had trained for months, he won the race with ease.

2. A relative pronoun accomplishes the same goal.

   Philip, *who* had trained for months, won the race with ease.

3. Changing the verb to a participle also creates a dependent clause.

   Having trained for months, Philip won the race with ease.

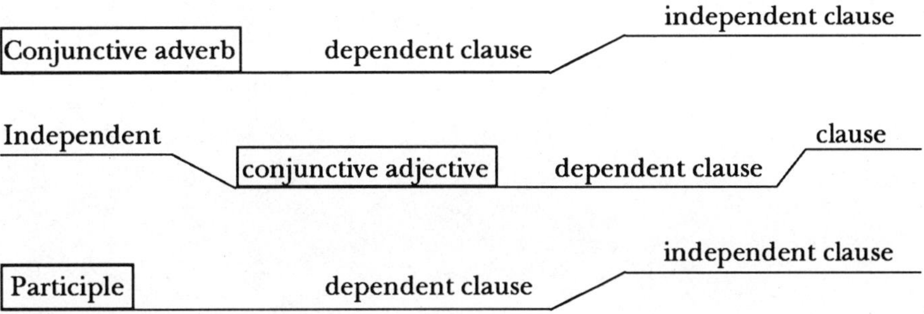

Name ______________________________ Score ____________________

Exercise 9d Subordination of long compound sentences

Subordinate one of the independent clauses in each of the following compound sentences by using a subordinating conjunction, a relative pronoun, and a participle. Make three revisions for each sentence.

1. The computer was quite inexpensive, but it suited Annie's needs.
   a.
   b.
   c.
2. Annie had never used a computer, so she was initially anxious.
   a.
   b.
   c.
3. She wrote several letters daily, and she also created graphics.
   a.
   b.
   c.

4. She enjoyed typing the letters, yet she dreaded creating graphics.
   a.

   b.

   c.

5. Annie increased her output, for the computer gave her additional time.
   a.

   b.

   c.

9e Reduce clauses to modifying words and phrases.

Reducing modifying clauses to phrases or single words will control focus and tighten style.

Common Problems

Sprawling clauses are ineffective in communicating the writer's point because they disperse the reader's attention and contribute to an unpolished style.

Examples

Clauses can be reduced in several ways.

1. Create a compound subject or predicate:

    Ricky washed the car, and David helped him.

    Ricky and David washed the car. [compound subject]

    Michael dribbled to his right, and then he faked left, and then he dunked the ball.

    Michael dribbled to his right, faked left, and then dunked the ball. [compound predicate]

2. Create participial phrases:

    The cat hopped to the table. She lapped up the milk. She mewed contentedly.

    Hopping to the table, the cat lapped up the milk, mewing contentedly.

3. Create appositives:

    The expansion team, which was named the Timberwolves, played hard defense and was exciting to watch.

    The expansion team, the Timberwolves, played hard defense and was exciting to watch.

Name ______________________________ Score ________________

Exercise 9e Reducing clauses

Revise the following paragraph by reducing clauses to phrases and words. Combine and rearrange sentences when necessary.

Albert Pinkham Ryder was an American painter. He lived from 1847 to 1917. He was a recluse for much of his life, but his paintings reveal a creative imagination. One of his most famous paintings is *Siegfried and the Rhine Maidens.* It portrays the maidens bathing nude in the water. Water was one of Ryder's favorite subjects. Siegfried watched the maidens. He was on a horse. The horse raised a front leg. The maidens looked startled. The sun blazed down. Moonlight was predominant in most of his works. Ryder's paintings reveal his interest in the intensity of light and the shadows it creates. A huge tree dominates the painting. It is in the center of the painting. Its branches swirl and twist in the wind. The branches extend to the upper corners of the painting. The sun shows through the branches. The maidens are to the left of the tree. They are in the lower left of the painting. Siegfried is to the right of the tree. He is on a path. The painting is in shades of brown and gold. Gold dominates the painting. The painting is very bright.

9f Avoid inverted subordination.

Inverted subordination places the main point in the dependent clause. In a complex sentence, the independent clause should contain the central point. Other information should be subordinated in a dependent clause or phrase.

Common Problems

Independent clauses that contain obvious or minor points or dependent clauses that carry major points or widely known information are misleading.

Examples

The following sentence buries the writer's central idea:

> The sun rose in the east as the army prepared for battle.

The major point is the army's preparation, not the obvious fact about the sun.

The inverted emphasis can be revised in two ways:

1. Make the subordinate clause the main clause.

   As the sun rose in the east, the army prepared for battle.

2. Make the independent clause a phrase.

   At dawn, the army prepared for battle.

Name ______________________________ Score ______________

Exercise 9f Avoiding inverted subordination

Revise each of the following sentences to emphasize the major point. In one revision, make the subordinate idea a clause. In a second revision, make the subordinate idea a phrase or a word. If a sentence emphasizes the major point, perform only the second revision.

1. The Superbowl, whose final score amazed the viewers, was finally over.

   a.

   b.

2. MADD, which is an acronym for Mothers Against Drunk Driving, has become a political force in the 1990s.

   a.

   b.

3. Charles Darwin did not originate the theory of evolution, although he did develop the mechanism of natural selection to explain how the theory works.

   a.

   b.

4. Although recent studies have revealed several benefits, coffee is considered a health hazard.

   a.

   b.

5. Second-hand smoke, which may be more dangerous to smokers than the smoke they inhale from their own cigarettes, refers to the fumes people inhale from the cigarettes of others.

   a.

   b.

9g Eliminate excessive subordination.

When writers create lengthy sentences that contain several subordinate ideas, they have created sentence sprawl.

Common Problems

Excessive subordination in a sentence can cause a reader to lose the main point among the myriad minor points.

Examples

The following sentence buries the independent clause and subordinates ideas which should be emphasized:

> Although in the United States opera does not attract a general audience, the film version of *La Traviata,* which starred Placido Domingo and Teresa Stratas, was a box office success, probably because of the appeal of the featured singers rather than of the opera itself.

The revision places emphasis where it belongs by creating simple and complex sentences out of the multiple clauses of the original.

> In the United States opera does not attract a general audience. But the film version of *La Traviata* was a box office success, perhaps because of the featured singers, Placido Domingo and Teresa Stratas. They might appeal more to viewers than does opera itself.

Name ____________________ Score ____________

Exercise 9g Eliminating excessive subordination

Revise the following complex sentences to reduce subordination and emphasize a central point. Create separate sentences when necessary.

1. When people want to control the mosquito population, they often erect bird hotels, which are actually elaborate bird houses designed to hold up to a dozen birds and which they hope will attract Purple Martins who have voracious appetites.

2. Because the Social Security withholding tax has created a surplus, which has grown to millions of dollars, some politicians want to use the fund to lower the national debt which is now the highest it has been in our history although the fund was never intended for any purpose other than protecting Social Security for future generations.

3. Speaking before a large group of people, one of the candidates for president of the student government, which requires candidates to address the major campus organizations, became visibly upset although she was certain beforehand that the crowd would not bother her because she had received an "A" in a course in public speaking.

4. After a decade of hearing about the benefits of jogging, we now learn that the supposed experts, who have made fortunes advocating this bone-jarring form of torture, have changed their tune and now favor a less demanding exercise, one which possesses the same benefits as jogging without the physical stress, one which even allows us to use the same equipment as before, and one which still allows us to compete against each other for the pleasure of wearing a tee shirt that advertises our obsession with healthy living—*walking*!

5. Because high schools are supported by local governments, which often fail to convince their constituents that the schools are properly using the funds allocated to them, most high schools rarely have enough resources to maintain their present standards, much less raise them, because the people are unwilling to accept a tax increase even though they want schools that will prepare students for the future, whether or not that future includes a college education.

CHAPTER 10

Improving Sentence Style: Emphasis

10a Use emphatic placement.

Writers create *emphasis* when they place key ideas in the most forceful positions, such as the beginning or end of a sentence. The choice of terms—those with precise meanings and even related sounds—also produces emphasis.

Common Problems

Writers overlook emphasis when they pay more attention to the content of a sentence than to the placement of ideas or to word choice. Writing only one draft of an essay is a principal cause of this problem.

Examples

USE PLACEMENT FOR EMPHASIS.

Building to the major point creates emphasis, whereas concluding with a qualifying phrase is anticlimactic. Consider these two sentences:

> According to a nationwide poll, the most popular TV program of the 1980s was *The Cosby Show.*
>
> The most popular TV program of the 1980s was *The Cosby Show,* according to a nationwide poll.

The first sentence builds to the important point. The second buries the most important point in the middle of the sentence and emphasizes a minor one in the concluding phrase.

The beginning of a sentence can also be emphatic, particularly if an interrupting phrase sets it off:

> *The Cosby Show,* according to a nationwide poll, was the most popular TV show of the 1980s.

Internal punctuation, such as a comma or a dash, can also function as an interrupter to achieve emphasis:

> The bill proposed a registration deadline of six weeks prior to the election—far too long.

> ***Note:*** Writers should avoid *overusing* internal interrupters, either by word, phrase, or punctuation. By definition, interruption slows the reader; used too frequently, interruption becomes boring rather than emphatic.

Reversing the normal order of a sentence also attracts reader attention. Like interrupters, though, overuse defeats the purpose:

> So very disappointed I was when I arrived too late to see the play.

Expletive structures (*there, what,* and *it*) are frequently unemphatic (and wordy). They usually bury the subject of a sentence in the middle or omit the subject from the sentence completely.

There are three stallions frolicking in the corral.

There had been plenty of time to make it to the play.

What needed to be done was to inoculate all the children for measles.

In earlier times, *it was* falsely thought that the porpoise was closely related to the shark.

In each case, the sentences would be more emphatic or more specific if the expletives were eliminated:

Three stallions are frolicking in the corral.

John had plenty of time to make it to the play.

The school needed to inoculate all the children for measles.

In earlier times, even *great scientists* falsely thought that the porpoise was closely related to the shark.

USE WORD MEANING AND SOUND FOR EMPHASIS.

Changing the meaning of a word, using a term in a different context, using a figure of speech, or even repeating a sound creates emphasis:

Lucinda had *a way* with a man, but someone got a*way* with hers. [The different meanings of *way* attract attention.]

A *grave* error while driving can lead to the *grave.* [The pun on *grave* is a serious use of the usually comic device.]

After working for his father all day, Bruce was *as weak as* a wet Kleenex. [The simile provides a concrete image of Bruce's lack of strength.]

The *w*est *w*ind *w*hipped the farmers as the day *w*ore on. [The repetition of the *w* sound suggests the sound of the wind and emphasizes the plight of the farmers.]

Name ______________________________ Score ______________

Exercise 10a Emphatic placement

1. Revise the following sentences to make the central point more emphatic.
   a. We would, if our lifespan were a million instead of seventy years, be afraid to cross the street, because we would, if the laws of probability apply, be very likely to be hit by a car.

   b. The year 1989 was a time of great turmoil in Eastern Europe, when the events are seen in the context of history.

   c. The movie received four stars, according to the ad in the newspaper.

   d. One of the favorite forms of literature is the western, which has been enjoyed for over a century.

   e. The decade of the 1990s will see animal rights emerge as a problem many are concerned with.

2. Create five sentences of your own, and briefly explain what you have done to emphasize important points.
   a. Sentence:

      Explanation:

   b. Sentence:

      Explanation:

c. Sentence:

Explanation:

d. Sentence:

Explanation:

e. Sentence:

Explanation:

3. Revise the following sentences to eliminate expletives.
   a. There are duties which all employees owe to their employers, but blind obedience is not one of them.

   b. What happened at the meeting was that the committee voted to have an office party.

   c. It is easy to say that we should improve education, but it is difficult to find the means of achieving that goal.

   d. There will be time after work for Betty to enjoy swimming.

Name ____

Exercise 10a (continued)

e. What the auto industry wants from the government is a fair trade agreement with foreign countries.

4. Using the techniques of creating emphasis through meaning, generate two emphatic sentences for each method:

   a. A word or phrase in two senses

      1)

      2)

   b. Reinforcing the meaning of an idea by using sound

      1)

      2)

   c. A metaphor or simile

      1)

      2)

10b Use strong, active verbs.

An effective writing style relies on verbs that reveal an action, in contrast to linking verbs (*be, am, is, were*) and auxiliary verbs (*have, has, had*). The active voice also provides an agent, or actor, who performs the action of the sentence.

Common Problems

The passive voice both removes an agent and adds a linking verb and thus makes it difficult for the reader to visualize the action of the sentence (see chapter **31**).

Examples

The following sentences bury the action of the sentence:

> The dance *had been* enjoyed.
>
> Hitting the game-winning home run *was* a great feeling.

The first sentence, written in the passive voice, contains no actor, and the verb *enjoy* is cluttered by vague verbs. The second sentence buries both actions, *hitting* and *feeling* in nominalizations (see **10c**) and links the ideas with a vague verb.

> *Eddie enjoyed dancing* with Dee at the prom.
>
> When she *hit* the game-winning home run, Sara *jumped* in the air and *raised* a *clenched* fist over her head as she *crossed* home plate.

Remedying the verb problem also allows the sentences to include more specific and vivid information.

Name ______________________________ Score ______________

Exercise 10b Active verbs

Underline the ineffective verbs in the following sentences, and rewrite them using strong verbs. If the action is in a noun, make the verb form of the noun the action of the sentence. If the sentence contains no actor, supply one (see **10c** and chapter **31** if necessary).

1. The climb to the top of the mountain was the highpoint of the vacation.

2. Thirty-eight points had been scored.

3. The gun is drawn, and running and hiding are occurring in the bank.

4. The discovery of the buried treasure had been pleasant for Long John.

5. There was singing at the party, and laughter was present.

6. The cat gave a howl as chasing was happening.

7. The test had been passed with a grade of 100.

8. Waterskiing is an exciting pastime.

9. The golf ball is in the cup after only one stroke.

10. The soaring of the hawk was a moving sight.

10c Avoid nominalizations.

Sentences are vibrant when they contain verbs that describe an action, rather than nouns that suggest the action (nominalizations).

Common Problems

Nominalizations cause two problems: they remove the real actor from the sentence, and they transform actions (verbs and adjectives) into abstract nouns. Using nominalizations generally makes a style wordy. When the subject of the essay is complex, nominalizations make the essay difficult to understand.

Examples

Some verbs and adjectives and their nominalizations are included below:

VERBS	NOMINALIZATIONS
act	action
implement	implementation
discover	discovery
study	study

(Note that *study* can be either a verb or a noun.)

ADJECTIVES	NOMINALIZATIONS
happy	happiness
sad	sadness
curious	curiosity

The following sentences display nominalizations:

The *determination* of an attendance policy was necessary.

The *discovery* of America occurred before 1492.

The *hope* was that the experiment would be a *success.*

No actor appears in these sentences, and each uses a weakened verb. Notice below how more vivid they are when rewritten with strengthened verbs:

The *dean* must *determine* an attendance policy.

The *Vikings discovered* America before 1492.

Edison hoped the experiment would *succeed.*

All three sentences now have actors, are specific, and contain fewer words than their nominalized counterparts.

Name ______________________________ Score ______________

Exercise 10c Nominalizations

1. Revise the sentences to eliminate the nominalizations (shown in italics). Add actors when necessary.
   a. There is a *need* to gather more data for the experiment.

   b. The *brightness* of the sun made the otherwise dreary land beautiful.

   c. The *glow* of the lightning bug showed in the dark.

   d. The *explanation* of how the rotary engine worked was necessary.

   e. The secretary's *explanation* of his absence satisfied his employer.

2. Revise the following nominalizations, supplying actors when necessary.

   a. Philip did a review of the play for his drama class.

   b. We all have a need for love.

   c. It was a curiosity to Dana why anyone enjoyed slasher films.

   d. It was a surprise for Roderick when his sister Madeline returned.

e. The average leap of an adult kangaroo is over fifteen feet.

f. There was a discussion of the homecoming.

g. The intention was to visit three museums in one day.

h. The committee showed its appreciation for the group's effort.

i. The revelation of the new models appealed to all at the auto show.

j. An erosion of player confidence caused the coach to be fired.

3. The following sentences have more than one nominalization. Revise the sentences and supply actors when necessary.

   a. Few people receive any enjoyment from the preparation for the writing of an essay, but they enjoy its completion.

   b. The failure to establish priorities causes the dismissal of many freshmen.

   c. Terry's enjoyment of fast cars is a source of worry to his mother.

   d. There was always a feeling of happiness during holiday visits to relatives.

   e. Even good friends feel resentment when asked for the loan of their homework.

CHAPTER 11

Improving Sentence Style: Variety

11a Use both loose and periodic sentences.

Loose sentences follow the natural word order: the sentence states a key idea, an action, and then the afterthoughts. Conversely, *periodic sentences*, which invert the normal word order, create suspense, a dramatic tension. They interrupt the flow and force readers to wait to the end of the sentence for the key idea. Varying loose and periodic sentences not only creates variety, but also emphasizes ideas and points by controlling the reader's anticipation.

Common Problems

Overusing loose sentences makes a style casual and fails to create points of emphasis. Too many periodic sentences create the opposite problem with a similar result: a series of highpoints emphasizing no single point. An excess of periodic sentences also creates a style that sounds unnatural in most situations—overly formal and stuffy.

Examples

A loose sentence:

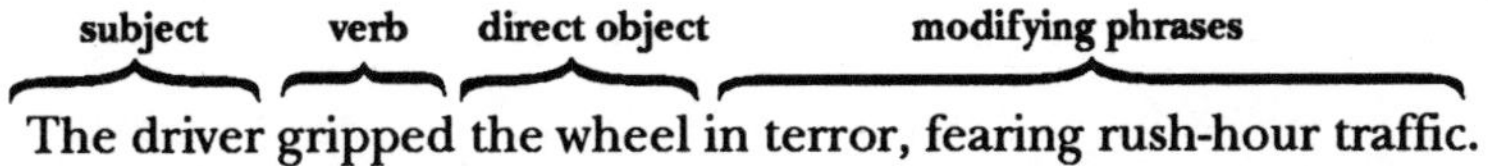

The driver gripped the wheel in terror, fearing rush-hour traffic.

A periodic sentence:

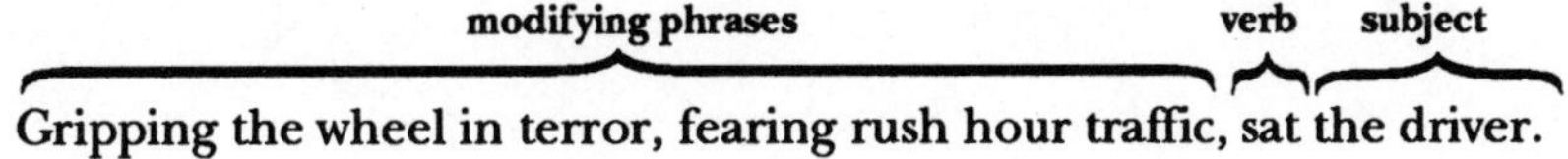

Gripping the wheel in terror, fearing rush hour traffic, sat the driver.

Name ______________________ Score ______________

Exercise 11a Loose and periodic sentences

1. Combine the following short sentences into loose sentences:
   a. Cats entertain their owners. Cats play by themselves. Cats are curious.

   b. Hermit crabs are clean. Hermit crabs learn simple tricks. Hermit crabs will eat from a person's hand. Hermit crabs are active.

   c. Spiders create beautiful webs. Many people hate spiders. Most spiders will not hurt people. Spiders eat insects.

   d. The *Tyrannosaurus rex* was not like today's reptiles. It moved quickly. It did not drag its tail. It was warm blooded.

   e. Lions make poor pets. They sleep many hours daily. They roar loudly. They eat their owners.

2. Revise the following short sentences into periodic sentences:
   a. Drama set to music occurred in ancient Greece. True opera began in Italy. *Dafne* was the earliest opera known. Jacopo Peri composed *Dafne* in 1597.

   b. Early opera plots came from Greek myths. These operas were serious. Later comic operas appeared. Comedies brought opera many followers.

   c. The structure became unified in the seventeenth century. The three-act opera eliminated irrelevant episodes. The new operas were called *opera seria.*

   d. Another kind of opera was *opera comique.* It contained spoken dialogue. This opera could be on any topic.

e. Spectacular melodrama typified opera after the French Revolution. This kind of opera became Grand opera in the nineteenth century. These operas dealt with historical subjects. The plots were often violent.

3. Revise the following sentences into a paragraph consisting of loose and periodic sentences to emphasize a particular point:
   a. Computers frighten many people.
   b. Computers can help students.
   c. Many word processing programs are easy to understand.
   d. Easy computer programs are called "user friendly."
   e. Writers can move sentences on a word processor.
   f. Writers can move entire paragraphs on a word processor.
   g. Revising sentences is easy on a computer.
   h. Writers can add or delete sentences from a draft.
   i. Writers can revise a draft before printing it.
   j. Some programs correct errors.

11b Use different types of phrases and clauses.

Writers provide variety to their sentences when they use different kinds of phrases and clauses.

Common Problems

Repeating the same sentence pattern creates an extremely dull style.

Examples

The following kinds of clauses (see chapter **23**) and phrases (see chapter **22**) add variety to style:

1. *Adverb clause:*
   Because he could not type well, Kevin wrote all early drafts by hand.

2. *Relative clause:*
   Susan, *who also could not type well,* had a word processor, *which enabled her to create typed drafts with ease.*

3. *Noun phrase:*
   Anita could write only in a certain arrangement: *three pens on her desk, a dictionary near her right hand, and a pad of paper to her left.*

4. *Verbal phrase:*
   Sitting relaxed in a chair, Rick jotted down lists *to form the basis for an essay.*

5. *Adjective phrase:*
   Marni liked to begin writing when she was most alert, *as alert as she could be after a full day's work.*

6. *Absolute phrase:*
   Hands poised above the keyboard, eyes riveted on the paper, and teeth clamped shut, Ernest attacked the typewriter and conquered his assignment.

7. *Prepositional phrase:*
   Norman always finished his assignments *at the last minute of the last hour of the final day.*

8. *Adverb phrase:*
   In the middle of the night, at the darkest hour, with wind howling, Edgar wrote his most effective pieces.

Use Different Types of Phrases and Clauses

Name ______________________ Score ______________

Exercise 11b Variety in phrases and clauses

Combine the following sentences by using the form of clause or phrase indicated.

1. Adverb clause
   a. The morning was cold. Marcia hated waiting for the bus.

   b. She looked down the street. The bus was not in sight.

2. Relative clause
   a. A young woman walked to the bus stop. She had come out of Marcia's building.

   b. The woman was shivering. She was wearing a very light summer coat. The coat had no buttons.

3. Noun phrase
   a. The wind blew the woman's hair. Her eyes were shut. Her lips were pursed. She held her light coat close to her.

   b. Marcia's hands were in her pocket. She clenched her hands. She turned her back to the wind.

4. Verbal phrase
   a. Marcia heard a horn honk several times. But she did not look at the car.

   b. The driver kept honking the horn. The driver shouted, "Marcia!"

   c. Marcia turned toward the voice. She wondered who the driver was.

5. Adjective phrase
   a. Marcia was happy to hear her name. She was the happiest she had been that morning.

   b. But she was wary of strangers. Her uneasiness caused her to hesitate.

   c. However, the voice was friendly. The friendliness reassured her.

6. Absolute phrase
   a. The voice was deep. It was throaty. Yet Marcia did not recognize it.

   b. Marcia stared at the driver. Marcia's eyes squinted. Her brow furrowed.

   c. She began walking toward the car. Her feet moved slowly. Her eyes looked at the woman in the light coat.

7. Prepositional phrase
   a. The woman smiled. The driver received the smile.

   b. The woman ran. Reaching the car was her goal.

   c. The woman's hand waved. The man was the object of the wave.

Name ____________________

Excercise 11b (continued)

8. Adverb phrase
   a. The two women stopped. They stared at each other. They seemed confused.

   b. The man's voice stammered. He said *to the woman in the light coat,* "Is this woman a friend of yours, Marcia?"

11c Write sentences of differing structures.

The four sentence types (simple, compound, complex, and compound-complex) either determine or reinforce meaning. Taking advantage of all of these functions not only enhances style with sentence variety, but also makes the meaning precise.

Common Problems

An overuse or random use of sentence types creates a monotonous style, and casual use of compound or complex sentences may create unintended emphasis.

Example

The paragraph below moves from two elaborate ideas and narrows to a straightforward statement in the fourth sentence. The fifth through eighth sentences shift from long to short structures, from intricate to direct, which focus on the ironic turnabout in the final sentence.

A state legislator had sponsored a bill that required high school	**Complex**
students to take an introduction to business course. Although the	**Complex**
schools now have many requirements, the representative thought his	
bill was justified. Many high school graduates can't manage their own	**Compound**
finances, and even fewer understand how capitalism works. He said	**Complex**
that his bill would solve both problems. After they had taken the	**Compound/complex**
course, students would have actual experience in managing money,	
and they would appreciate their country. He was wrong. When he put	**Simple, Complex**
the question to a vote at the local high school, the bill failed. That's	**Simple**
democracy!	

Name ______________________ Score ______________

Exercise 11c Variety in sentence structure

1. Revise the structure of the paragraph in the example above so that it begins with the concluding idea—the failure of the bill. Change the sentence types when possible to create variety in an effective paragraph.

2. Analyze the sentence variety in an introductory paragraph and a body paragraph that you have written. Justify the sentence types, or revise the paragraph so the sentences are more effective. If the sentence types differ from the introduction to the body paragraph, explain the difference.

11d Write sentences that express different methods of development.

Conventional development methods apply to sentences as well as to essays and paragraphs. Applying the appropriate form of development reinforces the sentence's function in the paragraph and guides the reader.

Common Problems

When content is expressed in only one or two of the traditional methods of development, the writing is thin and the style is uninteresting.

Examples

The following sentences reflect the traditional methods of developing sentences:

1. *Definition:*
   The Sonoran coral snake, one of two species of coral snake found in the United States, inhabits only New Mexico and Arizona.
2. *Narration:*
   I stumbled across a coral snake on my last visit to New Mexico.
3. *Description:*
   The coral snake, on average, is two and one-half feet long with a small blunt head and black, red, and yellow rings.
4. *Comparison:*
   The coral snake, like the king snake, has bands of black, red, and yellow.
5. *Contrast:*
   Whereas the coral snake's yellow and red bands touch each other, the red and yellow rings of the king snake are separated by black.
6. *Classification:*
   The coral snake is very poisonous.
7. *Cause and effect:*
   A person can die from the bite of a coral snake.
8. *Process:*
   After being bitten, a person should not try to suck out the poison but instead should apply a tourniquet above the bite, move as little as necessary, and go directly to a doctor.
9. *Example:*
   When I approached, the coral snake was coiled in the space between two rocks, its yellow, black, and red blending with the light of sunset so that I did not see it until my friend pointed it out to me.

Name ______________________________ Score ______________

Exercise 11d Sentence development

1. Using each of the nine modes indicated above, write a paragraph on one of the following subjects: a favorite pet, a place you like to visit, a favorite holiday.

2. Analyzing an essay you have written, indicate the type of sentences you have used.

CHAPTER 12

Correcting Misplaced Parts and Dangling Modifiers

12a Eliminate dangling modifiers.

A modifying word or phrase should be placed close to the noun, pronoun, or verb that it describes. This general rule is easy to apply when sentences are cast in active voice. Introductory verbal modifiers will then usually describe the actor in the sentence, as they should.

Common Problems

A modifier that does not clearly modify a noun, pronoun, or verb has no logical reason for being placed in the sentence. The modifier has nothing to attach to in the sentence; it dangles. Introductory verbal phrases can make sentences precise and add variety, but if they are not clearly connected, they become *dangling modifiers.* This danger is especially great if the sentence is cast in passive voice because the actor is either at the end of the sentence or removed completely.

Examples

The introductory verbal phrase of the following sentence modifies the first noun in the main clause:

> While sitting in a comfortable chair, Joe ate a peach.

Clearly, Joe is doing the eating. But if the main clause is written in the passive voice and the actor is omitted, the sentence looks like this:

> While sitting in a comfortable chair, the peach was eaten.

The phrase seems to modify the peach, but that is impossible, so the modifier dangles.

The following sentence makes clear that two people are involved:

> While Annie practiced her free throws, the coach nodded in approval.

But if the introductory dependent clause is changed to a verbal phrase, the coach seems to be approving of her own free throw practice:

> While practicing her free throws, the coach nodded in approval.

Correcting Misplaced Parts and Dangling Modifiers

Name ______________________________ Score ______________

Exercise 12a Dangling modifiers

Revise the following sentences to eliminate dangling modifiers. If a sentence contains no dangling modifier, place a check mark before the sentence.

1. While playing the piano, the audience listened attentively.
2. When traveling through Europe, it is entertaining to watch other tourists.
3. The cake was placed in the oven, smiling with satisfaction.
4. When studying for an exam, there are four techniques needed to be kept in mind.
5. The mail carrier was forced from the yard, baring his teeth and growling.
6. Listening to the music of Beethoven, the class felt calmed.
7. Just after being born, the mother felt much better.
8. After experimenting for several years, the structure of DNA was discovered.
9. Bored by long trips with no friends to accompany him, the radio became the only source of entertainment.
10. Purring softly, the mouse sat quivering in the corner.

12b Place modifiers where their meaning is clear.

Modifying words, phrases, and clauses placed close enough to the words they modify prevent ambiguity.

Common Problems

When modifiers are not close to the words they describe, they easily become misplaced and create confusion. The *squinting modifier,* for instance, may refer to more than one word. Passive voice may accentuate the problem because the actor is removed from its natural position or is omitted.

Examples

Adjectives should be next to the nouns they modify:

The *beautiful* snow fell on the house.

The snow fell on the *beautiful* house.

In both cases the modified word is clear: in the first example, the snow is beautiful; in the second, the house is.

Adverbs can appear in several positions in a sentence and still modify clearly, but they are usually most effective close to the word they modify:

Symbolically, the novel *Uncle Tom's Cabin* was very important.

The novel *Uncle Tom's Cabin* was very important symbolically.

The novel *Uncle Tom's Cabin* was symbolically very important.

In each case, *symbolically* clearly modifies *important* (the adverb tells "in what way").

Placement of some adverbs, such as *only, almost, just,* and *even,* can change the meaning of the sentence significantly:

I *only* ate one sandwich all day. [Ambiguous: did the speaker eat food other than a sandwich?]

I ate *only* one sandwich all day. [Clear meaning: one sandwich was all the speaker ate.]

Like single words, the placement of phrases, such as the verbal phrase below, can also affect meaning.

Standing on tiptoe, the child looked into the box and saw a snake.

But moving the modifying phrase creates an entirely different image:

The child looked into the box and saw a snake *standing on tiptoe.*

The next two sentences make clear what action was graceful, but the third is ambiguous because the modifier "gracefully" squints, "goes in both directions":

The receiver who *gracefully* caught the ball evaded three tacklers and scored a touchdown.

The receiver who caught the ball evaded three tacklers *gracefully* and scored a touchdown.

The receiver who caught the ball *gracefully evaded* three tacklers and scored a touchdown.

Name ______________________________ Score ______________

Exercise 12b Placement of modifiers

1. Explain the difference that the placement of the modifier makes in the following sentences:
   a. The young bird *almost* flew twenty feet from its nest.
   The young bird flew *almost* twenty feet from its nest.

   b. Fred *only* wanted to know if Barney would help him feed the animals.
   Fred wanted to know if *only* Barney would help him feed the animals.

   c. Ricky *just* came home from the club because Lucy asked him to.
   Ricky came home from the club because *just* Lucy asked him to.

   d. Donald *nearly* lost twenty million dollars because he made a foolish mistake in judgment.
   Donald lost *nearly* twenty million dollars because he made a foolish mistake in judgment.

   e. Mary had made several friends after working *barely* a week in Minneapolis.
   Mary had made several friends after *barely* working a week in Minneapolis.

2. Revise the following sentences so that the modifiers are well placed.
   a. The acrobat walked across the room to the people on his hands.

   b. Riding the subway during rush hour, time passes slowly for Geoff.

   c. Every day Arnold worked out with weights that he could remember.

   d. The movie *Glory* was nominated for several Oscars which dealt with little known facts about African-American soldiers.

   e. Beth was informed about the meeting on replacing several officers by the secretary.

3. Rewrite each of the following sentences twice to indicate the possible meanings of the sentences containing squinting modifiers.
   a. Frances has said when she was not tired she would wash the dishes.
      1)

      2)

   b. Cynthia's washing the car immediately surprised her father.
      1)

      2)

   c. Fred said after he ate dinner he would play with his brother.
      1)

      2)

   d. The guard who had been shooting hurriedly sat on the bench in disgust.
      1)

      2)

   e. Filling out all the forms completely frustrated the students.
      1)

      2)

12c Do not interrupt the flow of the sentence with modifiers.

A sentence flows smoothly if the writer places modifiers at the beginning or end of the main clause or verb phrase.

Common Problems

When modifiers are placed so they interrupt clauses and phrases, they restrict the flow of ideas and slow the reader.

Examples

The flow of the first sentence is interrupted because the subject is separated from the verb. The second sentence, in which the modifying dependent clause is placed first, leads the reader directly to the main point:

> The *Empanterias amplexus, although not as well known as Tyrannosaurus rex,* was every bit as ferocious and as big as the more familiar predator.
>
> *Although not as well known as Tyrannosaurus rex,* the *Empanterias amplexus* was every bit as ferocious and as big as the more familiar predator.

In the following sentence the verb phrase flows smoothly with no interruptions:

> If scientific estimates are correct, the *Empanterias may have preceded Tyrannosaurus* by thirty million years.

But if the modifying clause interrupts the verb phrase, it slows the flow:

> The *Empanterias may,* if scientific estimates are correct, *have preceded Tyrannosaurus* by thirty million years.

Although not as serious, split infinitives can also limit the flow of a sentence. The problem becomes evident in the following three sentences:

> *Empanterias* was able *to devour* a 1,400 pound cow in one gulp.
>
> *Empanterias* was able *to* easily *devour* a 1,400 pound cow in one gulp.
>
> *Empanterias* was able *to,* if it so chose, *devour* a 1,400 pound cow in one gulp.

The first sentence reads smoothly with no interruption. Although not ineffective, the second sentence would improve if *easily* were placed either before the verb phrase or after the infinitive. The third sentence would improve if the phrase interrupting the infinitive occurred either before or after the main clause.

Name ______________________ Score ______________

Exercise 12c Modifier interruption of flow

Revise the following sentences by moving interrupting modifiers. Place a check mark before the sentence if the interruption is justified.

1. Human intervention in insect control, even when it is intended to be beneficial, often has long-run negative consequences.
2. The 1980s has, with some justification, been characterized as a decade dominated by selfishness.
3. The United States wants to never be considered an aggressor.
4. The environment, which had not been a serious issue in the 1980s, may become one of the major political battles of the 1990s.
5. Effective speakers need to clearly state their ideas but at the same time recognize the attitudes of their audiences.
6. Politicians should, without hesitancy, tell the truth or say nothing at all.
7. Pilotless planes will explore, by 1991 at the latest, the ozone hole over Antarctica.
8. Women's bodybuilding, although still not appreciated by the general public, has been increasing in popularity.
9. Inexperienced people who wish to correctly wire a stereo system in order to save money need to keep the telephone number of their nearest service center available.
10. Hikers, when traveling through unfamiliar territory, need to tell forest rangers their itinerary.

CHAPTER 13

Grammatical Completeness

13a–13e Add the necessary words or phrases to complete a sentence grammatically and logically.

Words and phrases that might be omitted in speech often add precision in prose. Because prose is usually different from normal speech, writers must be careful to prevent confusing structures.

Common Problems

The level of usage between spoken English and written standard English often differs. Writers who are unaware of this fact or who fail to acknowledge this distinction create an unacceptable informality.

Examples

1. Omitting the articles *a, an,* or *the* will cause confusion and misreading:

   the? a? / the? an? / the? a?

   Ruth saw ^ boy who lived next door give ^ apple to ^ girl in his class.

Not only do the articles add grammatical completeness to the sentence, but also they can alter the meaning. (Recall that *a* appears before words that begin with a consonant sound, and *an* appears before words that begin with a vowel sound.)

2. Omitting the word *that* from subordinate clauses is grammatically acceptable, but when the omission can cause a misreading, *that* is essential:

   Josh knew baseball was his father's favorite sport.

   Joan learned a song she had heard on the radio had been popular when her parents were young.

The meaning of the first sentence is clear without a "that" after "knew"; Josh knows what sport his father likes. However, in the second sentence, the omission of *that* leads the reader to believe that Joan learned a song, not that the song had been popular years earlier. Readers should not be misled for even a split second, so the *that* is necessary.

3. Omitting prepositions, verbs, and pronouns can also be confusing, as in the following:

   by

   Ronald was threatened ^ and frightened of his older brother.

The preposition *by* prevents the misreading that Ronald was threatened *of* his older brother. *Threatened of* is not idiomatic.

Omitting the verb in the following sentence creates an agreement error:

has
Racing bikes *have* narrow tires; the trail bike ∧ wide, studded ones.

If *trail bike* were plural, then the verb could be omitted; *have* as the implied verb would be understood from the preceding clause.

When *who* or *whom* appears in the first part of a sentence, it can be omitted in the second part *only* if the understood word is the same case as the first:

who
Teachers *whom* others in the field respect and ∧ are admired by students are becoming an endangered species.

The pronoun *whom* is in the objective case, so readers would assume the omitted (understood) pronoun would be in the same case. However, the omitted word needs to be in the subjective case.

4. Omitting words and phrases that complete comparisons is ambiguous and misleading. In the following sentence the word *in* creates a parallel structure that makes the comparison clear:

in
The suspense *in* the movie was just as breathtaking as ∧ the play.

The addition of the concluding phrase in the following sentence determines the exact meaning:

than a noose?
than no tie at all?
than any of *your* other ties?
than any tie I have ever seen?
That tie is much nicer ∧.

5. Some intensifiers also require additional phrasing to complete a thought:

to eat dinner
Alexander was *too* tired ∧.

that I left after the first stabbing
The movie was *so* violent ∧.

Name ______________________ Score ______________

Exercises 13a–13e Grammatical completeness

Correct the following sentences by adding words or phrases to make the sentences grammatically complete and precise. Place a check mark before sentences that need no revision.

1. The first test of the semester was easier.

2. The corporation realized the cost of environmental protection needed to be part of the production costs.

3. Thomas goes to theater every Friday night with friend.

4. Richard was one whom his friends turned to in a crisis and paid little attention to the rest of the time.

5. The first cigarette Tammy smoked was terrible; the tenth wonderful.

6. Biff said that he would do better in the future.

7. The 1991 cars are going to be far roomier and less boxy.

8. Many pollsters were happy to see that more people voted in the last election.

9. The competition was just as intense in the semi-finals as the championship game.

10. In *Rainman,* the audience liked Dustin Hoffman more than Tom Cruise.

11. Without a doubt, students are better prepared in the 1990s!

12. An eagle is lifted and then glides on wind currents.

13. Danny was eager to ski as his brother.

14. The antlers of elk are smaller than a moose.

15. Seeing *Julius Caesar* performed by a professional company made the play more enjoyable.

16. It was the beat generation of the 1940s and 1950s who paved the way for the yippies of the 1960s and made being a nonconformist acceptable.

17. The captain recognized the team was exhausted.

18. Off-campus housing is often too expensive.

19. Looking out her window, Jeane saw man climbing over fence.

20. Fifty quarter horses were sold to the rancher and another given to him as a bonus.

CHAPTER 14

Correcting Mixed Constructions

14a–14c Correct mixed constructions.

Some errors are acceptable in speech but not in prose. Writers should take care to closely proofread for illogical or ungrammatical constructions, such as shifting from one grammatical pattern to another.

Common Problems

To create a natural style, writers often imitate speech, not recognizing that oral and written conventions differ. Another problem results when we think faster than we write. Changing direction in mid-sentence or not completing thoughts can create ungrammatical or illogical constructions.

Examples

1. Edit sentences for correct grammatical constructions. The following sentences are grammatically incomplete.

   When I have to run laps is punishment.

   The coach *ordering* me to run five laps.

   The first sentence is unacceptable because an adverb clause cannot be the subject of a sentence. The second is unacceptable because *ordering* is a participle, not a verb. In the revised versions below, the adverb clause is changed to a gerund phrase, and the participle to a verb:

   Having to run laps is punishment.

   The coach *ordered* me to run five laps.

   The following faulty example begins as a complex sentence (the first clause is subordinate) but seems to change to a compound sentence (a comma and a coordinating conjunction join the two clauses):

   When I finish track practice, *and* I go home and relax for an hour.

   Omitting the coordinating conjunction solves the problem by creating a complex sentence.

2. Avoid using *is when, is where,* and *the reason is because.*

   The verb *be* and its forms (*is, are, was, were*) require a noun or adjective complement, not an adverb. Using an adverb creates not only a grammatical but a logical problem:

   A geode *is when* a stone has a concave section lined with crystal.

The pseudoscience of phrenology *was where* the bumps on people's heads revealed their character traits.

The *reasons* most people in the Middle Ages thought the sun rotated around the earth *were because* they were on a moving planet and could not judge its movement and *because* they accepted the views of their scientists and theologians.

All three sentences are inaccurate. A geode does not refer to time, as *when* suggests: "A geode is a stone that has. . . ." In the second sentence, the pseudoscience is not a place, as *where* suggests: "Phrenology was the study of the bumps on people's heads to determine. . . ." In the third sentence, the reasons are not causes, as *because* suggests: "The reasons were that they were on a moving planet, . . . and that they accepted the views of their scientists and theologians."

3. Correct illogical connections.

The subjects and verbs in the following sentences don't make sense together:

The revelation of changes in one species of fossil animals can disclose how changes in another species might have occurred.

Tom Cruise, who starred in *Born on the Fourth of July,* provided a devastating indictment of the government's treatment of servicemen injured in Vietnam.

Because *reveal* and *disclose* are synonyms, the statement "revelations . . . can disclose" is circular. The sentence should be revised to indicate that "changes . . . can reveal." The movie *Born on the Fourth of July* provided an indictment, not the actor, Tom Cruise:

Changes in one species of fossil animals can disclose how changes in another species might have occurred.

Born on the Fourth of July provided a devastating indictment of the government's treatment of servicemen injured in Vietnam.

Name ______________________________ Score ______________

Exercise 14a–14c Mixed constructions

Eliminate the mixed constructions in the following sentences.

1. One of the best times for a brisk walk is because the sun is just rising.

2. It was because the groundhog saw his shadow that people feared a harsh winter.

3. While seeing *Driving Miss Daisy* provided insight into the subtle ways prejudice affects even those who think they have no prejudice.

4. The image of Ronald Reagan waving to onlookers as he boarded a helicopter created greater popular appeal than either Jimmy Carter who preceded him or George Bush who followed him.

5. After Marcus had eaten his Thanksgiving meal was the traditional time for a nap.

6. A comma splice is where two independent clauses are joined by a comma instead of a period, semicolon, or a colon.

7. Two reasons a greater percentage of people in Great Britain than in the United States attend concerts and plays are because doing so is part of the English tradition and the prices are low.

8. The similarity in the rules of American and Canadian football are not nearly as different they appear at first.

9. It is in doing the best possible job a person is capable of that gives job satisfaction to the majority of workers.

10. When the space shuttle successfully lands is always a joyous time for Americans.

11. The popularity of Tom Clancy's novels reveal actual technology which the United States and the Soviet Union possess.

12. Being a good citizen should register to vote and exercise that privilege.

13. To climb a mountain in the western states is more enjoyable than the scenery found in the eastern states.

14. In circling the mall for forty-five minutes looking for a parking spot takes away most of the pleasure of a shopping spree.

15. By visiting friends for a vacation is less expensive than staying at a motel, but runs the risk of being visited on their vacations.

CHAPTER 15

Correcting Shifts

15a Make verbs consistent in tense, voice, and mood.

A paper that displays a consistent tense, voice, and mood is easy to read and understand. Consistent tense makes time clear. A consistent voice within a sentence, usually the active voice, makes the actors and agents explicit. A consistent mood reveals the writer's purpose, whether factual, giving commands, or expressing a wish or condition.

Common Problems

An inconsistent tense, voice, or mood causes confusion, suggests a writer's lack of control of the essay and the conventions of English, and diminishes the writer's credibility.

Examples

1. *Tense:* A consistent tense maintains the time frame of an action.

   The leaves *covered* the freshly raked lawn when the wind *blows* through the trees.

   The mixture of past and present tense makes the sentence above imprecise. The verbs should be either past tense (*covered* and *blew*) or present tense (*cover* and *blow*).

   By convention, writers use the *present* tense in writing about literature or literary criticism:

   In "The Murders in the Rue Morgue," Poe's detective, C. Auguste Dupin, *explains* to the narrator that intuition *helps* him solve crimes.

   Convention also dictates that writers use the *past* tense when reporting historical events and personal narratives:

   The founding fathers *wrote* the Constitution to ensure rights that Great Britain and the Puritan colonial governments had denied.

   Where I *grew* up, neither my family nor I *knew* many of our neighbors.

   One way to remember these two conventions is to keep in mind that literary events are in the present for each new reader, and that events that take place in the historical or personal past remain in the past.

2. *Voice:* Sentences should maintain either the active voice or the passive voice. The following sentences are inconsistent:

   After the White House *was designed, George Washington chose the site.*

The White House *was completed* in 1792, but *workers restored it* in 1814 after it was partially destroyed in the War of 1812.

Because the first sentence emphasizes who did actions, both verbs should be in the active voice. Who completed and restored the White House is unimportant in the second sentence, so both verbs should be in the passive voice.

After *James Hoban designed* the White House, George Washington chose the site.

The White House *was completed* in 1792 but *restored* in 1814 after it was partially destroyed in the War of 1812.

3. *Mood:* Mood reveals a writer's attitude toward sentences. The *indicative mood* denotes factual material, the *imperative mood* denotes commands, and the *subjunctive mood* denotes possibilities or conditions contrary to fact or wishes. Mixing moods confuses readers about a writer's attitude.

If the Mississippi River *were* to follow its projected changes, New Orleans *is* under water in one hundred years. [subjunctive and indicative]

Painting with a roller assures best results; *use* a long stroke to avoid an uneven surface. [indicative and imperative]

The first sentence should be entirely in the subjunctive because it describes a possibility; the condition has not yet occurred. The second set of sentences could be expressed in either the indicative or the imperative mood, depending on the writer's intention:

If the Mississippi River *were* to follow its projected changes, New Orleans *should be* under water in one hundred years. [subjunctive only]

Painting with a roller assures best results; *using* a long stroke avoids an uneven surface. [indicative only]

Paint with a roller for best results; *use* a long stroke to avoid an uneven surface. [imperative only]

Note: Because the imperative mood is expressed in the second person, combining it with either the indicative or subjunctive also results in a shift in person (see **15b**).

Name ______________________________ Score ______________

Exercise 15a Consistent tense, voice, mood

1. Revise the following sentences to make the tenses consistent and to conform to conventional usage. Place a check mark before sentences that need no revision.
   a. The character Huckleberry Finn taught us to judge people by their actions, not by their race or social status.

   b. Twain tells of many of his own experiences in *Huckleberry Finn,* although he changes the names of actual characters.

   c. As a child in the 1970s, Heather and Buffy ride to school on a bus rather than walk.

   d. Their grandparents walked to school even in the coldest weather and do homework almost every night.

   e. The Vietnam war is the subject of many films of the 1980s.

   f. Frank wants to go to college and major in history after he graduates from high school while his younger brother Matthew will study medicine.

   g. Lyndon Johnson is responsible for expanding the United State's role in Vietnam and for furthering civil rights, actions for which he receives criticism and praise from the same groups.

   h. Mozart was regarded as a genius even in his own time because he was both a composer and a musician by the age of three.

   i. What surprises many people is learning that Michael Jordan doesn't make his high school team when he first tries out.

j. Many people enjoy seeing reruns of early television comedies, some of which were made more than thirty years ago.

2. Revise the following sentences to make the voice consistent. Place a check mark before sentences requiring no revision.
   a. After the car had been washed, Charles's father let him have it for the night.

   b. Watching the Super Bowl on TV, popcorn was passed around.

   c. The committee had been meeting to determine which students should receive scholarships.

   d. When patients are treated quickly, doctors find that their patients have better attitudes about them.

   e. Because the lone cowboy could not guard the entire herd, several hundred head of cattle were stolen over a two-week period.

3. Revise the following sentences to make the mood consistent. Place a check mark before sentences requiring no revision.
   a. If he were in better shape, Mike Tyson would have retained the heavyweight championship.

   b. Finish cleaning the fish; then they can be cooked and eaten.

   c. If he had been more pleasant, Bill might have had a chance of dating Hillary.

   d. Tammy told Jim to meet her at the party. Wear a tie too.

   e. Jem would fetch the ball all day when Marty threw it to him.

15b Avoid shifts in person.

Person in a sentence denotes who is speaking (first person: *I, we*), who is being spoken to (second person: *you*), or who is being spoken about (third person: *he, she, it, they*).

Common Problems

Inexperienced writers often shift from one person to another in a single sentence. Such shifts often confuse the reader and detract from the point that the writer is trying to make.

Examples

The first sentence below unnecessarily shifts from third to second person in an attempt to involve readers. The second and third are alternatives:

SHIFTING: The countries in Central America are moving toward democracy, and *you* can understand their reasons.

BETTER: The countries in Central America are moving toward democracy. *We* can understand their reasons.

OR

The countries in Central America are moving toward democracy, and *their* reasons are understandable.

In the second sentence, *We,* in a separate sentence, achieves the writer's purpose of involving readers. In the third sentence, *their* focuses on the countries.

Using the second person to refer to a general reader should be avoided when the context refers to a specific reader. Use the second person only for instructions.

> Being a baby sitter requires much more ability than most people think. First, *you* have to be responsible and recognize *your* limitations. *You* need to ask the parents where they will be, how *you* can reach them in an emergency, and what rules they want *you* to follow with their child. Then, *you* need to pay close attention to the child's interests and never leave the child unsupervised in a dangerous situation. And most important, *you* should never fall asleep while the child is awake.

Such a paragraph would be acceptable for baby sitters but not for general readers. The following paragraph broadens the audience:

> Being a baby sitter requires much more ability than most people think. First, *baby sitters* have to be responsible and recognize *their* limitations. *They* need to ask the parents where they will be, how they can be reached in an emergency, and what rules they want *sitters* to follow with their child. Then, *baby sitters* need to pay close attention to the child's interests and never leave the child unsupervised in a dangerous situation. And most important, *they* should never fall asleep while the child is awake.

Consistent Point of View:
Smooth, Clear

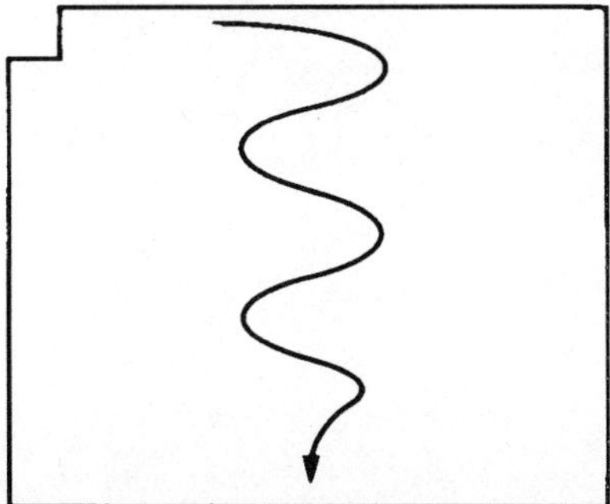

Shifting Point of View:
Rough, Confusing Flow

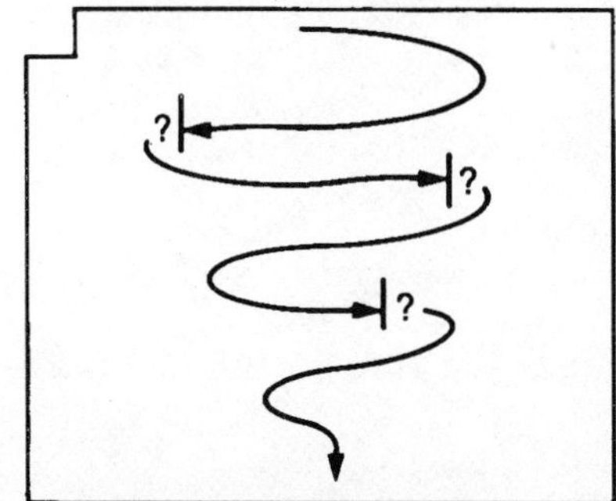

Name ______________________________ Score ________________

Exercise 15b Shifts in person

1. Revise the following sentences to make the person consistent. Place a check mark before sentences that do not need revision.
   a. Whenever I ice skate for more than a few minutes, your cheeks turn rosy red.

   b. Lawrence Olivier's portrayal of King Lear made you realize what a truly great actor he was.

   c. The TV shows about wars, whether comedies like *M.A.S.H.* or dramas like *China Beach,* don't let you know what war was really like.

   d. You can mark this sentence with a "✔" if you don't think it needs revision.

   e. When dunking a basketball, don't hang on the rim.

2. Revise the following paragraph so it applies to a general audience.

   Throughout the United States environmentalists are restoring endangered species to their natural habitats. You see this restoration in action in Colorado where whooping crane eggs have been placed in the nests of sand cranes, who raise the hatchlings as their own. Then the young whoopers are returned to their original habitats. You shouldn't be surprised that this procedure is successful. Put an infant with a new mother, and watch the nurturing instinct emerge. But when that doesn't work, you have to intervene and raise the animals yourself. Zoos have been particularly adept at this task. In more drastic cases, you see artificial insemination used to assure that a species doesn't die out. Don't assume that the entire problem is created by humans. Nature is not kind and causes extinction of species too. That just makes the problem more complex. But look on the bright side. We are winning some battles. You can succeed with effort. If you keep a sustained effort, you can win.

3. Revise the following paragraph using the second person to convey directions for making iced tea.

When I'm in the mood for a good cup of iced tea, I always follow a set routine. I start with very cold, fresh water, which I bring to a rolling boil. Then, I pour the water over a large spoonful of fresh tea. I don't use teabags because they aren't fresh enough for me, and I don't put the tea in any container inside the pot because I want the tea to spread out. I always use a heavy china pot to keep in the heat. Metal pots are particularly bad because they give the tea a metallic flavor. I let the tea steep for seven minutes (I want it strong because I will dilute it with ice). I strain the tea as I slowly pour half the mixture over crushed ice. This procedure cools the tea so that I don't have to use much ice and further dilute the mixture. After two minutes, I pour the remaining tea through the strainer into the glass holding the now cool tea. I then add one or two cubes. Some people may add lemon or sweetener, but I like the taste of tea. If I wanted lemonade or some sickly sweet drink, I wouldn't make tea! Then I stir the mixture to make it as cold as possible, add ice to fill the glass, and relax with a truly refreshing drink.

15c Be consistent in number.

A shift in number usually occurs when a singular noun or pronoun is changed to a plural one; it can be corrected effectively by using plural nouns and pronouns or by recasting sentences.

Common Problems

A shift in number often occurs as the writer tries to avoid sexist language—that is, to avoid using masculine pronouns to represent both genders.

Examples

The following sentences are inconsistent in number:

INCONSISTENT: *Everyone* should turn in *their* tests at the end of the period.

A fashion *model* has a difficult job; *they* put in long hours and endure uncomfortable conditions.

Correcting these shifts by substituting the traditional *his* in the first sentence and *he* in the second offends many. These pronouns would also be inaccurate if the majority of students or fashion models are female. Substituting *her* and *she* merely reverses the problem. The use of *his and her* and *he and she* solves the problem but is often awkward. Using the plural is one of the more effective options:

BETTER: *All students* should turn in *their* tests at the end of the period.

Fashion *models* have a difficult job; *they* put in long hours and endure uncomfortable conditions.

Sometimes recasting the sentence is an alternative:

BETTER: Turn in all tests at the end of the period. [imperative mood]

All tests should be turned in at the end of the period. [passive voice]

The *job* of fashion model is difficult; *it* requires long hours and the ability to endure uncomfortable conditions. [change to neutral subject]

Modeling is a difficult job; *it* requires long hours under uncomfortable conditions. [change to neutral subject]

Name ______________________________ Score ______________

Exercise 15c Consistency in number

Revise the following sentences to maintain consistency in number and to avoid sexist language. Place a check mark before sentences needing no revision.

1. Neither Ronald nor Nancy had heard whether their auditions had earned them roles in the school play.

2. The application said that anyone who wanted a job at McDonald's should turn in his application before March 1st.

3. Somebody had parked their car in front of the service entrance.

4. Each employee was asked to turn in their suggestions for making customers more satisfied with the service they receive.

5. The newspaper reported that either President Bush or Vice President Quayle would give their response to the elections in Europe.

6. Everyone at the conference offered their opinions of the problem.

7. Neither Dan Rather nor Tom Brokaw gives his personal view of the causes of the problems they report.

8. Sometimes nobody wants to tell their answers to the entire class.

9. A physical education teacher must teach his students just as those in traditional classrooms do.

10. "Will someone tell me if they enjoyed the concert?" the teacher asked her students.

15d Avoid shifts between direct and indirect discourse.

Direct discourse relates what is said; *indirect discourse* paraphrases what is said. Quotation marks are necessary to show direct discourse. Questions in direct discourse also require question marks, but they take a period in indirect discourse.

Common Problems

To avoid overusing one form of discourse, writers sometimes shift from one form to the other in a single sentence. In doing so, they may fail to distinguish between a person's actual words and the idea expressed—that is, they may not put the direct discourse in quotation marks and thereby mislead the reader about who is speaking.

Examples

The following sentences include distracting shifts from indirect discourse to direct discourse and from indirect questions to direct questions:

INCONSISTENT: Sam told Bob *that he should come to his room* [indirect discourse] and *make sure to bring your books* [direct discourse]

The next day their teacher asked *if they had completed the assignment* [indirect question] and *will you read your first answer to the class, Sam* [direct question].

Both sentences can be revised in two ways to make the discourse consistent:

INDIRECT DISCOURSE: Sam told Bob *that he should come to his room* and *that he should make sure to bring his books.*

The next day their teacher asked *if they had completed the assignment* and *if Sam would read his first answer to the class.*

DIRECT DISCOURSE: Sam told Bob, *"Come to my room, and make sure to bring your books."*

The next day their teacher asked, *"Have you completed the assignment?"*

"Will you read your first answer to the class, Sam?"

Name ______________________________ Score ______________

Exercise 15d Shifts between direct and indirect discourse

1. Revise the following sentences to maintain indirect discourse throughout.
   a. The Senator asked if we wanted improved roads and social services, and will you be willing to pay the taxes required to support them.

   b. The Johnsons' neighbor told them keep the dog from barking and to make sure he doesn't get out of their yard.

   c. The announcer screamed come on down and that we could win great prizes.

   d. The customer asked the clerk if he would wait on her and if I have a coupon, can I use it.

   e. Joan's father told her to bring the picnic basket and put it in the back seat.

2. Revise the following sentences to maintain direct discourse throughout.
   a. Francie's English teacher asked her did you help Bill with his homework?

   b. George's grandmother told him I would never have let your father grow his hair as long as yours!

   c. Betty loved reading, but I hate reading when I'm tired or when I'm not in the mood, she said.

   d. Sometimes taking a break from work allows a person to return to a task with renewed vigor, Norm said as he shot the basketball.

   e. Get off the table. I'm going to put you outside if I catch you there again, Florence screamed at her dog as he looked at her in confusion.

PART

4

Words and Language

CHAPTER 16

Appropriate Language

16a Match the level of formality to your subject and audience.

The level of formality is influenced by both the writer's purpose and the subject, but especially by evaluating correctly the expectations of the audience. The level of formality for graded college essays is most often informal.

Common Problems

Although writers may understand their purposes, their subjects, and the necessary degree of formality, they are frequently unaware of the audience for college writing. As a result, they are often too informal and occasionally too formal. Inappropriate or mixed levels of formality may confuse or irritate the audience.

Examples

Because the levels of formality in prose overlap, they might be represented more accurately by a continuum than by distinct categories. These levels are as follows:

Formal

SUBJECTS (serious and complex): legal briefs, technical reports, scholarly articles, scientific reports
AUDIENCE: specialized, knowledgeable, intellectual
PURPOSE: to inform or persuade
WRITTEN CONVENTIONS: specialized terminology, usually third person, few contractions, passive voice, nominalizations

> The discovery of and naming of *Australopithecus afarensis* could not have been accomplished without the contributions of many paleoanthropologists.

Informal

SUBJECTS: college essays, magazine articles, sermons, news articles, memos
AUDIENCE: general
PURPOSE: to inform, persuade, or entertain
WRITTEN CONVENTIONS: general terminology, third or first person, standard contractions, verbal style

> I enjoyed my trip to the Field Museum where I saw many new fossil exhibits—exhibits that wouldn't have been possible fifteen years ago.

Very informal

SUBJECTS: personal letters, journal entries, notes

AUDIENCE: close friends, the writer

PURPOSE: to entertain, inform, persuade, record thoughts, work out ideas

WRITTEN CONVENTIONS: loose diction, slang, abbreviations, usually first person, sometimes shifting to second person, contractions

> Fred, you should've seen the old bones at the museum. It would've blown your mind.

Name ____ Score ____________________

Exercise 16a Formality

1. Indicate the level of formality and a possible audience and purpose for the following passages. Explain the reasons for your choices.
   a. Water skiing is one of the things I really like doing a lot. You forget about everything as you glide over the water with a cool breeze blowing in your face.

   b. It has been said that philologists thrive on perusing the corpus of their favorite author.

   c. Pick up sport coat at the cleaners. Order corsage. Find out color of Tammy's dress. See if George'll drive. Make reservations at Ember's or Antonio's. Be at Tammy's at 7:15. Practice dancing with Mom at 4:30.

   d. Experiments conducted upon drosophila have been successful in creating specimens far different from the progenitors.

   e. The most well known and successful proboscideans are the elephantidae whose habitat was once extensive but now includes only sections of Africa and India.

2. Rewrite the preceding sentences to make them informal. When necessary, use your dictionary to determine a more common meaning for formal terms. Supply actors when you convert the passive voice to the active, and change nominalizations to verbs.
   1.

   2.

   3.

   4.

   5.

16b, 16c, 16e Use jargon, slang, colloquialisms, and neologisms sparingly.

Jargon, slang, colloquialisms, and neologisms are inappropriate for the informal style of most college assignments. These terms may reduce the range of the audience and often conflict with the purpose or subject of the essay.

Common Problems

Any kind of nonstandard diction or other unfamiliar terminology risks confusion. These diction problems in writing may be the result of a carryover from speech. The level of formality in speech is often inconsistent and may be appropriate for a special audience, but informal college writing strives for consistency and a general audience.

Examples

Jargon: In the following sentence, *jargon*—technical terms from particular disciplines, such as accounting and computer technology—is less effective than general standard diction:

> The *bottom line* of the survey was that administrators need abundant *input* if they want faculty members to accept their *output.*
>
> The main point the survey revealed was that administrators need a wide range of faculty opinions if they want the faculty to accept their conclusions.

Bottom line refers to the place on a balance sheet indicating net income or loss; *input* and *output* refer to the data entered in a computer and the resulting product.

Slang, colloquialisms, and regionalisms: Slang is the language of a social group that helps unify it; a *colloquialism* is language more appropriate to speech than to writing; and *regionalisms* are the colloquialisms of a particular geographic region that, like slang, help define a group. The narrow appeal and extreme informality of slang, colloquialisms, and regionalisms make such diction generally inappropriate for college writing, as illustrated below:

> We were just having fun, but the *Five-O* put an end to that. [slang for "the police arrived"]
>
> Three *guys* in my history class tried *to talk me into* attending a lecture on Vietnam with them. [colloquial for "three men tried to persuade me"]
>
> I was *fixin' to* write my essay when my friend asked me to go to a movie. [regionalism for "preparing to write"]

Neologisms are newly invented words.

> They *dialogued* for over an hour.
>
> Tricia has become a *soapaholic* during her spring break.

The conversion of the noun *dialogue* to a verb offers no advantage over *spoke.* In some informal writing the blending of *soap opera* and *alcoholic* might be acceptable to indicate a person addicted to watching soap operas, but writers must be wary of such creations and should avoid overusing them.

Name ______________________________ Score ______________

Exercise 16b, 16c, 16e Jargon, slang, colloquialisms, regionalisms, neologisms

Identify the problems in each of the following sentences and revise them to remove jargon, slang, colloquialisms, regionalisms, and neologisms. Some sentences may have more than one type of problem.

1. The dispatcher sent two uniforms to investigate the complaint of disorderly conduct.

2. Every time she thought about her psychology midterm, Jill became uptight; she was certain she would come unglued during the actual test.

3. Susan was not for sure whether she would go to the concert with her friends from school or with her parents.

4. The fact of the matter is that taxes will be increased in the next two years.

5. Rick woke his sister Gayle at 6:00 a.m. just so he could be the first to happy birthday her.

6. When my roommate and I went to Orlando, we had a really fun time, but we ran out of money after only three days.

7. After having set the parameters for the discussion, the moderator let the debate begin.

8. The committee wanted feedback from local residents on the pros and cons of a minimum security prison being built in the area.

9. I feel like that we'll have a tough row to hoe next year because every team in the conference will have more experience and depth than us.

10. When students prioritize their time well, they improve gradewise.

16d Avoid pretentious and bombastic language.

Readers gain an impression of the writer from the diction as well as from the ideas expressed. Writers whose prose is simple and straightforward make the most favorable impression on the readers.

Common Problems

Words that are too formal for the subject, purpose, or audience and synonyms unfamiliar to the reader that the writer used to achieve variety often create an awkward rather than a fluent style. Inflated synonyms do not make ideas significant.

Examples

The following sentences contain inappropriate diction:

> *One* could do far worse than choose either a *canine* or a *feline* as a *domestic companion.*
>
> Because he lived only a mile from his office, Charles *strolled* to work whatever the weather.

In the first sentence, *one* is an overly formal way of saying "a person," or "you." The words *canine, feline,* and *domestic companion* are not only too formal for the purpose of the sentence, they are also too general: wolves are also canines, tigers are also felines, and people are also domestic companions. In the second sentence, the word *strolled* is too formal and probably inaccurate; few would walk leisurely, as *stroll* implies, in stormy weather. Far more appropriate would be the following:

> *A person* could do far worse than choose either a *dog* or a *cat* as a *pet.*
>
> Because he lived only a mile from his office, Charles *walked* to work whatever the weather.

The following sentence uses archaic words that unnecessarily increase the formality of the sentence:

> The morning was so *beauteous* that *ere* she knew it, Susan had missed the train for work.

The revised sentence uses contemporary, natural diction:

> The morning was so *beautiful* that *before* she knew it, Susan had missed the train for work.

Another form of pretentious language is the use of *euphemisms,* which are phrasings that replace terms considered unpleasant. Most people accept euphemisms designed to protect another's feelings or sensitivities—for example, "Jane's mother *passed away* recently" or "The *rest room* is down the hall." But euphemisms should not be used to deceive:

> The advertisement announced a sale on *preowned automobiles.*
>
> The information you were given is *inoperative.*

Both sentences are intended to mislead readers and could be stated more accurately:

> The advertisement announced a sale on *used cars.*
>
> I *lied* to you.

Name ______________________________ Score ______________

Exercise 16d Pretentious language

Rewrite the following sentences removing the pretentious language.

1. Because she could not remember what her customers had ordered and because she enjoyed talking to her fellow workers more than cleaning tables, Laura was let go.

2. It is of paramount importance that Daniel find gainful employment, or he will be unable to fulfill his obligatory financial responsibilities.

3. The executive branch has proposed several revenue enhancing programs to reduce the deficit.

4. Jean said that just because she was under the influence was no reason for her driver's license to be suspended.

5. The disputes between my sibling and myself over the program offerings available on television have driven our progenitors to the extreme measure of denying the machine alternating current.

6. If only Lisa's efforts regarding her academic pursuits equalled those she puts forth for her social enterprises, she would earn the highest evaluations of her scholarly facilitators.

7. Oliver thought it more prudent to withhold an accurate rendition of the events in which he had participated than to incur possible incarceration for admission of his culpability.

8. Mrs. Baker had been in a family way for four months before she had to buy new clothing.

9. Grant tried to convince his mother that she would enjoy her golden years more fully in a retirement community of her peers than in his home.

10. Reggie told Veronica that her ocular orbs were an indication to him that she had fallen under the spell of his oratory skill, but she assured him she was only suffering from an allergic reaction to his inexpensive *eau de toilette.*

CHAPTER 17

Using the Exact Word

17a Use the dictionary to find the correct form of a word.

Among the many benefits of a dictionary, other than providing definitions and spellings, is the assistance it provides in selecting precise diction, an essential feature of an effective style. The following are excellent college-level dictionaries:

The American Heritage Dictionary (Second college edition, 1985)
The Random House College Dictionary (Revised edition, 1984)
Webster's New World Dictionary (Third college edition, 1988)
Webster's Ninth New Collegiate Dictionary (1988)
Webster's II, New Riverside University Dictionary (1984)

Common Problems

Vague, imprecise, or inaccurate terms undermine all other virtues a piece of writing might possess. Although pocket-sized dictionaries provide correct spellings and brief definitions, they do not offer the advantages of a college-level dictionary.

Example

In addition to defining terms, dictionaries indicate correct spelling, syllabication, pronunciation, parts of speech, etymology, usage, synonyms, and antonyms, and they provide information on language, individuals, and places. Check the table of contents and several entries before deciding which dictionary to purchase.

Name ______________________________ Score ________________

Exercise 17a Correct word forms

1. Choose one of the collegiate dictionaries listed on the previous page (check with your teacher if you wish to use another dictionary), and complete the following exercises.
   a. Using the table of contents, list its major sections.

   b. Compare the table of contents from two dictionaries of your choice. How do they differ?

   c. What pronunciation(s) are acceptable for *suite?*

   d. Translate the following foreign phrases: *ex libris, vox populi, ars longa, vita brevis, eureka, lapsus linguae.*

   e. Why should the word *irregardless* be avoided?

   f. What does the word *gaol* mean, and why is it spelled as it is?

g. Write in your own words two opposing definitions for the word *trip*.

2. Using *The Oxford English Dictionary* (your library will have a copy), answer the following questions:
   a. How has the word *toilet* changed since its earliest usage?

   b. How has the word *stench* changed its meaning over the years?

   c. How has the word *bead* changed its meaning?

17b Use a dictionary and a thesaurus to discover appropriate synonyms.

A thesaurus helps writers choose words with precise connotations for the context, replace overworked phrasing, avoid repetition, maintain a consistent level of formality, and discover new, provocative terms.

Common Problems

Inappropriate choices from a thesaurus create an inconsistent tone and level of formality and an imprecise, often pretentious style. Therefore, some teachers caution students on overusing a thesaurus, a valuable tool when applied correctly.

Examples

Synonyms, antonyms, and idioms add great variety to prose style; however, writers should be careful when using a thesaurus to avoid choosing terms with inappropriate connotations. Because a thesaurus does not define terms, a writer should keep a dictionary readily available. Consider the following use of *mutual* and *common*:

> We had a *mutual* interest in gambling.
>
> We had a *common* interest in gambling.

In this context, both words suggest shared interests. But *common* can also suggest "base" or "low," connotations not intended in the original sentence.

Name ______________________________ Score ______________

Exercise 17b Appropriate synonyms

1. Using a dictionary, explain in your own words the differences between the italicized word and its synonyms.

   a. *friendly*, outgoing, gregarious, amiable, cordial

   b. *lonely*, forlorn, lonesome, solitary, aloof

   c. *loud*, noisy, obstreperous, vociferous, blatant

   d. *childish*, childlike, immature, infantile, puerile

   e. *funny*, droll, jocular, comical, facetious

   f. *cheap*, inexpensive, low-priced, modest, poor

g. *informer,* tattletale, stool pigeon, blabbermouth, talebearer

h. *job,* profession, vocation, trade, occupation

i. *purpose,* aim, goal, objective, end

j. *stop,* cease, quit, halt, desist

2. Write a sentence for *each* word in the following pairs of synonyms, making certain that your sentences reflect the connotations of the specific term.
   a. gregarious

      cordial

   b. vociferous

Name ______________________________

Exercise 17b (continued)

blatant

c. childlike

infantile

d. droll

facetious

e. vocation

trade

17c Use the word with the correct meaning.

Carefully chosen words communicate ideas clearly and reinforce style.

Common Problems

Homophones (words that sound the same but are spelled differently—see section **47b**), words that appear to have the same meaning, or nonidiomatic terms dilute the intensity of sentences.

Examples

The terms in the following sentences do not communicate the writer's intended meaning:

FAULTY: Corinne's daily aerobic workout *enervated* her, making her heavy schedule possible.

Although she went to football games with Annie, Jean was completely *disinterested* and spent much of her time watching the crowd.

When she surprised her parents by marrying Barry, Anita's mother said that she would be happy to *except* him in the family.

The company sent people to Alaska *in search for* oil.

In the first sentence, Corinne should be "energized" or "invigorated," not "weakened," as *enervate* suggests. Jean was "uninterested," not "impartial," the meaning of *disinterested.* Because of the context, the third sentence is ambiguous; Anita's mother may have wished to "exclude" Barry, a meaning of *except,* rather than "welcome" him, a meaning of *accept.* In the last sentence, the correct idiomatic usage is "in search *of*" rather than "in search for."

BETTER: Corinne's daily aerobic workout *energized* her, making her heavy schedule possible.

Although she went to football games with Annie, Jean was completely *uninterested* and spent much of her time watching the crowd.

When she surprised her parents by marrying Barry, Anita's mother said that she would be happy to *accept* him in the family.

The company sent people to Alaska *in search of* oil.

Name ______________________ Score ______________

Exercise 17c Correct meaning

1. In the following sentences, circle the appropriate term. Check your answers by referring to a college-level dictionary.
   a. Biologists examined the desert to determine the (affect/effect) of the nuclear explosion on the environment.

   b. The lawyer asked that the defendant receive the maximum penalty because of the (enormousness/enormity) of the crime.

   c. From the tone of his father's voice, Darwin (implied/inferred) that he could not go to the midnight showing of *The Rocky Horror Picture Show.*

   d. By driving a truck across it, the engineer (assured/insured) the crowd that the bridge was safe.

   e. The wind, the warm sun, and the roar of the waves provided Rita with one of the most (sensual/sensuous) experiences she had had in years.

   f. Before he bought his computer, Norm sought the (advice/advise) of his friend Jeff.

   g. Just as the play reached the (climatic/climactic) scene, someone in the audience had a fit of sneezing.

   h. A group of parents wanted to (censor/censure) a book that their children had been assigned in school.

   i. Laura asked her parents how much (farther/further) they had to drive before they would arrive at the zoo.

   j. The telethon had been on (continually/continuously) for twenty-four hours.

2. In the following sentences, circle the appropriate idiom. Check your answers by referring to a college-level dictionary.
   a. Professor Jonas asked her students to (try and/try to) finish the test in thirty minutes.

   b. Stella wanted Stanley to (come by/come to) her house before they went to the party.

   c. One of the central issues in the question of abortion (centers on/centers around) is not whether a collection of cells is living but whether the collection is a human life.

   d. The baseball owners (differed with/differed from) the players' association on the question of free agency.

   e. Fred was annoyed because the class didn't (agree to/agree with) his plan.

17d Understand connotations and denotations.

A *connotation* is the suggested or implicit meaning; a *denotation* is the direct or explicit meaning. Connotations and denotations affect readers by appealing to their senses, beliefs, prejudices, and fears.

Common Problems

Writers sometimes try to move an audience unfairly through connotation by appealing to prejudice and fear.

Examples

The connotations of the terms in the following sentence reinforce the writer's meaning, that the gathering was tasteful:

> The *bouquet* [not *odor*] of the wine *accented* [not *stressed*] the *elegance* [not *grandeur*] that typified the entire *celebration* [not *party*].

The connotations in the following sentence attempt to conceal the fact that a person committed a crime:

> As a *war hero* [not *soldier*] and a *patriot* [not just a *citizen*], the defendant deserves *leeway* [not *special privileges*] for his *actions* [not *disregard of laws*].

These sentences use connotative language for different purposes—purposes whose ethical implications writers must seriously consider.

Name ______________________ Score ______________

Exercise 17d Connotations and denotations

1. Revise each of the following sentences, creating two additional versions. First, substitute neutral words for the italicized words. Next, substitute words with the opposite connotations.

   a. Philip thought the movie was *gushy* and *sentimental.*

   ____

   ____

   b. The official said, "We should call those *replacement drivers* what they are—*scabs.*"

   ____

   ____

   c. Terry's *social drinking* often led to *aggressive* behavior.

   ____

   ____

   d. Lance disliked Dwight because he was a *wimp* and an *apple polisher.*

   ____

   ____

e. Carolyn was a threat to the men in the office because she was *masculine* and *forceful.*

____

____

2. Indicate the different connotations of the following pairs of words.

a. studious ____

bookish ____

b. woman ____

lady ____

c. svelte ____

lean ____

d. accept my gratitude ____

thanks ____

Name ______________________________

Exercise 17d (continued)

e. guy ______________________________

lad ______________________________

f. bumpy ______________________________

jagged ______________________________

g. athlete ______________________________

jock ______________________________

h. old ______________________________

elderly ______________________________

i. independent ______________________________

rebellious ______________________________

j. courage____

guts ____

17e Use concrete and specific words.

Words that appeal to the senses (sight, touch, hearing, smell, taste) rather than abstract, general terms help readers understand and envision what the writer is saying.

Common Problems

General examples with abstract terms make prose confusing, dull, and lifeless.

Examples

The following sentences use abstract, general language:

I had a great sandwich for lunch today.

We had a lot of fun at school.

Making these sentences concrete adds interest and zest and makes the writer's point clear:

With the melted Swiss cheese dripping off the corned beef and the smell of the sauerkraut, my mouth began to water, but when I sunk my teeth into the crisp, toasted rye bread, I thought I would go out of my mind with joy.

When Mr. Mongerson's experiment in science class with static electricity made Stacy's hair stand on end, Jackie and I laughed until we had tears in our eyes.

Name ______________________________ Score ______________

Exercise 17e Concrete and specific words

1. Revise the following abstract terms by supplying first a specific example and then an actual example.
Example:
Hamburger
SPECIFIC EXAMPLE: *A MacDonald's Big Mac*
ACTUAL EXAMPLE: *The Big Mac I had yesterday with the torn bun and with mayonnaise dripping from the lettuce hanging over the side.*

a. A brand of athletic shoe

SPECIFIC EXAMPLE: ______________________________

ACTUAL EXAMPLE: ______________________________

____

b. A bird chirping

SPECIFIC EXAMPLE: ______________________________

ACTUAL EXAMPLE: ______________________________

____

c. An animal's coat (or hide, or skin)

SPECIFIC EXAMPLE: ______________________________

ACTUAL EXAMPLE: ______________________________

____

d. A confrontation between two people

SPECIFIC EXAMPLE: ______________________________

ACTUAL EXAMPLE: ______________________________

____

e. A refreshing drink

SPECIFIC EXAMPLE: ______________________________

ACTUAL EXAMPLE: ______________________________

____

f. An unpleasant morning

SPECIFIC EXAMPLE: ______________________________

ACTUAL EXAMPLE: ______________________________

____

g. An untidy room

SPECIFIC EXAMPLE: ______________________________

ACTUAL EXAMPLE: ______________________________

____

h. A favorite article of clothing

SPECIFIC EXAMPLE: ______________________________

ACTUAL EXAMPLE: ______________________________

____

i. An experience involving water

SPECIFIC EXAMPLE: ______________________________

ACTUAL EXAMPLE: ______________________________

____

Name ______________________________

Exercise 17e (continued)

j. A memorable odor

SPECIFIC EXAMPLE: ______________________________

ACTUAL EXAMPLE: ______________________________

____

2. Revise the following paragraph using specific details or, if possible, actual details to make the style vivid.

Gazing down from the high point, I saw several pretty places in the foreground and some in the distance. As I watched I also saw interesting things happening. I could hear what was going on, too, and that made me more anxious to get there. As I walked closer, I noticed details I hadn't seen or heard before. It was not nearly as boring as I had thought it would be.

17f Avoid sexist or biased language.

Language that reveals an awareness of reader sensitivities creates a bond between writers and readers and reinforces the writer's credibility.

Common Problems

Historically, the masculine pronoun *he,* (and *him, his*) has referred to the combination of males and females as well as just to males. But since the 1960s, use of the traditional, all-encompassing *he* has become regarded as sexist and discriminatory. Contemporary writers cope with the problem in various ways.

Examples

Avoid words that inappropriately imply gender, that patronize, or that demean.

1. Use plural nouns and pronouns, use first-person plural, or recast sentences completely to avoid sexist language.

   Such sentences as

   > A writer must consider the effect of *his* language on *his* audience.

   should be revised in one of the following ways:

   > *Writers* must consider the effect of *their* language on *their* audiences.
   >
   > *We* must consider the effect of *our* language on *our* audience.
   >
   > *A* writer must consider the effect *of language* on *an* audience. [A shift in emphasis is one way of recasting the sentence.]
   >
   > *Eudora Welty* always considered the effect *her* language had on *her* audience. [Making the sentence specific also removes the pronoun problem.]

   The options of using "he or she," or "one" create grammatically correct sentences. But the former is awkward, and the latter is stilted. Coining new words, such as "s/he" creates other problems.

2. Instead of using the word *man* to refer to the human race, use *humanity, people,* or *human beings.*
3. Avoid implying a single gender for a job or role filled by either sex. Use *salesperson* instead of *salesman* or *saleslady.*
4. Do not precede a job title with the gender; use the term *secretary,* not *male secretary,* or *lawyer,* not *female lawyer.*
5. Do not use patronizing terms. If in a similar situation a male would be referred to as a *man* (not a *gentleman*), then use the term *woman* rather than *lady* to refer to a female. If a male would be referred to as a *man,* refer to a female as a *woman,* not as a *girl*).
6. Do not use demeaning terms. A person who makes a living by writing is a *writer,* not a *woman writer,* an *African American writer,* or a *Hispanic writer.* Terms like *poet, artist,* and *soldier,* should be treated similarly (the obvious exception to this point occurs when the specific gender, race, or nationality is the issue discussed). Also avoid terms such as *girl* or *gal* or *boy* to refer to adults. Use *baggage carrier,* not *bellboy.*

   Some demeaning terms referring to gender, race, religion, nationality, or geographic background are, unfortunately, so well known that they do not need mention here. They should never be used in speech, much less in writing. Aside from being intrinsically offensive, they destroy a writer's credibility.

7. When no agreed-upon term is available, use a label that describes the job rather than the person. An *office boy* or *office girl* might be a *messenger* or an *assistant.* A *bus boy* is a *person who clears tables.*

Name ______________________ Score ______________

Exercise 17f Sexist or biased language

1. Using the methods suggested on the previous pages, create *two* revisions of the following sentences to remove sexist language or ineffective solutions to the problem of sexist language.
   a. The teacher asked everyone to turn in his examination.

   ____

   ____

   b. Cindy asked each of her parents what they wanted her to give them for their anniversary.

   ____

   ____

   c. Everybody who attended the leadership conference said that he had profited from it.

   ____

   ____

   d. If one wants to buy tickets for the concert, one can buy them at three locations beforehand, unless one wants to take one's chances at the door.

   ____

   ____

e. When somebody first tries to write at a word processor, he or she usually thinks that they will have more problems than he or she does.

____

____

2. Supply substitutes for the inappropriate terms in the following sentences.
   a. Ever since she was a little girl, Megan wanted to be a policeman.

   b. At the square dance the men stood in a line, and the ladies faced them.

   c. Saul Bellow is a great Jewish writer whose novel *Seize the Day* was made into a successful movie.

   d. The chairman rapped the gavel and called the meeting to order.

   e. Bob was annoyed that his male nurse woke him to administer a sleeping pill.

   f. One of the most serious problems mailmen face is unchained dogs.

   g. The girls at the office gave a party for the office boy who was retiring.

   h. If a man does his best, he may not be rich, but he should be happy.

Name ____

Exercise 17f (continued)

i. The weatherman predicted that a hurricane would hit the coast during the night.

j. Lillian Gish and Bette Davis played two old maids in *The Whales of August.*

CHAPTER 18

Concise Language

18a Avoid long generalizations, and edit and cut unnecessary words.

An engaging style is brief and direct and avoids empty expressions.

Common Problems

Wordy phrasings obscure important information, bury the point of the sentence, and deflate the verve of prose style.

Examples

Writers must identify the audience they are writing for and must assume that their readers have some general knowledge of the subject.

WORDY: Because many farmers use pesticides, *which are aimed at parasites and other organisms destructive to cash crops,* to eliminate these creatures, beneficial insects are also destroyed.

Even a general audience should know what pesticides do.

REVISED: Because many farmers use pesticides to eliminate harmful creatures, beneficial insects are also destroyed.

A sentence is not weak simply because it is long, it is weak when the sentence is made wordy through empty phrasing. *Compressing* clauses to phrases and phrases to single words is an effective first step in editing.

WORDY CLAUSE: Gardening provides a release from the tensions of living *that we encounter every day.*

REVISED: Gardening provides a release from the tensions of *everyday* living.

WORDY PHRASE: Many climatologists are concerned that forests *in tropical regions* are being cleared for pasture and crop production.

REVISED: Many climatologists are concerned that *tropical* forests are being cleared for pasture and crop production.

Deadwood is empty phrasing that contributes little to a sentence. Becoming attuned to deadwood is important in avoiding it.

DEADWOOD: Employees will be paid *on a bi-weekly basis.*

Due to the fact that grizzlies are nearly extinct in the lower 48 states, conservation efforts have been concentrated in Alaska's national parks and forests.

REVISED: Employees will be paid *bi-weekly.*

Because grizzlies are nearly extinct in the lower 48 states, conservation efforts have been concentrated in Alaska's national parks and forests.

Redundant terms repeat unnecessarily, not for emphasis or rhetorical effect.

REDUNDANT: No drastic changes occurred in the *three-decade period* of the fifties, sixties, and seventies.

The cooperation of each member is necessary for *complete* unity.

REVISED: No drastic changes occurred in the fifties, sixties, and seventies.

The cooperation of each member is necessary for unity.

Some *intensifiers* and *qualifiers* add nothing to the description or level of feeling and are thus meaningless.

MEANINGLESS: The teller reported that Mrs. Barnes was *really* upset about the $52 charge for overdrafts.

The young lieutenant recalled his blue-eyed girl back home, whom he'd almost forgotten but liked *a lot.*

In addition to being a weak intensifier, the phrase *a lot* is imprecise, overused, and often too informal for its context.

Unnecessary qualifying phrases do not actually cushion the writer's position, and the additional phrasing only weakens the sentence.

UNNECESSARY: *In my opinion* Gwen Verdon in *Damn Yankees* sparked the 1955 Broadway bonanza.

In movie musicals, *it is clear that* Fred Astaire is a more accomplished dancer than Gene Kelly.

Expletive structures, such as *it is* and *there is* are invariably wordy and delay the point of the sentence.

EXPLETIVE: *There are* many stories in the naked city.

It is here in this lush prairie setting that the story of the immigrants continues.

There had been no desire on Roderick's part to get himself out of his melancholy mood.

REVISED: The naked city has many stories to tell.

The story of the immigrants continues in this lush prairie setting.

Roderick had no desire to get himself out of his melancholy mood.

Name ______________________________ Score ______________

Exercise 18a Generalizations, wordiness

1. Recast the following sentences with more succinct phrasings.
   a. In spite of the water on its surface, Monterey Bay, off the coast of California, might look like the Grand Canyon, which is located in Arizona.

   b. This large chasm is being explored with vehicles which reflect an advanced state of technology, are not manned, and are operated by remote control.

   c. The depth to which these vehicles can sink is almost 3,000 feet, and at that level life grows and thrives in the dark.

   d. As water becomes darker and darker, fish begin to make their own light, which scientists have come to label as "bioluminescence."

   e. Besides the glows cast by the fish, the creatures of these diving vehicles were put into use.

   f. In addition to the fish and crustaceans that enjoy the deep waters of Monterey Bay, marine scientists have also learned in recent years that some sea mammals, such as the elephant seal, also have been known to reach great depths.

   g. The elephant seal has been known to descend to more than 3,600 feet, and scientists can only speculate on the reasons, which to humans is almost defying death, including the food available at that depth.

   h. Monterey Bay also contains a forest, which is usually thought of as tall trees forming a canopy with lower growing trees and shrubs to fill in, but this forest is one of kelp growing just a little way off the shore.

i. For the fish that live in the bay and for the other forms of animal life to be found here, this kelp forest is an important source of food at the same time that it creates myriad hiding places for tiny creatures which need to escape from predators.

j. The wonders of Monterey Bay may be seen in a compact way at the Monterey Bay Aquarium, an institution that gathers plant and animal life to exhibit, including a unique kelp forest and other indigenous ecosystems of the bay.

2. Recast the following sentences to eliminate wordiness or repetition.
   a. A plant that is to be particularly enjoyed in the landscaping efforts of all interested gardeners is *hosta,* which has a tendency to spread well in shady areas and comes in so many varieties.

   b. There's a possibility that we could finally determine that SDI (or the "Star Wars" laser system) is a somewhat less feasible alternative than we think of it now, and we would thus be enabled to enter into other research programs as the U.S. seeks to develop defensive systems in the nuclear arena which are more cost effective.

   c. There are many basic similarities between the film version of Shaw's *Pygmalion* and Lerner and Loewe's *My Fair Lady.*

   d. For one thing, Eliza is a flower seller in both the film and the play who is uneducated and really talks with a Cockney accent.

   e. There is another similar scene which is included in both works when Eliza really practices her vowels that she can't say by reciting "The Rain in Spain."

   f. The film and the musical play also have exactly the same concluding end with Eliza returning to the flat of Henry Higgins.

Name ______________________________

Exercise 18a (continued)

g. The movie version, which relies heavily on the Broadway musical produced earlier, kept two of the first and foremost important actors, in my opinion—Rex Harrison and Stanley Holloway.

h. However, it's certainly true that this ending is very different than the ending of Shaw's play, which has Eliza going off to marry Freddy and Professor Higgins laughing in a sarcastic way about the future prospects of this marriage.

i. Due to the fact that Eliza is both something Higgins creates and a person who fights back, I believe that her conflict with him is basically an indication that she likes him a lot.

j. Basically, the play appearing on Broadway portrays in a comedic way how love can cross class lines, but this can happen only at the point when the professor learns some humility and Eliza realizes that she is a human being who is entitled to respect from him.

3. Revise the following paragraph to eliminate unnecessary phrasings.

It has been shown that the government was really searching for a way that was painless in a political sense to reduce the deficit of the federal budget. To do this Congress enacted the Balanced Budget and Emergency Deficit Control Act of 1985. This act is better known as Gramm-Rudman-Hollings. The president signed this bill. The goal of GRH was to achieve a budget at the federal level which was very balanced. Under this law there are lower and lower ceilings on deficit spending in each fiscal year. The budget which is agreed upon and approved by Congress and the president must be within $10 million of the target which is specified by the Balanced Budget and Emergency Deficit Control Act. When this target is not reached and met, there are cuts in spending which the Congress and the president must begin across the board.

18b Use positive constructions for clarity.

Positive constructions allow prose to flow smoothly, without curious phrasing to puzzle the reader.

Common Problems

Affected prose style may be peppered with negative constructions in an effort to appear understated and witty. In most cases, however, the reader must usually ponder the writer's real intention—always a deadly event.

Examples

CONFUSING: Windsor, Ontario, is not unlike its neighbor across the border, Detroit, Michigan.

BETTER: Windsor, Ontario, is like its neighbor across the border, Detroit, Michigan.

In the sentence "The sky was not cloudy," readers do not know whether the sky was deep blue or sunny or heavily overcast.

Name ______________________________ Score ______________

Exercise 18b Positive constructions

Revise the following sentences to state the main point positively. Add details if necessary.

1. *Blue Steel* was not the best film of 1990.

2. Dee was surprised to find that her blind date was not 5'10".

3. The walls of the classroom were not green.

4. John did not have a happy expression on his face when he received his examination.

5. Broccoli is not George's favorite vegetable.

6. Sports are sometimes a not inexpensive way of keeping fit.

7. However, compared to such exercise, gardening offers a not costly and a not inefficient way to metabolize calories.

8. Such chores as mowing, raking, and weeding expend not less energy than swimming.

9. As with any strenuous activity, it's not incautious to do the easy jobs first.

10. Your garden and your body will both be not ungrateful for this regular maintenance.

CHAPTER 19

Figurative Language

19a Use both metaphor and simile.

When a *tenor* (a subject) is compared to a *vehicle* (a second, dissimilar subject), the similarity suggested guides reader response and gives insight into the writer's mind. *Similes* make a bold, explicit comparison by using *like* or *as*. *Metaphors* make a subtle, implicit comparison without labels to guide readers.

Common Problems

Both similes and metaphors are ineffective if the similarity between the tenor and the vehicle is not evident or if the vehicle is unfamiliar. Overworked similes or metaphors are deadening because they substitute for, rather than support, ideas.

Examples

Using *as,* the simile in the following sentence explicitly compares Ralph's chance for an A (the tenor) to catching a trout bare-handed (the vehicle):

> Ralph's chance for an A on his final exam was as remote *as* his catching a trout with his bare hands.

The following sentence *implies* the same vehicle as the sentence above (a fish escaping a person's grasp) to clarify the implied tenor (Ralph's attempt for an A):

> Ralph *grasped* for an A on his final exam, but it *slipped* between pen and the paper and *escaped.*

The verbs *grasped, slipped,* and *escaped* imply the vehicle.

The simile in the following sentence is ineffective:

> The leaf floated on the stream like the earth on the Milky Way.

The vehicle, the earth's movement in the Milky Way galaxy, is less familiar to most readers than the tenor, a leaf floating on a stream.

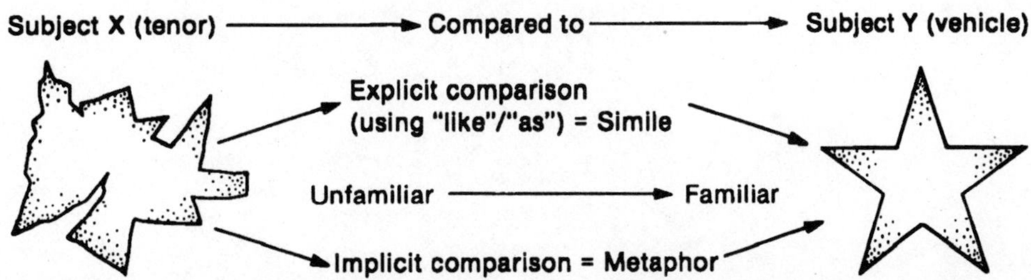

Name ______________________________ Score ______________

Exercise 19a Metaphor and simile

Identify whether or not the following sentences contain similes or metaphors. In those that do, identify the tenor and vehicle. If the vehicle does not narrow the tenor, explain why that is the case. If no similes or metaphors are present, place a check mark before the sentence.

1. After arguing with Suzanne, Joe felt like a crumpled Kleenex.

2. At midnight, the campfire still glowed like burning embers in the dark.

3. A clear night was a map for early seafarers.

4. Modern writers use dirty words as a means of creating realism.

5. Terry was as frustrated as a diabetic in a candy factory.

6. Many sports writers think that David Robinson is the Park Avenue of NBA centers.

7. Stegosauruses were the rhinos of the Mesozoic age.

8. Sam's mother complained that he ate like a bird—a vulture!

9. Cindy thought Mel Gibson was a hunk, but Hilary thought he was like many other contemporary actors.

10. Jim's careless errors drove a knive in the heart of his English teacher, and his penmanship twisted it.

19b Use figurative language to sway opinion, view life, and surprise the reader.

Figurative language uses connotative meanings to reinforce the literal, denotative meanings.

Common Problems

Figurative language is ineffective when it fails to reinforce the literal meaning or creates connotations that conflict with that meaning.

Example

The images that similes create can determine reader response to a denotative statement:

The pedestrian ran as quickly

a. as an embattled deer.

b. as an embattled rhino.

As vehicles both *a* and *b* succeed in the *primary* goal of connoting quickness, but the images have *secondary* connotations: the image of a deer might connote timidity, a victim; whereas the image of a rhino might suggest aggressiveness, an attacker.

Name ______________________ Score ______________

Exercise 19b Figurative language

Describe the primary and secondary connotations of the following similes and metaphors and explain whether the secondary connotations reinforce the goal of the sentence, detract from it, or are neutral.

1. Government should provide a safety net for all American citizens.

2. The center on Titanic State's basketball team runs the court like a gazelle.

3. The cigarette smoke coiled around Chuck's body and crushed the air from his lungs.

4. The senator attacked his opponent's arguments one at a time and completely demolished them.

5. When the president addressed the group, all eyes were riveted on the podium.

6. The Doberman faced the terrified intruder and growled like a finely tuned engine.

7. Geoff grasped the meaning of Eve's expression and put his pet tarantula back in its cage.

8. Books are windows into the minds of their authors.

9. The sun spread over the valley like an oil spill over the ocean.

10. Anne swept all unpleasant facts under a rug in the corner of her consciousness.

19c Create fresh similes and metaphors.

Fresh similes and metaphors can be created by comparing humans and human features to nonhuman things—animals, vegetables, minerals, actions—and by comparing the nonhuman to humans and human features (the latter is called *personification*).

Common Problems

Overused similes and metaphors are ineffective, as are figurative expressions when the dissimilarity between the tenor and the vehicle is too great.

Examples

The following sentences create a simile or a metaphor by likening elements in essentially dissimilar things:

> Rumors slither into people's minds and poison friendships. [a human action/a snake]
>
> Dean and Jerry were the peanut butter and jelly of the basketball team. [a relationship/food]
>
> The mosquito accepted Gail's bare arm as an invitation to dinner, enjoyed the feast, and wandered home in a gluttonous stupor. [an animal action/a human action]

The following figures of speech are ineffective:

> In her new outfit, Buffy was as pretty as a picture.
>
> Herb's mouth was as dry as the Sahara Desert.

The simile in the first sentence is worn out, while in the second it is exaggerated.

Name ______________________ Score ______________

Exercise 19c Fresh analogies

1. Complete the following phrases *twice,* using similes or metaphors to create a positive and a negative image.
   a. Getting my driver's license was

      1) ______________________.

      2) ______________________.

   b. I treat my mother like

      1) ______________________.

      2) ______________________.

   c. Entering college was like

      1) ______________________.

      2) ______________________.

   d. Eating a large pizza

      1) ______________________.

      2) ______________________.

   e. A letter from a friend

      1) ______________________.

      2) ______________________.

2. Explain the connotations of the following metaphors (vehicles) and how they enhance the tenor. You may wish to use a dictionary to look up the literal meanings.
   a. Henri wanted to *blow off* the test.

   b. The movie was really *gross.*

c. By the Christmas break, Dee was *burned out.*

d. When Adriane left Rock, he became *unglued.*

e. After a day's work, Gerry was often *uptight.*

19d Do not mix metaphors or make strained comparisons.

A mixed metaphor uses two or more conflicting comparisons. The metaphor in the vehicle must be consistent with the tenor; that is, the similarity must be greater than the dissimilarity.

Common Problems

A metaphor that shifts from one image to a conflicting image suggests that the writer's thoughts are inconsistent. Strained metaphors also seem to force figurative language rather than enhance the tenor.

Examples

The following sentence contains two metaphors that seem to conflict:

> The committee *dug up* new information that *added fuel* to the investigation.

"Digging up" suggests investigation, but while some fuel, such as coal, might be dug up, that image doesn't relate to an investigation. A sustained metaphor would achieve that goal:

> The committee *dug up* new information that *revealed a solid foundation* for the investigation.

"Digging up" and "revealing a foundation" are consistent.

In the next sentence the simile in the vehicle is inappropriate for the tenor:

> The lion attacked its prey like a rabbit tearing into a fresh piece of lettuce.

The vehicle conveys the voraciousness appropriate to the tenor, but the connotation of a rabbit is not suitable to that of a lion.

Name ______________________ Score ______________

Exercise 19d Mixed metaphors, strained comparisons

1. Revise the following sentences to eliminate mixed analogies or strained comparisons. If the image is effective, place a check mark before the sentence.
   a. The rain gushed from the gutter like a waterfall of bubbling lava.

   b. The ship split the sea like a comb through matted hair.

   c. The television dominated the room, and all present gave their complete attention to it.

   d. Ken overstepped the boundaries of good taste, so he swallowed his pride and admitted his error.

   e. When the Lakers were eliminated from the playoffs, fans crept from the Forum like sheep.

2. Create five sentences of your own that include mixed metaphors and similes or strained comparisons. Then revise each of the sentences so the figurative language is effective.

   a. ______________________

   b. ______________________

   c. ______________________

   d. ______________________

e. ______________________________

f. ______________________________

g. ______________________________

h. ______________________________

i. ______________________________

j. ______________________________

PART

5

Basic Grammar

CHAPTER 20

The Parts of Speech

20a Nouns

Nouns name a person, place, or thing. They may be concrete or abstract, proper or common.

Common Problems

Writers who lack knowledge of their subjects or wish to make their essays more general than their subjects permit often use abstract and common nouns rather than concrete and proper nouns.

Examples

The first example below, which contains *proper nouns* (those that name a *particular* person, place, or thing and always begin with a capital letter) is preferable to the second sentence, which uses *common nouns:*

> **proper noun** **proper noun**
> *John D. Rockefeller* founded the *University of Chicago.*

> **common noun** **common noun** **common noun**
> A *philanthropist* founded a famous *university* in the *Midwest.*

Sometimes, however, common nouns provide all the necessary information:

> **common noun** **common noun**
> The *scissors* are on the *table.*

The brand names are unimportant to the meaning of the sentence.

Concrete nouns, those perceived through the senses, are also generally preferable to *abstract* nouns, those that name ideas and qualities:

> **concrete nouns**
> *Penicillin* saved *thousands* of lives in *1990.*

> **abstract nouns**
> *Medicine* saved *many* lives last *year.*

But as with common nouns, sometimes abstract nouns are not only preferable but necessary:

> Superman fights for *Truth, Justice* and the *American Way.*

The sentence requires naming the concepts.

Name ______________________________ Score ____________________

Exercise 20a Nouns

1. Underline the nouns in the following sentences and label them as proper, common, concrete, or abstract.

   a. Marshall Williams invented the carbine rifle while in prison.

   b. Tourists enjoy the beauty of the Grand Canyon.

   c. Cigarette smoking is the most easily preventable threat to health in the United States.

   d. Farmers in Arkansas now farm catfish in addition to their traditional crops of cotton, rice, and soybeans.

   e. *Lethal Weapon II* was one of the biggest hits of 1989, and Mel Gibson was one of the most popular stars of that year.

2. Revise the following sentences so they include both proper and concrete nouns.

   a. My favorite television show provides my family with entertainment in the middle of the week.

   b. A teen takes delight in driving a car around town.

   c. Time in the mountains brings great joy to many.

   d. The girl was proud of the fish she caught on her trip to the lake.

   e. The truth of the matter is that most politicians demonstrate honesty.

20b Pronouns

Pronouns substitute for nouns. Effective use of pronouns avoids repetition, intensifies diction, clearly relates parts of a sentence to one another, and creates cohesion within sentences and paragraphs.

Common Problems

A series of sentences that don't contain pronouns is usually repetitious. Ineffective use of pronouns also creates confusion. When some pronouns function as adjectives, they are occasionally difficult to identify.

Examples

Pronouns are divided into seven types:

1. *Personal pronouns* refer to a *specific* person or to *specific* people and things:

	SINGULAR	PLURAL
First person	I, me	we, us
possessive	my, mine	our, ours
Second person	you	you
possessive	your, yours	your, yours
Third person	he, she, it, him, her	they, them
possessive	his, her, its	theirs

The following sentences reveal the problem in labeling personal pronouns:

Grace handed the paper to *her.* [pronoun]

Grace handed the paper to *her* friend. [adj.]

In the first sentence *her* substitutes for a noun, an unnamed female, so it is a pronoun. In the second sentence, *her* functions as an adjective because it modifies the noun *friend.* It is therefore a *possessive adjective.* (One of the anomalies of traditional grammar is that the personal pronouns *my, our, your,* and *its* always function as adjectives yet are also classified as personal pronouns. See section **20d.**

2. *Relative pronouns* introduce dependent clauses to the main clause; they relate the clauses. *Who, whom, whoever, whomever,* and *whose* refer to humans, and sometimes to animals and things:

John sold his bike to Phil, *who* then lost it.

Who substitutes for *Phil* and relates the clause that follows it to the main clause. *That, which, whichever,* and *what* (as a substitute for *that which*) refer to things, inanimate objects:

Phil lost the bike *which* John had sold him.

NOTE: While *that, which, whichever,* and *what* sometime refer to people and more often to animals, most writers prefer the *who* personal pronouns when referring to people or animals.

3. *Interrogative pronouns—who, whom, whose, what, which—*introduce questions:

Who is at the door?

Whom do you think is at the door?

See section **28g** for the use of *who* versus *whom.*

4. *Reflexive pronouns*—the *-self* pronouns—indicate that the subject of the sentence receives the action:

   Bill wrote *himself* a list of places to visit.

5. *Intensive pronouns*—the *-self* pronouns—emphasize the preceding noun or pronoun:

   I *myself* will capture the villain!

   NOTE: Do not use the "-self" pronouns in place of personal pronouns.

   Sara and *I* [not *myself*] visited the ocean.

   Bill went with Sara and *me* [not *myself*].

6. *Demonstrative pronouns* indicate which nouns receive or perform an action; they summarize a previous action. *This* and *these* refer to something near, and *that* and *those* refer to something distant. Demonstrative pronouns are often confused with demonstrative adjectives; only the function distinguishes one from the other:

   This was very important. [pronoun]

   That phone call was very important. [adjective]

   The first sentence refers to a call that has just occurred; the second, to one that had occurred in the past. However, in the first sentence *this* is a pronoun because it substitutes for an unidentified noun or pronoun. (When the noun following the demonstrative pronoun is omitted, reference errors often result. See chapter **27**.) In the second sentence, *that* modifies *phone call* and is therefore a demonstrative adjective. (See section **20d**.)

7. *Indefinite pronouns* refer to *unspecified* people or things. Some of the indefinite pronouns are *all, any, anything, each, everyone, nothing, several, someone,* and *something.* Like possessive and demonstrative pronouns, an indefinite pronoun's function in the sentence determines whether it is an indefinite adjective:

   All should turn in their papers. [pronoun]

   All students should turn in their papers. [adj.]

   Because *all* substitutes for a noun or pronoun in the first sentence, it is a pronoun; because *all* modifies *students* in the second sentence, it is an adjective. (See section **20d**.)

Name ______________________ Score ______________

Exercise 20b Pronouns

1. Underline and label the pronouns in the following sentences. Be aware that some words that appear to be pronouns are in fact adjectives.

   a. The writer e. e. cummings, who writes his name without capital letters, is one of the century's most creative poets.

   b. Not many people use automatic weapons for hunting, but they are popular with collectors.

   c. The committee praised itself for its efforts in saving each taxpayer hundreds of dollars.

   d. Michael Jordan himself makes the Chicago Bulls capable of beating any team on a given night.

   e. Who do you think will be elected president in 1996?

   f. Victory belongs to those who work to achieve it.

   g. When will the car that was brought in Monday be ready?

   h. Cynthia asked herself if she had practiced enough for her piano recital.

   i. How the deficit will be solved—that is what all Americans want to know.

   j. Ted saw himself as a wit, but he was only half right.

2. Create ten sentences that contain pronouns. Be sure that your sentences are sprinkled with pronouns from all seven categories listed above. Underline and label all pronouns.

   a. ______________________

   b. ______________________

   c. ______________________

   d. ______________________

e. ______________________________

f. ______________________________

g. ______________________________

h. ______________________________

i. ______________________________

j. ______________________________

20c Verbs

Verbs indicate an action or a state of being. Those that indicate an action enable readers to visualize. State of being verbs—linking verbs—do not reveal action. Therefore, their use should be minimized.

Common Problems

Nouns made from verbs (nominalizations—see section **10c**) force the use of linking verbs. The passive voice (see section **10b**) removes the actor and weakens the force of verbs.

Examples

Verbs appear in five forms:

Infinitive	We *kick* the can.
Present tense	Barry *kicks* the can.
Past tense	Barry *kicked* the can.
Past participle	We *have kicked* the can.
Present participle	We *are kicking* the can.

Action verbs are either *regular* or *irregular.* Regular verbs have past tense and past participle forms that end in *-ed* or *-d,* such as *touched* and *cared.*

Irregular verbs take varied forms in the past tense and past participle, such as *go: went, gone* or *begin: began, begun.*

The most common state of being verb, or *linking verb,* is *be* (*am, are, is, was, were, being, been*). Others are *appear, smell, feel, taste.*

Some verbs precede other verbs and "help" them. These verbs are *auxiliary verbs.* Verbs such as *can, will, shall, should, could, would, may, might,* and *must* can only be auxiliary verbs. Others such as forms of *be, do,* and *have* can be either main verbs or auxiliary verbs:

Teri has left town. [auxiliary]

Teri has Phil's car. [main verb]

Name ______________________________ Score ______________

Exercise 20c Verbs

Underline the verbs in the following sentences.

1. Tyrone had driven his father's car and then washed it.
2. The bear might have seen the sleeping camper.
3. The fraternity might not have won the float competition except for the fact that three of the judges had been former members.
4. When he wrote of Gaul, Julius Caesar said, "I came, I saw, I conquered."
5. The agreement was finalized after a three-hour meeting.
6. The owl dove and would have caught the mouse, but a hawk had reached the prey first.
7. Computers are going to replace televisions by the year 2000.
8. Francis had fun watching his dog play with a squirrel.
9. The practice of gene splicing appears to be a major benefit to humanity.
10. Athletes improve their performance greatly by practicing many hours daily.

20d Adjectives

Adjectives, which modify nouns and pronouns, make writing precise and lively. Identifying adjectives that are identical to some pronouns requires attention to the function of the word in the sentence. If it substitutes for a noun or pronoun, the word is a pronoun. If the same word modifies a noun or pronoun, it is an adjective.

Common Problems

Omitting essential adjectives can create unidiomatic sentences. Overusing adjectives diminishes the role of the verb, which is to communicate the action of the sentence. Focusing on the word rather than its function may result in mislabeling some classes of adjectives.

Examples

1. Adjectives can modify by describing or specifying qualities of nouns or pronouns:

   The *beautiful, red,* and *gold* sunset. [descriptive]

   The *last* day of my *freshman* year. [specifying]

2. Some adjectives modify in particular ways:
   a. *Articles* specify whether a noun or pronoun is definite or indefinite. The words *a* and *an* are *indefinite articles* (*a* is used before words beginning with a consonant sound; *an,* before words beginning with a vowel sound). The word *the* is a *definite article:*

      Both *a* hawk and *an* owl are predators.

      The elf owl lives in cactus plants.

   The first sentence deals with hawks and owls in general; the second, with a particular type of owl.

   b. *Predicate adjectives* follow linking verbs and limit, or specify, the subject:

      The Mississippi River is *high* this spring.

   The adjective *high* specifies a quality about the Mississippi River.

3. Three groups of adjectives have the same form as pronouns, but they *follow* a noun rather than *substitute* for a noun:
   a. *Demonstrative adjectives:* As with demonstrative pronouns, *this* and *these* refer to something physically or temporally near, and *that* and *those* refer to something distant. Unlike the demonstrative pronoun, the demonstrative adjective modifies a noun or pronoun that follows it:

      This phone call was very important.

      That phone call was very important.

   The first sentence refers to a call that has just occurred; the second, to one that had occurred in the past. In both sentences, *this* and *that* modify *phone call.* If *phone call* were eliminated, both *this* and *that* would be pronouns.

   b. *Possessive adjectives* are the same as their pronoun counterparts (*my, mine, our, ours, your,* and so on). Yet they often function as adjectives:

      Gina loaned *her* book to Arlene.

      Gina loaned the book to *her.*

   In the first sentence, *her* modifies *book,* so it is an adjective. In the second, *her* substitutes for the proper noun *Arlene* and is a pronoun.

c. *Indefinite adjectives:* Some indefinite adjectives are the same as indefinite pronouns: *all, any, each, every, several, some,* to name a few. The difference between the two is the function the word performs in the sentence. The pronoun substitutes, the adjective modifies:

All students should turn in their papers.

In this sentence, *all* modifies *students,* so it is an adjective. Eliminating *students* would make *all* a pronoun.

Name ______________________________ Score ______________

Exercise 20d Adjectives

1. Underline and label the adjectives in the following sentences. In addition, underline and label the demonstrative, possessive, and indefinite *pronouns.*

   a. The entire team enjoyed a steaming hot pizza with everything on it as a celebration of its first victory.

   b. It was one of those rainy fall days which make the most avid football fans wish they were in their living rooms instead of being in a windy, bone chilling stadium.

   c. *Our Town* was performed at a local theater.

   d. This year will see countless explanations of the tremendous changes occurring in Eastern Europe.

   e. The great, white stallion reared on its hind legs and whinnied as the masked man urged him forward.

   f. Buffy asked her favorite teacher if anything important happened when she was absent.

   g. Ted punctuated his speech with colorful metaphors, but not many people in the audience understood them.

   h. The English Bulldog was ecstatic when his owner brought a soup bone home from the store.

   i. A sun-powered automobile will be an affordable option for consumers in the next decade.

   j. In the next few years, scientists will know if their theories about global warming are valid.

2. Write a paragraph in which you describe an actual visit to a restaurant you have enjoyed. Use descriptive adjectives that appeal to each of the five senses. Underline and label all adjectives in the paragraph.

20e Adverbs

Adverbs modify verbs (and verbals), adjectives, and other adverbs. Like adjectives, adverbs add precision by indicating or clarifying time, place, manner, and degree; they also affirm or deny.

Common Problems

Adverbs can be confused with adjectives (see chapter **33**) if their function in a sentence is unclear.

Examples

An adverb gives information about time, place, manner, and degree:

When: again, always, early, never, forever, often

Where: above, below, up, down, here, there, everywhere

Why: why, therefore, wherefore, then

How: badly, easily, foolishly, how, not, no, surely

To what degree: almost, much, more, most, little, less

Adverbs also affirm or deny: yes, no, maybe, perhaps

Adverbs can modify verbals (verbs that function as nouns, verbs, or adjectives—see section **22c**), entire phrases, and clauses:

verbal **adverb**

Walking quickly, Millicent avoided the rain.

adverb **prepositional phrase**

Robert Novak is *frequently on news shows.*

adverb **independent clause**

Unrealistically, she planned her law school education.

Phrases or clauses can function as adverbs if they give information about time, place, manner, or degree:

adverb **clause**

Norm *did* his homework *before he watched television.*

The clause modifies the verb *did* and answers the question *when?*

Adverbs frequently derive from adjectives, often adding *-ly* to the adjective, as *frequently* does in this very sentence. *Frequently* modifies the verb *derived* and tells to what degree or when. But a major problem in adverb use occurs when writers use adjectives in place of adverbs (see chapter **33**):

NOT: I feel *real* good. [adjective]

BUT: I feel *really* good. [adverb]

Name ______________________ Score ______________

Exercise 20e Adverbs

Underline the adverbs, including phrases and clauses that function as adverbs, and indicate what information they give and what words, phrases, or clauses they modify. Also, revise the sentences in which adjectives incorrectly serve as adverbs.

1. Early in the morning is the best time to catch fish—or cold.

2. Because he had a date, Joe washed the family car without his father even asking him.

3. The bill easily passed in the House, but it lost badly in the Senate.

4. "Yes," Tom's mother said earnestly, "you may rent the Jim Varner movie—if you keep the sound down."

5. Perhaps, the Lakers and the Celtics will be in the NBA finals again next year.

6. Marilyn is rarely late for school.

7 *Love Me Tender* was Elvis's first movie, and his character died at the end.

8. Almost everyone had a real good time at the concert; therefore, the group planned to go again next year.

9. Eating just before going to bed can cause nightmares.

10. Very often, parents are more conservative than their children, but that has not been true in recent years.

20f Prepositions

Prepositions are used with a noun or pronoun (and its modifiers) to form a phrase that indicates place, position, time, or means. The function of prepositional phrases is the key to identifying them. Because they modify nouns or verbs, prepositional phrases function as adjectives or adverbs.

Common Problems

Overusing prepositional phrases, like the overuse of adjectives and adverbs, suggests that a style may rely too heavily on linking verbs and not enough on action verbs.

Examples

A prepositional phrase is composed of a preposition, modifiers (if any), and a noun or pronoun (the object of the preposition):

modifier
prep **object of prep**

Thoreau went *to the woods.*

Determining what the prepositional phrase *tells* indicates whether the phrase is adjectival or adverbial. *Adjectival prepositional phrases* tell which one and what kind of:

pronoun **prep phrase** **noun** **prep phrase**

One of the deer spotted the *hunter in the woods.*

The first prepositional phrase tells what kind of; the second tells which one. *Adverbial prepositional phrases* tell when, where, why, and under what circumstances:

prep phrase **prep phrase** **prep phrase** **prep phrase**

Despite the heavy rain, Terry went *to the library at 11:30 p.m.* and studied *for a history test.*

The first prepositional phrase tells under what circumstance; the second, where; the third, when; and the fourth, why.

Prepositions can be either single words or phrases:

about	below	in	onto	up
above	beneath	in addition to	out	upon
according to	beside	in case of	outside	with
across	besides	in front of	over	with respect to
after	between	in place of	past	with the exception of
against	beyond	in spite of	rather than	within
ahead of	but	inside	since	without
along	by	inside of	through	
among	concerning	instead of	throughout	
around	despite	into	till	
as well as	down	like	to	
at	during	near	toward	
because of	except	of	under	
before	for	off	underneath	
behind	from	on	until	

Name ______________________________ Score ______________

Exercise 20f Prepositions

Underline the prepositional phrases in the following sentences and indicate whether they are adverbial or adjectival and what they tell.

1. Because of the slick roads, Martha drove more slowly than other drivers on the highway.
2. Tammy was dressed for a picnic in fuchsia walking shorts and hiking shoes.
3. In spite of himself, the professor was a fan of Sylvester Stallone movies.
4. In the middle of the summer of 1980, the middle section of the nation was hit by a persistent and dangerous heat wave.
5. With a swipe of his powerful front claws, the anteater ripped the top off the termite mound.
6. The Indians of the Northwest are struggling for the right to fish along the Columbia River.
7. Throughout history adults have sought in vain to pass on the lessons they learned to young people.
8. Michael Jordan played for the University of North Carolina before he was drafted by the Chicago Bulls.
9. John did not ordinarily like to attend weddings, but he decided that it might be wise to appear at his own.
10. With the exception of four days in May, the area received some rain every day in the spring.

20g Conjunctions

Conjunctions connect words, phrases, and clauses and indicate a relationship between them. Effective control of conjunctions creates cohesion within sentences, paragraphs, and essays by connecting, creating junctions as the word *conjunction* suggests. *Coordinating conjunctions* indicate equality, and *subordinating conjunctions* indicate inequality of parts within and between sentences.

Common Problems

Imprecision is the usual result of ineffective conjunctions, especially the overuse of coordinating conjunctions. Writers cannot create emphasis if they overuse coordinating conjunctions.

Examples

Coordinating conjunctions join words, phrases, and clauses in grammatically equal relationships. The particular meaning of each conjunction indicates the difference in these relationships:

and: an addition
but, yet: a contrast
for, and *so:* causation
or, nor: positive and negative alternatives, respectively

NOTE: When a coordinating conjunction joins two independent clauses, a comma must precede the conjunction (see chapter **8** and section **25b**).

Correlative conjunctions also join elements in a grammatically equal relationship, but they always occur in pairs: *not only . . . but also, neither . . . nor, both . . . and.*

After graduation from high school, James will *either* enter the military *or* enroll in college.

The paired conjunctions guide readers and define the relationship between the elements they join. (See section **8b** for a discussion of parallel structures.)

Subordinate conjunctions join elements in an unequal relationship. Some common subordinating conjunctions follow:

after	even though	than	where
although	how	though	wherever
as far as	if	till	whether
as soon as	now that	unless	while
as if	once	until	
because	since	when	
before	so that	whenever	

These conjunctions make whatever follows them dependent, or subordinate, on another part of the sentence. For example, the two sentences "The cat leapt" and "The mouse ran" are grammatically equal; both are simple sentences, independent clauses, capable of standing alone. But if the subordinate conjunction *when* is placed before one of the sentences, the sentence becomes a fragment, a dependent clause:

When the cat leapt. [fragment]

When the mouse ran. [fragment]

When two sentences are joined by the subordinate conjunction, the result is a complex sentence: an independent and a dependent clause. Which clause the conjunction precedes determines the meaning of the sentence:

> The cat leapt *when the mouse ran.*
>
> The mouse ran *when the cat leapt.*

The dependent clause can occur before the independent clause or after it:

> *When the mouse ran,* the cat leapt.
>
> *When the cat leapt,* the mouse ran.

Note that when the dependent clause occurs first, it is followed by a comma (see section **36d**).

Conjunctive adverbs (*therefore, however, thus, moreover, nevertheless,* and others) connect words, phrases, and clauses. Like other conjunctions, they indicate relationships between sentences or parts of sentences. But like adverbs, they give the information that adverbs give. Also, their position in a sentence varies, which is more typical of adverbs than of conjunctions:

> Fred will, *however,* buy a new tennis racquet.
>
> *However,* Fred will buy a new tennis racquet.
>
> Fred will buy a new tennis racquet, *however.*

Unlike coordinating conjunctions, conjunctive adverbs cannot join two sentences with a comma (see section **25e**).

Name ______________________ Score ____________

Exercise 20g Conjunctions

1. In the following sentences, insert an appropriate coordinate conjunction in the spaces provided.

   a. Jon's high school basketball team won the playoff game, __________ he had a great time.

   b. Tonya dislikes Diet Coke, __________ she bought a case of them.

   c. Larry will try out for the debate team, __________ he will audition for the play.

   d. Neither Sandra and Bill __________ Susan and Don enjoyed the movie.

   e. The football game was fun, __________ our team won.

   f. Jimmy played with his dog, __________ it bit him.

2. Create four sentences using correlative conjunctions.

   a. ______________________________

   b. ______________________________

   c. ______________________________

   d. ______________________________

3. Complete the following sentences with clauses that reflect the meaning of the subordinate conjunctions.

   a. Henry Thoreau went to the woods

      after ______________________________.

      because ______________________________.

      although ______________________________.

b. Computers are going down in price

which ____.

as ____.

c. Jeanne wants to buy an American car

unless ____.

while ____.

if ____.

d. Congress will not raise taxes

when ____.

since ____.

4. Rewrite the following sentences *twice*, placing the conjunctive adverbs in different positions. Revise punctuation when necessary.

a. Jill feared dogs. Ted, therefore, left Killer at home.

1) ____

2) ____

Name ______________________________

Exercise 20g (continued)

b. Smoking is dangerous. Nevertheless, it is increasing among teens.

1) ______________________________

2) ______________________________

c. The speed limit has been increased; consequently, people are once again buying large cars.

1) ______________________________

2) ______________________________

d. The ozone layer is threatened. Many people doubt the threat, however.

1) ______________________________

2) ______________________________

e. Dogs are often affectionate. Similarly, cats endear themselves to some owners.

1) ______________________________

2) ______________________________

20h Interjections

Interjections indicate emotion or surprise. Although they make dialogue lively, formal writing and even informal college writing require special reasons for including interjections.

Common Problems

Overuse of interjections diminishes their usefulness. The emotional outburst implied in the interjection is usually inappropriate in formal writing.

Examples

Interjections serve no specific grammatical function. They can be a sound, a word, a phrase, or even a short sentence. They are set off from a sentence by a comma but may also be punctuated as a sentence using a period or an exclamation point:

> *Argg!* I hate broccoli. [a sound, not a real word]
>
> *Oh,* we won in overtime. [a single word]
>
> *Holy Mackerel!* [a phrase]
>
> *I'm finished!* [Sentences such as this one can be considered an interjection.]

Name ______________________ Score ______________

Exercise 20h Interjections

Write five sentences of dialogue using an interjection in each.

1. ______________________

2. ______________________

3. ______________________

4. ______________________

5. ______________________

CHAPTER 21

The Parts of the Sentence

21a Subjects

The *subject* is the part of a sentence that performs the action. The normal position for the subject is near the beginning of the sentence and before the verb. In most cases, the subject of a sentence tells *who* or *what* does the action of the sentence.

Common Problems

The subject may be difficult to identify when it is not in its normal position or when it is a phrase or clause.

Examples

A *simple subject* is a noun or pronoun without its modifiers:

The *plane* left.

The *complete subject* is a simple subject and its modifiers:

The huge jet plane from France left.

A noun phrase or clause can also be the complete subject of a sentence (see chapters **22** and **23**):

Whoever is late will miss the plane.

A *compound subject* has two or more simple subjects joined by *coordinating conjunctions* or *correlative conjunctions* (see section **20g**):

The *plane and bus* left at the same time.

The subject of a sentence does not precede the verb in questions, when expletives (forms of *there is* and *it is*) are used, when word order is inverted for stylistic purposes, and in imperative sentences in which the subject *you* is understood:

verb **subject**
Is the *plane* leaving on time?

verb **subject**
There *are* many *reasons* for the plane being late.

verb **subject**
Into the sky *flew* the *plane.*

verb
(You) *Leave* now!

Name ______________________________ Score ______________

Exercise 21a Subjects

Underline the complete subject once and the simple subject twice.

1. The horse is the animal that helped tame the American West.

2. It is time to mow the lawn.

3. Get out of my yard right now.

4. Who will win the election is impossible to tell.

5. The Geo Prizm, which is made by General Motors, an American company, and the Corolla, which is made by Toyota, a Japanese company, are forms of the same car.

6. Who can tell which teacher will succeed with which student?

7. When walking at night, people should wear bright clothes.

8. Recently, hang gliding has become a popular hobby.

9. Why people prefer a particular animal as a pet seems to be an unsolvable mystery.

10. "Thank all the people who sent in money for making this fund drive a success," said the host of the fund drive.

21b Predicate

The *predicate* tells what the subject is doing or what is being done to the subject, or it comments on the subject. It conveys the action of the sentence and usually follows the subject (for exceptions, see section **21a**).

Common Problems

The predicate may be difficult to identify when it is not in its usual position. Identification of the complete predicate may be troublesome when noun or pronoun modifiers are confused with verb modifiers.

Examples

The *simple predicate* consists of the verb alone:

Go! [an imperative sentence consisting of a single verb]

The mule *kicked* the dog. [past tense]

Tom *was eating* his lunch. [past progressive tense]

The *complete predicate* consists of the verb and its modifiers, objects, and complements (see sections **21c–21d**):

The dog *bit the mule.* [verb and direct object]

Tom *gave the dog a slap.* [verb, indirect object, and direct object]

The dog *had been Tom's best friend.* [a verb and predicate noun]

A *compound predicate* consists of two or more verbs joined by a coordinating conjunction and modifiers:

Rover *ran to the house and hid under the porch.* [two verbs each with a prepositional phrase joined by a coordinating conjunction]

Name ______________________ Score ______________

Exercise 21b Predicates

Underline the simple predicate twice and the complete predicate once. If a sentence has more than one clause, follow the same procedure for all clauses.

1. Menlo Park's major claim to fame was that Thomas Edison's workshops were located there.
2. Now, people think of Menlo Park only as a small city south of San Francisco.
3. The major reminder of the past is a memorial tower, which commemorates the man who made the city famous.
4. Edison used to sleep very little and work very hard.
5. Edison is an American hero because he started with very little, worked diligently, and became rich.
6. Edison is an example of the American Dream.
7. But he did not succeed alone.
8. Many people worked by his side, carried out his plans, and sometimes offered their own.
9. That idea is not often emphasized.
10. The American Dream stresses individualism, not cooperation.

21c Objects

Objects receive the action either directly or indirectly or restate the subject by completing or complementing it. Direct and indirect objects tell information about the subject of the sentence. Object complements tell information about objects. Distinguishing between transitive and intransitive verbs helps identify objects.

Common Problems

Identifying objects depends on differentiating transitive and intransitive verbs. Distinguishing objects and complements can also be confusing.

Examples

1. *Direct objects* tell who or whom or what the subject does:

subject / **transitive verb** / **direct object**

The doctor removed the stitches.

The direct object, *stitches,* tells what action the subject, *the doctor,* did. However, only *transitive verbs* are capable of carrying or transferring (as the prefix *trans-* suggests) the action from the subject to the object. *Intransitive verbs* cannot carry the action or transfer meaning. For example, the intransitive verb *vanish,* although close in meaning to *remove,* cannot transfer the doctor's action to a direct object:

subject / **intransitive verb** / **direct object**

The doctor vanished the stitches. [ungrammatical]

2. *Indirect objects* tell to whom or for whom something is done:

subject / **verb** / **indirect object** / **direct object**

The nurse gave the patient a bill. [tells to whom]

subject / **verb** / **indirect object** / **direct object**

The doctor promised the patient a quick recovery. [tells for whom]

NOTE: The indirect object always appears before the direct object.

3. *Retained object* is the object that remains when a sentence written in the passive voice uses the indirect object as the subject. Compare:

subject / **verb** / **indirect object** / **direct object**

ACTIVE: The nurse gave the patient a bill.

subject (indirect object) / **passive verb** / **retained object** / **prepositional phrase**

PASSIVE: The patient was given *a bill* by the nurse.

4. *Object complement* is either a noun that renames the direct object or an adjective that modifies the direct object:

   subject **verb** **direct object** **object complement**
   The doctor called the patient a fortunate *man.*

   subject **verb** **direct object** **object complement**
   The bill made the patient *dizzy.*

Man renames *patient; dizzy* describes *patient.*

Name ______________________________ Score ______________

Exercise 21c Objects

In each of the following sentences, circle and label the different objects and complements.

1. The British call a television a *telly.*

2. Students are given a two-month vacation.

3. Elmer shot a rabbit.

4. Daisy gave Donald a brand new sailor suit.

5. Some people falsely label Billy the Kid a hero.

6. The birds picked the cherry tree clean.

7. The fortunate young woman had been given four bridal showers.

8. Henry built a small house near a pond.

9. Ivana once called her husband a generous man.

10. Olive offered her dinner guest a spinach salad.

21d Predicate nouns and predicate adjectives

Also called subject complements, the predicate nouns and predicate adjectives complete a linking verb by renaming or describing the subject. Predicate nouns and predicate adjectives make the subject of a sentence identifiable. Linking verbs are also a clue that a subject complement might follow (see section **20c**).

Common Problems

Predicate nouns and predicate adjectives might be mislabeled if their referents are not clear. Object complements refer to the object, and subject complements refer to the subject.

Examples

Predicate nouns rename:

subject	linking verb		predicate noun
Arkansas	is	the	Natural State.

Predicate adjectives modify:

subject	linking verb	predicate adjective
Arkansas	is	beautiful.

In both sentences, the subject complements, *Natural State* and *beautiful,* complete or add to the subject by renaming or modifying it.

Name ______________________________ Score ______________

Exercise 21d Predicate nouns and predicate adjectives

Label the predicate nouns and predicate adjectives in the following sentences, and underline all linking verbs. Place a check mark before sentences that do not contain subject complements.

1. The food in the cafeteria smells terrible.
2. This semester has been the best one yet.
3. The oldest building on campus is being remodeled.
4. The introductory math course is very difficult for most students.
5. The cheerleaders sounded great at the pep rally.
6. The president gave the outstanding students awards.
7. Three starters were sick, so the team lost the tournament.
8. The team may have lost anyway because it didn't look good in practice.
9. Some teachers don't seem happy about the emphasis on athletics.
10. Fraternities and sororities become second families for some students.

21e Sentence constructions

The number and types of clauses in a sentence determine whether a sentence is simple, compound, complex, or compound-complex.

Common Problems

Compound subjects, verbs, and objects, lengthy modifiers, or dependent clauses might make a sentence appear to have more clauses than it actually has.

Examples

1. *Simple sentences* have only *one* clause, regardless of their length:

   Go!

   Jackie drove a jeep.

   Driving through the night, Jackie, Teri, and Jill drove down the road, turned off at a dirt path, and found a cabin with large rooms and a view of a beautiful lake.

   All three examples are simple sentences. The first is a single word, an imperative sentence with the subject *you* understood. The second has a simple subject, a verb, and a direct object. The third has an introductory participial phrase, and compound subject, verb, and object and prepositional phrases.

2. *Compound sentences* comprise two or more independent clauses (no dependent clauses) and are joined by a comma and coordinating conjunction or by a semicolon:

   independent clause | **comma and coord conj** | **independent clause**
   Jackie like to fish, but Teri liked to sunbathe.

   If either or both independent clauses were longer, the sentence would still be compound.

3. *Complex sentences* contain one independent clause and one or more dependent clauses (see chapter 9):

   dependent clause | **independent clause** | **dependent clause**
   Because Teri had stayed in the sun too long, she got a bad sunburn, which ruined the trip for her.

   The sentence begins and ends with dependent clauses, the first an adverbial clause, the second a noun clause. The dependent clause can also interrupt the independent clause:

   dependent clause
   Jill, *whose skin was fair,* sat in the cabin and read.

4. *Compound-complex sentences* contain at least two independent clauses and at least one dependent clause (that is, they combine compound and complex sentences):

   independent clause | **dependent clause** | **independent clause** | **independent clause**
   Jackie was the only one who really enjoyed nature, but Teri and Jill liked to relax, so they went with her.

Name ______________________ Score ______________

Exercise 21e Sentence constructions

1. Identify the construction of the following sentences. Place a *1* before simple sentences, a *2* before a compound sentence, a *3* before complex sentences, and a *4* before compound-complex sentences.
   a. The tank rolled down the hill, hit the water, roared its engine, and went on as if it were on dry land.

   b. Bill changed his major, for he knew he would never understand philosophy well enough to make it his career.

   c. If he tries, Arnold can be more than a fine athlete.

   d. Trying to become a true democracy has been difficult for the Soviet Union and will require years of effort on the part of all citizens and government officials.

   e. Many children are frightened by cartoons and have nightmares about them, but parents rarely see any danger in letting their children watch cartoons for hours at a time.

   f. People can't say they hurt only themselves if they don't wear seatbelts; automobile deaths raise insurance rates.

   g. When very tired, a person shouldn't drive.

   h. The game ended in a tie after far too many hours.

   i. In recent years, Congress's role has diminished and lost favor with the public.

   j. Who will be the Democratic nominee for president in 1996 is a question many will ask in upcoming months.

2. Write ten simple sentences of varying lengths. Then combine them into a series of sentences that contain compound, complex, and compound-complex structures.
   a.

   b.

   c.

   d.

e.

f.

g.

h.

i.

j.

21f Sentence patterns

Sentences are generally arranged in five different patterns. These patterns help create effective sentences and cohesion between sentences.

Common Problems

Failure to recognize the parts of sentences can make identifying the patterns difficult, if not impossible.

Example

The following five basic patterns can each add single words, phrases and clauses:

1. Subject-verb.

   Ted thought.

2. Subject-verb-object.

   Ted wrote a letter.

3. Subject-verb-subject complement.

   Ted was exhilarated.

4. Subject-verb-indirect object-direct object.

   Ted mailed Betty the letter.

5. Subject-verb-direct object-object complement.

   Betty thought the letter wonderful.

Name ______________________________ Score ________________

Exercise 21f Sentence pattern

1. Identify each of the following sentence patterns.
   a. Tom's old car rode like a new model.

   b. The Chicago baseball teams, the Cubs and the White Sox, are rarely contenders during the same season.

   c. Most word-processing programs can check spelling errors.

   d. The entire senior class thought the prom the most successful in many years.

   e. The television ad promised viewers a free gift just for calling an 800 number.

2. Create five sentences, one for each of the five sentence patterns. Add words, phrases, and clauses to create mature sentences. Then underline and identify the basic elements—the subject, predicate, objects, and complements.
   a.

   b.

   c.

   d.

   e.

CHAPTER 22

Phrases

22a–22e Use a variety of phrases.

Because all *phrases* contain a subject *or* a verb—not both—and might contain grammatically related words, they appear in a variety of forms. Functioning as single parts of speech, different types of phrases provide interesting detail in sentence development.

Common Problems

Confusing phrases with clauses (see chapter **23**) or confusing the types of phrases makes sentences less fluent or even ungrammatical.

Examples

A phrase may be categorized (a) by form (its structural components) and (b) by function (its use in a sentence as one of four parts of speech):

1. *Verb phrases* consist of a main verb and auxiliary or helping verbs (*am going, have said, might have left*):

   By 2:00, the team *will have begun* practice.

2. *Noun phrases* consist of a main noun and modifying words and may be structured as gerunds, appositives, and sometimes infinitive phrases. The form and function of these types will be discussed later in this chapter.

3. *Adjective phrases* tell which one or what kind about a noun that immediately precedes or follows a phrase:

   The best time *of the day* is early morning.

   Participial phrases always function as adjectives, while prepositional phrases and infinitive phrases sometimes act as adjectives.

4. *Adverb phrases* tell why, where, when, how, under what conditions, and to what degree to describe a verb, adjective, or another adverb and function just like a single adverb.

These four grammatical functions may also be expressed in the following phrase forms:

1. *Prepositional phrases* consist of a preposition and its object and generally function as adjectives or adverbs. As an adjective, it modifies a noun or pronoun and appears next to the word it modifies:

   Jeremiah is a friend *of mine.* [The prepositional phrase modifies the noun *friend.*]

As an adverb, a prepositional phrase tells how, why, where, when, under what conditions, and to what degree to describe a verb, adjective, or another adverb. It need not appear next to the verb, adverb, or adjective it modifies:

> *Late at night,* the Adamses take a family walk.
>
> The Adamses take a family walk *late at night.*
>
> The Adamses, *late at night,* take a family walk.

In each case, the phrase modifies the verb *take.*

2. *Verbal phrases* contain verb forms and are of three types:
   a. *Gerund phrases,* in which the verb ends in *-ing,* always function as nouns and are usually subjects or objects of sentences:

      > *Driving in traffic* is tiresome. [subject]
      >
      > Most drivers hate *sitting in traffic.* [object]

   b. *Participial phrases* function as adjectives and appear immediately before or after the noun or pronoun they modify:

      > Drivers *tired from a traffic jam* are irritable.

   c. *Infinitive phrases* combine *to* with the base form of the verb and usually take an object (*to drive home*) or an adverb (*to drive quickly*). Sometimes *to* is implied (*The radio helped the driver [to] pass the time*). Infinitive phrases function in the same way as any noun, adjective, or adverb:

      > *To drive in traffic* is boring. [a noun as subject of a sentence]
      >
      > The driver had nothing *to do with himself* but wait in silence. [an adjective modifying *nothing*]
      >
      > He drove slowly *to avoid an accident.* [an adverb modifying *drove*]

3. *Absolute phrases* are formed by a noun and a participle and modify an entire clause rather than one word:

   > *The score being 100 to 71 with one minute remaining,* most fans left the game.

   The phrase modifies the entire main clause.

4. *Appositive phrases* rename or add information about a noun and appear next to the noun they modify:

   > Michael J. Fox's three related movies, *the Back to the Future series,* have made Marty McFly a household name.

Name ______________________________ Score ______________

Exercise 22a—22e Phrases

Circle the prepositional phrases, verbal phrases (indicate whether they are gerund, participial, or infinitive), absolute phrases, and appositive phrases in the following sentences. Also indicate the function each serves in the sentence—noun, adjective, verb, or adverb. Sentences may have more than one phrase.

1. Mark Twain wrote about the Mississippi River as no other author has ever done.

2. Caring for a dog teaches children to be responsible.

3. Skipping a meal, some dieters overcome with hunger will eat more than they might have if they had eaten three regular meals.

4. To have freedom means that a person has choices.

5. Ronald's favorite horse, a palomino, required patience for other people to control him.

6. The music rising to a crescendo, the audience applauded until the stirring strains subsided.

7. Beaten for the first time, in his fiftieth fight, Larry Holmes lost his chance to eclipse Rocky Marciano's record in the heavyweight division.

8. The wild turkey, the bird Benjamin Franklin favored as the national bird, would now be extinct if environmentalists had not fought to save it.

9. Storm warnings being in effect, schools were dismissed early.

10. For many people, watching television has replaced going to the movies.

CHAPTER 23

Clauses

Clauses are a group of grammatically related words that contain *both* a subject and a predicate. They are either independent (a complete sentence) or dependent (subordinate). Recognizing this distinction enables writers to emphasize ideas and punctuate appropriately.

Common Problems

Punctuating dependent clauses as sentences creates fragments, and ineffective use of subordinate clauses obscures the proper emphasis. Failing to recognize the features of the two types of dependent clauses makes identification difficult.

Example

1. An *independent clause* is a complete sentence that can be brief with no modifiers or extensive with many modifiers:

   Accidents happen.

   In the morning, birds chirping awakens us to a bright new day and to all the pleasure and pain accompanying the everyday tasks before us.

2. *Subordinate clauses* enhance sentences but are not themselves complete sentences:

   a. They *depend* on another clause because they are introduced by relative pronouns (*that, which, who*) or by subordinating conjunctions (*unless, when, after*):

   Rob, *who* was a good athlete, rarely lost.

   But *because* he was a good sport, Rob lost with grace.

   The coordinating conjunction *who* substitutes for Rob and makes the clause *who was a good athlete* dependent on the sentence in which it is embedded. In the second sentence, the subordinating conjunction *because* makes the clause *he was a good sport* dependent on the independent clause that follows it.

   b. Subordinate clauses function as nouns, adjectives, or adverbs in the independent clause they become a part of.
   Noun clauses appear as subjects or objects of a sentence:

   That fact that walking is as beneficial as jogging has increased its popularity. [subject of sentence]

   The coach liked *what he saw.* [object of sentence]

   Noun clauses usually begin with words such as *that, who, which, what, why, when, where,* and *how.* Sometimes the word *that* can be omitted:

Cindy knew *that* her check would arrive.

Cindy knew her check would arrive.

Adjective clauses modify nouns and pronouns and usually follow immediately the word they modify:

Sigmund Freud, *who revealed great sympathy to women's problems,* is now criticized by women's organizations. [The clause modifies the noun *Freud.*]

Adjective clauses usually begin with relative pronouns such as *who, whom, whose, which,* and *that* but can also begin with conjunctions such as *when, where,* and *why.*

Adverb clauses tell when, where, why, under what conditions, or to what degree:

Although he was very frightened, Roger was calm *when he spoke to Jessica.*

The first clause tells under what condition, and the second tells when. Adverb clauses begin with subordinating conjunctions such as *after, when, where, while, as, since, although, because,* and *if.*

Name ______________________________ Score ______________

Exercise 23 Clauses

Underline the subordinate clauses in the following sentences and identify them as noun, adjective, or adverb clauses. Place a check mark before any sentence not containing a subordinate clause.

1. If Jack goes to his fraternity's picnic, he will ask Jill, whom he has known for years, to go with him.

2. Peter wanted to prove to his friends that he could pass Mr. MacGregor's botany test.

3. Linguists believe that the term *GI,* which was coined in World War II, comes from the abbreviation for "government issue."

4. Even before the Vietnam War was over, movies revealed the divided opinion that existed in this country.

5. When Dick Tracy first wore a two-way wrist radio, most people thought they would never be practical.

6. Why so many comic strip heroes have become the subject of movies is difficult to explain.

7. The time when all entering freshmen will have word processors available to them is not far off.

8. Struggling with a full-time job while taking a full course load is now commonplace for many college students.

9. The opportunity for success is there for whoever is willing to work for it.

10. Trains that will travel over two hundred miles an hour will connect our large cities, if urban planners have their way.

PART

6

Editing Grammar for Style and Correctness

CHAPTER 24

Fragments

24a Attach fragments to sentences.

Fragments are incomplete sentences. Recognizing dependent clauses and phrases and attaching them to relevant clauses or phrases prevents fragments.

Common Problems

Writers may overlook fragments when they punctuate a dependent clause or phrase as a sentence. Sometimes intentional fragments (see section **24c**) are simply used ineffectively.

Examples

Introductory or concluding subordinate clauses should be connected to the independent clause:

> FRAGMENT: *Because they had been friends ever since elementary school.* Barbara and Lita dreaded graduation from high school. *Especially after they realized they would be attending different colleges.*

Both the introductory and concluding clauses are dependent (see chapter **23**) and should be connected to the independent clause:

> SENTENCE: Because they had been friends ever since elementary school**,** Barbara and Lita dreaded graduation from high school**,** especially after they realized they would be attending different colleges.

The dependent clauses are now part of a single complex sentence with only commas necessary to set them off.

Phrases, like dependent clauses, need to be connected to an independent clause:

> Carey worked very hard. *Polishing her father's car.*

Here the fragment can be joined to the independent clause by removing the period and lowercasing *polishing:*

> Carey worked very hard polishing her father's car.

NOTE: Fragments often result when the dependent clause or the phrase is preceded by phrases such as *for example, such as,* or *for instance,* or words like *especially,* or *particularly:*

Laura was very tired. *Particularly* because she had been at the beach all day. [fragment as a dependent adverb clause]

Laura's mother often became annoyed with her in the summer. *For example,* the time that she stayed at the beach too long, got sunburned, and could not help with the chores when she got home. [fragment as a dependent adjective clause]

Name ______________________________ Score ______________

Exercise 24a Attaching fragments

Correct the following fragments by joining clauses and phrases to independent clauses. Place a check mark before sentences that require no revision.

1. I enjoy hiking in the woods. But not when the temperature is in the 80s. That's too hot.
2. Hanging precariously from a vine and howling at the top of his lungs. The monkey seemed frightened. It was as if he feared he would fall.
3. Indiana Jones was an unusual figure to be a hero. Unusual because teachers aren't often thought of as being heroic. Jones being a college anthropology professor.
4. Many of the actors in *Dick Tracy* were not immediately recognizable. For example, Dustin Hoffman and Al Pacino who wore very heavy facial make-up.
5. Soccer has become very popular in the United States. Despite the fact that several soccer leagues have failed. Soccer is played in most elementary schools.
6. Cigarette advertisements no longer appear on TV. In an attempt to reduce smoking among teenagers. Yet smoking is increasing. Often among those who watch TV the most. Teenagers.
7. A cat playing with a ball of yarn. Not even the most ardent dog lover can resist that.
8. The genius. That title has stayed with Ray Charles. Since the beginning of his career.
9. When Lew Alcindor changed his name to Kareem Abdul Jabbar. The center for the Chicago Bulls, Tom Boerwinkle, a poor scorer, said he was going to change his name. To Lew Alcindor. Boerwinkle didn't.
10. Flying across the Atlantic Ocean in three hours. The giant French jet, the Concorde, has still not been a financial success. Especially in the years when oil prices have been high.

24b Turn fragments into sentences.

Fragments can be converted into sentences by adding or substituting words in phrases.

Common Problems

Distinguishing phrases and dependent clauses from independent clauses is the key to avoiding fragments. Using verbals, particularly *-ing* verbs, as verbs creates fragments (see section **22c**).

Examples

Dependent clauses can be converted to sentences by deleting the subordinate conjunction or substituting a noun for a relative pronoun:

FRAGMENT: Many people who don't watch public television say they do. *Because* they want to appear intelligent.

SENTENCE: Many people who don't watch public television say they do. They want to appear intelligent.

FRAGMENT: Hillary was eager to see her favorite group. *Which* surpassed all her expectations when it performed on campus.

SENTENCE: Hillary was eager to see her favorite group. *U2* surpassed all her expectations when it performed on campus.

Phrases often require more revision than clauses to change them to sentences:

FRAGMENT: The hunter saw a bear cub. Eating wild berries.

SENTENCE: The hunter saw a bear cub. *The cuddly little thing was* eating wild berries.

A subject, modifiers, and an auxilliary verb convert the fragment to a sentence and add precision.

Name ______________________ Score ______________

Exercise 24b Turning into sentences

Convert the fragments in the following paragraph into sentences. Add words when necessary, but do not eliminate the fragments by joining them to other sentences, the procedure required in **24a.**

Racquetball appeals to many people. Even those who don't necessarily consider themselves athletic. Unlike tennis, racquetball can be played all year round. Even in cold or rainy weather because it is played indoors. Another advantage is that players of very different abilities can play against each other. Because a skilled player can improve her ability by placing the ball so her opponent *can* return it. Which is just as difficult as placing the ball where an opponent *can't* return it. Although strength is an advantage in most sports. The ability to place the ball is more important then hitting it hard. Especially when an opponent knows how to get good position. Staying in the middle of the court, having the ability to move forward or backward or from side to side. Racquetball also provides aerobic exercise. Which is far more important than exercise which merely stretches or builds muscles. Players also get a complete workout. For example, using all major muscle groups and increasing the heartbeat for a sustained period. But most of all, racquetball is fun. Fast moving, easy to learn, and beneficial too.

24c Use some fragments for stylistic purposes.

Intentional fragments left as such should be used sparingly, or they defeat their purpose—attracting attention by breaking a convention. The context must make clear that the fragment is purposeful and not an error.

Common Problems

A fragment is ineffective if it seems to be unintentional. Overusing fragments creates a loose style and reduces paragraph cohesion.

Examples

Fragments can create a series of images:

> *A silence that was almost palpable. Humidity so heavy that it clogged the lungs. Flies gathering on a screen door.* These were the signs that warned of a summer storm.

Fragments can create emphasis:

> None of Phyllis's friends came to her piano recital. *Not one!*
>
> The attic was filled with mementos of a long happy life together. *A wing chair, their first new piece of furniture; their son's first musical instrument, a trumpet; pictures that had hung on their walls; old clothes; children's toys; and, most important, photo albums.*

In the first sentence, the brief phrase gains emphasis by being separated from the main sentence. In the second, the series elaborates the previous sentence. In both instances, a dash or a colon might be preferred to link the fragments to the sentence.

Fragments can capture dialogue accurately:

> "Why can't I go?" Susan pleaded.
>
> "Because!" her mother said with finality.

Name ______________________________ Score ______________

Exercise 24c Stylistic uses

On a separate page, convert ten sentences from an essay you have written into effective fragments. The context will determine their effectiveness. (Note: Under normal circumstances, you would never have ten fragments in an essay.)

CHAPTER 25

Fused Sentences and Comma Splices

25a–25f Identify and revise fused sentences and comma splices.

Joining two independent clauses with no punctuation between them (fused sentences) or linking them by a comma (comma splice) confuses the meaning of sentences.

Common Problems

Inappropriate methods for linking sentences—fusing them or joining them with a comma—are often used because their ideas seem closely related.

Examples

Fused sentences and comma splices can be eliminated in a variety of ways, depending on the writer's purpose:

Rhonda likes Michael Jackson all her friends do too. [fused sentence]

He is a great singer, he can dance too. [comma splice]

1. The independent clauses can be made into separate sentences, thereby emphasizing the independence of each.

   Rhonda likes Michael Jackson. All her friends do too.

   He was a great singer. He could dance too.

2. A comma and coordinating conjunction (*and, but, or, nor, for, so, yet*) indicate a close relationship, as defined by the conjunction. (See chapter 8.)

   Rhonda likes Michael Jackson, but all her friends do too.

   Rhonda likes Michael Jackson, and all her friends do too.

   In the first sentence, *but* diminishes the distinction of Rhonda's preference by likening her to her friends. The *and* in the second sentence relates the two sentences closely and offers further information.

3. A semicolon joins two sentences closely but implies rather than states the relationship. (See section **38a.**)

   Rhonda likes Michael Jackson; all her friends do too.

   He is a great singer; he can dance too.

4. A colon between independent clauses suggests that the second clause either summarizes or explains the first.

   Rhonda is just like all her friends: she likes Michael Jackson.

   He is a great performer: he sings and dances well.

   In the first sentence, the colon suggests how Rhonda is like her friends. In the second, the colon summarizes in what way Jackson is a great performer.

5. A semicolon and a conjunctive adverb (such as *moreover, therefore, then*), like a comma and a coordinating conjunction, indicate that sentences have a close relationship: the semicolon indicates the closeness; the conjunctive adverb indicates the type of relationship. (See section **38b.**)

   Rhonda likes Michael Jackson; similarly, all her friends do too.

   He is a great singer; moreover, he can dance too.

   Note that a comma follows the conjunctive adverb. The difference between conjunctive adverbs and coordinating conjunctions is that conjunctive adverbs do not always begin the sentence.

   He is a great singer; he can, moreover, dance too.

   A comma separating the independent clauses here would create a comma splice. Because conjunctive adverbs can appear in places other than the beginning of the clauses they join, a semicolon rather than a comma is necessary when used with a conjunctive adverb to join clauses.

6. Two independent clauses can also be joined with a subordinating conjunction to make one clause dependent.

   Rhonda likes Michael Jackson because all her friends do.

   Although he is a great singer, he can dance too.

   These sentences now emphasize the independent clauses. Note that the dependent clause can either follow or begin the sentence and that, when the dependent clause appears first, it is followed by a comma.

   Because all her friends like him, Rhonda likes him too.

   Michael Jackson is a great singer although he can dance.

Exercise 25a–25f Fused sentences and comma splices

Identify the fused sentences and comma splices and then revise each using *two* of the methods suggested above. Place a check mark before any sentence that does not need revision.

1. Although he knew very little about cars, Gene enjoyed watching drag races at the track, he found the races exciting.
   a.

   b.

2. More and more, people are finding unusual ways to exercise some walk around malls early in the morning others run up and down steps in tall buildings.
   a.

   b.

3. Photography is both an art and a science, it offers the opportunity to be creative and doesn't require the hand-eye coordination of other arts it also requires a knowledge of photographic technology to transfer the creativity into a finished product.
   a.

   b.

4. Punctuation is more than just rules, different writers punctuate the same sentences in various ways then they achieve much different results.
   a.

   b.

5. The first Americans rarely refer to themselves as "Indians," they either use the name of their tribe or a more accurate term than "Indian," they call themselves "Native Americans."
   a.

   b.

6. The National Rifle Association has many advocates it opposes most restrictions on gun ownership.
   a.

   b.

7. Cordless telephones offer great mobility, which explains why so many people want to own them, they also reduce privacy.
   a.

   b.

8. Many students begin drinking coffee in college, it helps them stay awake when studying late, moreover, it helps them wake up for 8:00 classes.
   a.

   b.

9. Soft lenses have made contacts much more popular than they were when only hard lenses were available people with fair complexions often couldn't wear hard lenses.
   a.

   b.

10. Some fads last for years others last for only a few weeks, consequently, those who wish to make money by investing in a fad should be careful, they may lose money.
   a.

   b.

CHAPTER 26

Subject-Verb Agreement

26a–26j Revise sentences so the subjects and verbs agree.

Singular subjects take singular verbs, and plural subjects take plural verbs. The subject and verb must also agree in person (first, second, or third).

Common Problems

When the subject and verb are separated (especially by a noun or pronoun that differs in number from the subject), even native speakers of English can be confused by agreement. Compound subjects and collective nouns also can cause confusion.

Examples

1. Make the verb agree with the subject even when the two are separated.

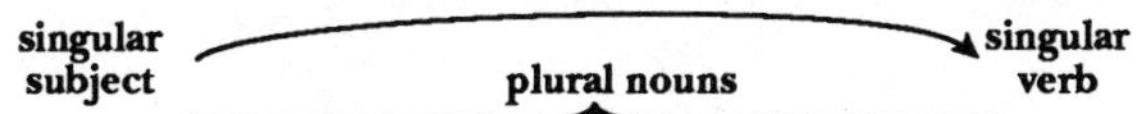

The *use* of *tools* by *apes* and some other *animals* *is* important to anthropologists in exploring animal intelligence.

The singular verb *is* must agree with the singular subject *use,* despite the plural nouns that separate the two terms.

2. Make the verb agree with the subject, not with a predicate noun (see section **21d**).

The *fights* that so often occur in hockey games *are* Tom's *reason* for not liking the sport.

The verb must agree with the plural subject, not the singular predicate nominative.

3. Make the verb agree with the subject even when the subject follows the verb (this usually occurs with expletives—*there is, there are*).

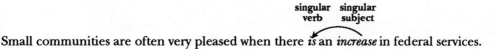

singular verb **singular subject**

Small communities are often very pleased when there *is* an *increase* in federal services.

This potential problem can be avoided by editing to remove the expletive.

4. Use plural verbs for most compound subjects joined by *and.*

   compound subject **plural verb**

   An infant's *health and intellectual potential are* hindered if its mother smoked during her pregnancy.

   However, when a compound subject forms a single idea, use a singular verb.

   subject—one person

   The *publisher and chief executive officer* of *Lear's* magazine *deserves* credit for his role in initiating this publication.

   When a compound subject begins with *each, every, no,* or *such a,* use a singular verb.

   Each man and woman *receives* the same benefits.

5. When a compound subject is joined by *or, nor, either … or, neither … nor,* or *not … but,* make the verb agree with the nearer part of the subject.

   plural subject **plural verb**

   Neither Bart nor his *sisters pay* attention to their parents.

   singular subject **singular verb**

   Neither his sisters nor *Bart pays* attention to their parents.

6. Use a singular verb with most indefinite pronouns, such as *each, none, neither, everyone,* and *nobody,* take singular verbs. (See section **20b.**)

   Each of the cottages *has* windows facing east.

   However, some pronouns (*none, some, part, all*) take either singular or plural verbs, depending on the noun or pronoun that follows in a prepositional phrase.

   Some of the *food is* missing. [singular]

   Some of the *students are* missing. [plural]

7. *Who, that,* and *which* require verbs that agree with the antecedent.

   Norm went to see his *friend* who *lives* in San Diego. [singular]

   Norm went to see his *friends* who *live* in San Diego. [plural]

8. Use a singular verb with a collective noun unless a plural meaning is clearly intended.

   The *committee is meeting* in the auditorium. [singular]

   The *committee* [members] *are meeting to cast their votes.* [plural]

9. Use a singular verb with nouns having a plural form but singular meaning.

   The *news was* on at 8:00 a.m. this morning.

Some nouns, although singular, are conventionally given plural verbs.

The *scissors are* on the table.

Bill's *pants fit* loosely after he began jogging regularly.

10. Use singular verbs with titles of works used as words.

Cats is one of the most successful musicals in recent years.

Even the word *taxes frightens* most politicians.

Name ______________________________ Score ______________

Exercise 26a–26j Subject-verb agreement

1. Circle the correct verb in the following sentences, and write the number of the item on the list that applies before each sentence.

   a. The senator's concern (is/are) the citizens of her state.

   b. Measles (is/are) more serious for adults than for children.

   c. *The Days of Our Lives* (has/have) been less popular with teenagers than *All My Children.*

   d. There (happen/happens) to be more to life than making money, Donald thought to himself.

   e. Classes with a great deal of activity (pass/passes) quickly for most students.

   f. Buffy's family (decide/decides) early in the fall where to spend Christmas vacation.

   g. In England, Gilbert and Sullivan plays often (introduce/introduces) children to opera.

   h. Japan creates cars that (has/have) high reliability ratings but low safety ratings when compared to American cars.

   i. Neither Hawaii nor its neighboring islands (has/have) any indigenous snakes.

   j. Each of the major biblical religions—Judaism, Christianity, and Islam—(has/have) shrines in Jerusalem.

2. Correct the agreement errors in the following sentences. Write the number of the applicable item on the list before each sentence and place a check mark before correct sentences.

   a. On the top shelf is the book you are looking for.

   b. No student, teacher, or administrator want a tuition increase.

   c. A herd of horses represent years of work for a horse rancher.

   d. *Reds* were Warren Beatty's most ambitious film, even moreso than *Dick Tracy.*

   e. None of the candidates represents the majority view.

f. The United States, as well as the Soviet Union, fears the reunification of Germany without strong limitations.

g. Joeys is the name given to young kangaroos.

h. Jack Nicholson's facial expressions is his greatest physical asset as an actor.

i. Mathematics are not emphasized as much in the United States as in Europe and Japan.

j. Politicians want to know if abortion, flag burning, or pornography are going to be the major emotional issue of the next election.

CHAPTER 27

Pronoun Agreement and Reference

27a–27h Make pronouns agree with their antecedents.

So the reader understands the point that the writer is trying to make, a pronoun must agree with its antecedent (the noun that the pronoun refers to) in number, gender, and person. In addition to agreeing, the pronoun must refer to a specific antecedent.

Common Problems

Because English has no ungendered singular pronoun referring to people (we have only *he* or *she*), writers may create agreement errors when they try to avoid sexist language. Unfamiliarity with conventions also creates some agreement errors.

Examples

1. Use a singular pronoun to refer to a singular antecedent.

 Brittany bumped *her* nose on the mirror.

 Many people have found the traditional convention offensive—that is, using masculine pronouns to refer to all members of a group regardless of the gender of the group:

 TRADITIONAL: *Each* nurse turned in *his* report.

 Since nurses can be either male or female, the modern convention uses other methods to avoid sexist language:

 a. Make both the noun and the pronoun plural.

 All nurses turned in *their* reports.

 b. Edit to eliminate the problem or to make the pronoun unnecessary.

 Ralph Smith turned in *his* report.

 The nurses turned in *the required* reports.

NOTE: Avoid overusing *he or she.* Frequent use is awkward to read and creates additional problems.

2. Make pronouns refer to a specific antecedent.

 Poe relies heavily on meter in *his* most famous poem, "The Raven."

 In the above sentence *his* clearly refers to the antecedent *Poe.*

?

In Poe's "The Raven," *he* relies heavily on meter.

In this sentence, the antecedent should be *Poe,* not the possessive *Poe's,* which modifies "The Raven" and *implies* the antecedent.

Often *this, that,* and *which* modify nouns and so act as adjectives rather than as pronouns. When used as pronouns, make sure their antecedents are clear (see section **20d**).

Sarah snickered. *This* made the teacher nervous.

Pronouns must also avoid ambiguous references.

Professor Dorman read "The Raven" with emotion and dramatic gestures. His students liked *it.*
?

What did the students like? The poem? The performance? Or both?

Pronouns that have no function or antecedent should be deleted.

UNCLEAR: Studying Poe's poetry, *it* is enjoyable.
It was great to hear the poem read aloud because *it* made the meaning clear.

In the first sentence *it* is unnecessary; in the second, having *it* appear twice with different meanings creates confusion.

REVISED: Studying Poe's poetry is enjoyable.
The students enjoyed hearing the oral reading because *it* made the meaning of the poem clear.

Using the second person (*you*) in formal writing is usually ambiguous or remote (and too informal for most college writing) because writers aren't referring to a single reader (see section **3b**).

UNCLEAR: When listening to an effective reading of Poe's poetry, *your* hair stands on end.

Does *your* refer to the writer or to most readers?

REVISED: When listening to an effective reading of Poe's poetry, *my* hair stands on end.
When listening to an effective reading of Poe's poetry, *the audience's* hair stands on end.

3. Use singular pronouns to refer to most indefinite pronoun antecedents (*any, anyone, each, either, everybody, none, something*).

Even critics who enjoyed *Batman* and *Dick Tracy* said that *neither* lived up to *its* advance publicity.

The pronouns *both, many,* and *few* are plural.

4. Use plural pronouns to refer to compound antecedents joined by *and.*

Bert and Ernie enjoyed eating caviar while listening to *their* favorite opera.

5. With compound antecedents joined by *or, nor, either … or, neither … nor, not only … but also,* use a pronoun that agrees with the nearest antecedent.

Neither Donald nor his nephews brought *their* swimsuits to the picnic.

Neither his nephews nor Donald brought *his* swimsuit to the picnic.

6. Consider collective nouns as singular if you refer to the group as a whole and as plural if you refer to the individual members.

   The debate *team* won *its* third straight tournament. [singular]

   The debate *team* listened to each other's arguments as *they* went to the tournament. [plural]

   In the first sentence, *team* refers to the group as a whole; in the second, *team* is a synonym for "team members."
7. Use relative pronouns appropriately: *who, whom,* and *whose* refer to people; and *that, which,* and *what* refer to things.

   Alan, who collects old books, went to an *auction that* promised to have some first editions.
8. Use *-self* pronouns (reflexive and intensive pronouns) only with clearly stated antecedents.

   Shirley created the problem *herself.*

   I, myself, will solve the problem, thought Shirley.

   This rule is another way of indicating that *-self* pronouns should never substitute for *I* or *me.*

   George and *I* [not *myself*] asked for our tests.

   Ms. Morton handed the tests to George and *me* [not *myself*].

Name ______________________________ Score ________________

Exercise 27a–27h Pronoun agreement

1. Revise the following sentences to eliminate *agreement* errors. Place a check mark before correct sentences.
   a. A police officer must do his best to project a friendly image to young children.

   b. The Geo Prizm and the Geo Metro made its appearance in 1990, but both appeared earlier under Japanese names.

   c. None of the women brought their golf clubs to the conference, but three of the men brought theirs.

   d. Neither the bride nor her attendants thought they would cry at the wedding, and only the bride did.

   e. The home crowd cheered when their team entered.

   f. Each teacher was responsible for his or her class doing well on the proficiency exam.

   g. Someone was supposed to offer their house for the party.

   h. Sharks or a killer whale ate their fill of the fish.

   i. Every first-year anatomy student is shocked when they discover that a bat is more closely related to an elephant than to a hummingbird.

   j. Pool and pocket billiards is the same pastime; the label is socioeconomic.

2. Revise the following sentences to make the *references* clear and to remove pronoun errors. Place a check mark before correct sentences.
   a. Tony's high school guidance counselor was the person that convinced him to attend college.

   b. The Detroit Pistons, they won back-to-back championships.

   c. In Michael Crichton's *Sphere,* he reveals the potential danger in advances in technology.

   d. Philosophers need to help scientists distinguish between life and human life because they have knowledge essential to the abortion issue.

   e. It is difficult for meteorologists to tell a particular area whether it will be hit by a tornado even if conditions make it likely.

   f. The fog was so thick that you couldn't see more than a few feet in front of the car.

   g. Stephen Hawking seems to be a person for which no problem in physics is too great a challenge.

   h. The Simpsons are unlike the Huxtables because they don't exhibit positive family values.

   i. Montana faked a pass to his tight end; then he passed long.

   j. Winning the lottery will allow my mother, father, and myself to buy anything we want.

CHAPTER 28

Case

28a–28g Use the appropriate case.

Case refers to the change in form that pronouns and some nouns undergo to show their grammatical relationships in a sentence. The *nominative* case (also called the *subjective*) is used for subjects or their equivalents, predicate nouns. The *objective* case is used for objects, and the *possessive* case indicates possession.

Common Problems

Most confusion in case results from pronouns that appear in compound subjects or objects. Other problems result when conventions are unfamiliar.

Examples

Nouns and some indefinite pronouns change case only in the possessive, adding **'**, or **'s**.

James's Halloween costume got *everyone's* attention, especially the *clown's* makeup.

Pronouns change case often:

Personal Pronouns

	Nominative	*Objective*	*Possessive*
Singular			
First person	I	me	my, mine
Second person	you	you	your, yours
Third person	he, she, it	him, her, it	his, her, hers, its
Plural			
First person	we	us	our, ours
Second person	you	you	your, yours
Third person	they	them	their, theirs

1. Use the *nominative* case of pronouns for subjects and predicate nominatives.

   I went to the store.

   Native speakers would almost always use *I* in the above sentence, but a compound subject may present a problem for some:

   My sister and *I* went to the store. [not "my sister and *me*"]

   Because many speakers fail to use the nominative case for predicate nominatives, writers must pay close attention to this usage.

   It was *I* [not *me*] who went to the store.

   The best students were *they* [not *them*] who studied consistently.

2. Use the *objective* case for pronouns that are used as a direct object, an indirect object, or an object of a preposition:

   Ted reminded *me* about a math test. [direct object]

   Professor Tuffy gave *us* a test. [indirect object]

   We returned it to *her*. [object of preposition]

Compound elements in the objective case may be confusing at times:

Ted reminded Buffy and *me* [not *I*] about the math test.

NOTE: *With, among,* and *between* are prepositions, so their objects are *always* in the objective case: "Between *you* and *me,* Watson, we will solve the crime."

3. Use the *objective* case of a pronoun for both the subject and the object of an infinitive (*to* plus the base form of a verb: "to walk"—see section **22c**).

   Ken's poodle wanted *him* to feed *her.*

   Because infinitive phrases *with a subject* can *only* function as objects, *him,* which is the subject of the phrase, is part of a larger unit, an object. *Her* is the object of the infinitive phrase. Therefore, both pronouns are in the objective case.

4. Use the same case for a pronoun used as an appositive as the word it renames (see section **22e**).

   The homecoming king and queen, Betty and *I,* were given a limousine ride and a free dinner.

   The homecoming committee awarded its king and queen, Betty and *me,* a limousine ride and a free dinner.

   King and queen is the subject of the first sentence and the object of the second. The pronouns reflect that difference.

   Similarly, when a noun renames a pronoun, the case depends on whether the noun is a subject or object.

   "*We* marines can handle the problem," Ollie volunteered.

   "Leave the problem to *us* marines," Ollie volunteered.

5. After *than* or *as* in elliptical expressions, use a pronoun that agrees with the unexpressed words.

   Nancy liked Ronnie more than *I* [liked Ronnie].

   Nancy liked Ronnie more than [she liked] *me.*

   In the first sentence, the pronoun is the subject of the understood phrase "I liked Ronnie"; in the second, the object of "She liked me."

6. Use the possessive case with gerunds, the *-ing* verb form used as a noun (see section **22c**).

   Sarah awoke to the *cat's* yowling. [not "*cat* yowling"]

NOTE: If the *-ing* word is a participle—a verb that functions as an adjective—do not use the possessive: "I smiled at *Sarah chasing* the cat."

7. Use *who (whoever),* and *whom (whomever)* correctly: *who* for nominative functions, *whom* for objective functions.

   Americans *who* support the U. S. Constitution should defend its ideas for others, even those people for *whom* the Constitution means little.

   Who is the subject of its clause and must be in the nominative case. *Whom* is the object of the preposition *for* and must be in the objective case.

Name ________________________________ Score ________________

Exercise 28a–28g Case

1. Circle the correct pronoun in the following sentences, and place the number of the applicable item on the list before each sentence.

    a. Professor Boynton and (we/us) biology students went on a field trip to collect specimens.

    b. Between Bill and (I/me), we ate the whole pizza.

    c. The conservative candidates were happy that it was (they/them) who were elected to the board.

    d. Diane and Sam were delighted that Carla and Nick had invited (they/them) to their picnic.

    e. I don't care (who/whom) you are, Donald; we don't accept credit cards.

    f. Natalie wanted Jo to join a sorority with Blair and (she/her).

    g. His landlord objected to (Kermit/Kermit's) croaking all night long.

    h. (We/Us) Simpsons stick together in a crisis.

    i. Tammy wanted to go fishing more than (I/me).

    j. Lana was annoyed to see (Clark/Clark's) staring at her.

2. Revise the following sentences to correct case errors. Place a check mark before any correct sentences.

    a. Marie hated to hear Arnold whimpering because he didn't make the team.

    b. The players and the managers were happy that the coaches and them were going to eat together.

    c. Our English teacher said he was happy to have we athletes in class.

    d. It is we who will pass the grammar test, not they.

    e. Mr. Ed and me voted nay on the leash law.

f. I want the debate to be between you and I.

g. The option is for her to wait at the student union and for he to meet her there, or she can go to her dorm and wait for him there.

h. Come to the gym to work out with Isaiah and I.

i. That was her you saw me with last night.

j. Kelly's father wanted she to wash the car.

CHAPTER 29

Verb Forms

29a Understand the basic verb forms.

Verbs are either *regular,* forming the past tense and past participle by adding standard endings (*-d, -ed,* or *-t*), or *irregular,* changing form in various ways, usually by altering internal vowels.

Common Problems

Because they often follow no pattern from one verb to the next, writers must memorize the various forms of individual irregular verbs. To avoid errors with the irregular verb *be,* writers must pay special attention because the verb occurs frequently in speech and writing.

Examples

Verbs have three forms: the *infinitive,* the *past tense,* and the *past participle.* In regular verbs, the infinitive takes *-d, -ed,* or *-t* to form the past tense and past participle:

Infinitive	***Past tense***	***Past participle***
taste	taste*d*	taste*d*
kick	kick*ed*	kick*ed*
burn	burn*t*	burn*t*

But irregular verbs are not predictable:

Infinitive	***Past tense***	***Past participle***
be	was	been
go	went	gone
swim	swam	swum

NOTE: College-level dictionaries list principle parts of verbs.

Name ______________________________ Score ______________

Exercise 29a Verb forms

Circle the proper verb form in the following sentences. Use a dictionary when necessary.

1. Charles (dealed/dealt) the cards.
2. The calf had (drank/drunk) the milk.
3. The group had (rode/ridden) in a small car for hours.
4. The phone (rang/rung) at 3:30 a.m.
5. Tarzan first (saw/seen) Jane when she was in danger.
6. Jane had (forgave/forgiven) him for his poor manners.
7. The thief had (stole/stolen) a new car.
8. The *Titanic* (sank/sunk) on its maiden voyage.
9. He had (went/gone) swimming early in the morning.
10. Carmen had (chose/chosen) to take her sister to the zoo.

29b Understand the function of auxiliary verbs.

Auxiliary verbs, also known as *helping verbs,* join with both regular and irregular verbs to indicate tense, voice, and mood. The correct use of auxiliary verbs is essential to writing and speaking standard English.

Examples

While some verbs can be only helping verbs, others can act as both main verbs and auxiliaries. The following can be only auxiliary verbs:

can will shall should could would may might must

The following can be both main verbs and helping verbs:

be am is are was were being been do does did have has had

Name ______________________________ Score ______________

Exercise 29b Auxiliary verbs

Underline all auxiliary verbs once and the main verbs twice.

1. The committee will be meeting at Pizza Hut.
2. The package should have arrived yesterday.
3. The economy might not be as healthy as had been thought.
4. Terry told his brother that he could have been a contender.
5. The store did not open on time, so people were waiting in line.
6. If he were willing to work hard, Winston could be a great musician.
7. Money has been designated for building roads, but it hasn't been released yet.
8. *The Lord of the Rings* has been very popular in the past and should be popular again when new readers become involved in the trilogy.
9. Air bags had not been available on moderately priced cars until Chrysler made them available on the Shadow and Sundance.
10. The parade might have been planned for many months, but no one could have imagined that snow would fall in Georgia in May.
11. The line "We shall overcome" inspired a generation.
12. Archie thought that he ought to do his homework before he called Veronica, but he did not do so.
13. Dick Francis has been able to interest mystery readers in horse racing, a feat few would have thought possible before he had accomplished it.
15. Wagner's masterpiece, *Der Ring des Nibelungen,* which has been introduced to many Americans through public television, may reawaken an interest in opera.

CHAPTER 30

Verb Tenses

30a Know the basic verb tenses.

Correct use of verb tense, which indicates the time of an action or a state of being, is necessary for accurate expression of ideas. Because the three tenses (simple, perfect, and progressive) each share the same subcategories (present, past, and future), nine variations are possible. *Simple* tenses merely indicate a time relationship. Remembering that one meaning of *perfect* is "complete" (as in a completed, or perfected act) helps to understand that tense. The *progressive* tense indicates a continuous action.

Common Problems

The uses and nuances of the perfect and progressive tenses require practice for skillful application.

Examples

The following chart illustrates each tense in the first person, using a regular and irregular verb and the most commonly used irregular verb, *be.*

Simple tenses

Present

I talk, write, am.

Past

I talked, wrote, was.

Future

I will talk, will write, will be.

Perfect tenses (an auxiliary form of *have* and past participle)

Present perfect

I have talked, have written, have been.

Past perfect

I had talked, had written, had been.

Future perfect

I will have talked, will have written, will have been.

Progressive tenses (a form of *be* and the present participle)

Present progressive

I am talking, am writing, am being.

Past progressive

I was talking, was writing, was being.

Future progressive

I will be talking, will be writing, will be being.

Name ______________________________ Score ______________

Exercise 30a Basic tenses

Rewrite the following model sentences in each of the other eight tenses. Maintain the same person as the original sentence.

1. Martina returns the volley.

   a. Martina ________________ the volley.

   b. Martina ________________ the volley.

   c. Martina ________________ the volley.

   d. Martina ________________ the volley.

   e. Martina ________________ the volley.

   f. Martina ________________ the volley.

   g. Martina ________________ the volley.

   h. Martina ________________ the volley.

2. You drive your car.

   a. You ________________ your car.

   b. You ________________ your car.

   c. You ________________ your car.

   d. You ________________ your car.

   e. You ________________ your car.

   f. You ________________ your car.

   g. You ________________ your car.

   h. You ________________ your car.

30b–30f Use verb tenses appropriately.

Using the tenses consistently and according to conventions is essential to a precise and effective style.

Common Problems

As sentences become more complex, writers may inadvertently shift tenses and create confusion. Novice writers are sometimes unaware of tense usage which is determined strictly by convention.

Examples

1. Keep tenses consistent. Shifting from one tense to another inaccurately describes the point and can confuse readers.

   SHIFT: Nelson Mandela *came* to the United States, and he *visits* important political figures.

   As written, the sentence has Mandela visiting *before* he came to the United States. The revision describes the event accurately.

   REVISED: Nelson Mandela *came* to the United States, and he *visited* important political figures.

2. Edit for special uses of the *present tense.* In addition to explaining contemporary action, the present tense, not the past tense, is used to discuss historical information, artistic creations, and scientific principles.

   When it *fails* to sign the Geneva Peace Treaty, the United States *initiates* its future involvement in Vietnam.

   When he *describes* the bleak environment, the narrator of Poe's "The Fall of the House of Usher" also *reveals* his own view of life.

   Darwin's theory of natural selection *explains* one way in which evolution might occur.

   This convention, which uses the present tense to discuss past events, is called the "historical" or "literary" present.

3. Use the past tense appropriately. The *past tense* relates information about the past and is therefore conventionally used for personal narratives because the events have already occurred.

   I *threw* my books in the back seat because Annie *forgot* to return my phone call.

   The past tense is also used for ideas that are now rejected (compare the use of the historical present).

   Most of Columbus's contemporaries *thought* the earth was flat.

4. Use the perfect tenses appropriately. The *perfect tenses* reveal that events have been "perfected" or completed before other events.

   Rachael *had eaten* four helpings of ice cream before realizing that it was not low cal.

   The simple past tense does not emphasize the sense of completion that the perfect tense does.

5. Use verbals in the correct tense (see section **22c**). Use the simple *infinitive* when the action it conveys occurs simultaneously or after the action of the main verb.

   Curtis had wanted *to go* to camp last summer.

   Despite the fact that *had wanted* is in the past perfect tense, the convention is not to use the past perfect infinitive ("Curtis had wanted *to have gone* to camp last summer") because the "going" had taken place *after* the "wanting." The past perfect infinitive would be correct if its action occurred *earlier* than that of the main verb.

Curtis would have liked *to have gone* to camp early.

Use the present participle to indicate an action that occurs simultaneously to that of the main verb.

Eating her pizza, Cathy rushed out the door.

Use the perfect participle to indicate an action that precedes another action.

Having eaten her pizza too quickly, Cathy felt uncomfortable.

Name ______________________ Score ______________

Exercises:

1. Revise the following sentences to correct tense errors. Place a check mark before sentences that need no revision. Sentences may contain more than one error.
   a. Yesterday, I see Annie at the mall, and I ask her if she wants to help me pick out a new outfit.

   b. When my cousin visits me during the summer, we went swimming every day.

   c. Gary painted the chair, and when it dried completely, he gave it another coat.

   d. President Eisenhower's farewell address warned America about the growth of the military-industrial complex.

   e. Plate techtonics explains how continents move and cause earthquakes.

   f. The speaker approached the podium and adjusts the microphone before she began her presentation.

   g. The black Labrador retriever became a successful show dog because she was well trained as a pup.

   h. Benjamin Franklin's autobiography formulated the American Dream of working hard, becoming successful, and being happy.

   i. Early astronomers tell us that the sun circles the earth.

j. Warren Beatty relies heavily on comic strip techniques to achieve many of the effects in *Dick Tracy*.

2. Circle the appropriate verbal in the following sentences and indicate after each sentence whether the action of the main verb *precedes* the action of the verbal, *follows* it, or *occurs simultaneously*.

   a. Tonya had expected (to pass/to have passed) her final in college algebra.

   b. (Carrying/Having carried) his computer to his car, Lou slipped on the ice and fell.

   c. Nelson Mandela was to meet with African-American leaders in New York (to assure/to have assured) continued support for sanctions against South Africa.

   d. (Hitting/Having hit) the game-winning home run, Jackson jogged to the dugout a happy man.

   e. For as long as he could remember, Barry had wanted (to own/to have owned) a Corvette.

CHAPTER 31

Voice

31a–31b Identify the active and passive voices and use them appropriately.

Sentences that contain transitive verbs can be written in either the active or passive voice. In general, *active voice* is preferred because it is concise, provides vivid actors, and creates cohesion between sentences.

Common Problems

Because the passive voice eliminates the actors that relate one sentence to another, overuse of the passive voice creates vague, abstract constructions.

Examples

1. Use the active voice to emphasize the subject and the action the subject performs:

   ACTIVE: The *principal appointed* our class president.

   We can rewrite the same sentence to have the object perform the action:

   PASSIVE: Our class *president was chosen* by the principal.

   This second example de-emphasizes the actor and adds the helping verb *was* and the preposition *by*. Passive sentences can also eliminate the actor completely:

   PASSIVE: Our class *president was chosen.*

   This third example, while grammatically correct, is more abstract than its active voice counterpart. Readers don't know how the class president was chosen or by whom.

2. Use the passive voice only to emphasize the receiver and occasionally to add sentence variety. Sometimes the actor is unimportant to the sentence, in which case the passive voice is preferable:

   PASSIVE: The Wilson Building *was erected* in 1903.

   Readers probably don't need or want to know the company or the workers who constructed the building.

   Sometimes the passive sentence is more effective than its active voice counterpart:

   PASSIVE: Any passive *sentence can be stated* in the active voice.

   ACTIVE: A *person can state* any passive sentence in the active voice.

In this case, the subject of the active sentence is unimportant.

Name ______________________________ Score ______________

Exercise 31a–31b

Change the following sentences into active voice, supplying an actor when necessary. If the passive voice is more appropriate than the active voice, place a check mark before the sentence.

1. Susan was called on by her teacher to answer five questions.

2. The field was plowed in early April.

3. No explanation of why she broke up with Ken was given by Barbie.

4. Don't worry; the dishes will be done when you get home.

5. Roger Rabbit was murdered!

6. When Joe's father arrived home, the car had been washed and polished.

7. George Bush was elected president in 1988.

8. Social Security benefits have been cut.

9. The course was designed to challenge even the most skilled golfer.

10. Mistakes were made.

11. Oil was discovered off the coast of Washington in the 1970s.

12. To evaluate the recent movies about Vietnam, the history of the war must be examined.

13. The question of what constitutes human life, not just life, has been ignored by both sides in the abortion issue.

14. The senator said the road project had been canceled.

15. This set of exercises is finished!

CHAPTER 32

Mood

32a–32b Use the subjunctive mood effectively.

Of the three moods in English—indicative, imperative, and subjunctive—only the subjunctive creates problems for writers. The *indicative mood* asserts facts and asks questions, the *imperative mood* issues commands, and the *subjunctive mood* expresses wishes or statements contrary to fact. The subjunctive uses only *were* (never *was*) to create the past tense or the simple form of the present tense in the third-person singular (that is, the *-s* is dropped).

Common Problems

Because writers use the subjunctive infrequently, they often incorrectly substitute the indicative for the subjunctive.

Examples

1. Use the subjunctive mood in *if* clauses that express conditions contrary to fact:

   If he *were* [not *was*] a good student, Jon could earn a scholarship.

2. Use the subjunctive mood in *that* clauses following words such as *ask, request, desire, insist, recommend, wish:*

   The president *asked* that Congress *support* [not *supports*] the war on drugs.

   Her music teacher *suggests* that Gena *be* [not *is*] thoroughly prepared for her audition.

   In *that* clauses, the subjunctive uses the simple, present tense form of the verb in third-person singular.

Name ______________________________ Score ______________

Exercise 32 Mood

Revise the following sentences to correct errors in the subjunctive mood. Place a check mark before correct sentences.

1. If I was Larry King, I would ask that my guest prepares for the interview by thinking of potential questions.

2. Michael Jordan's coach suggests that he do nothing differently in the next season, and the Bulls will win more games because last year's rookies will improve.

3. Professor Turgidson insists that all homework is turned in at the beginning of class.

4. Marty would buy a new DeLorean if money was no object.

5. The president demanded that the prisoners be released.

6. Sylvester Stallone realizes that his portrayal of Rocky and Rambo demands little acting ability.

7. Her parents wished that if Barbie was to stop dating Ken, she finds another boy just as polite and well mannered.

8. The coach insisted that the team does not care who it faces in the playoffs.

9. It has been said that if the Bill of Rights was put to a vote, it would be defeated.

10. The student council recommended that each student receive free admission to all school-sponsored events.

CHAPTER 33

Adjectives and Adverbs

33a–33e Identify adjectives and adverbs and use them appropriately.

Whether a word, phrase, or clause serves the function of an adjective or an adverb depends on the word being modified (see sections **20d–20e**).

Common Problems

Although speech often ignores the distinction between adjectives and adverbs, writing retains the distinction.

Examples

1. Understand the difference between adjectives and adverbs.

   Certainly Romeo *loved* Juliet. [adverb modifying the verb *loved*]

   Juliet was *certain* Romeo loved her. [adjective modifying the noun *Juliet*]

   Writers often confuse the adjectives *good, bad,* and *well* with the adverbs *well* and *badly.*

   Calvin was *good* after his mother spoke to him.

   The adjective *good* refers to Calvin's behavior, but that is not the case in the next sentence:

   Calvin *did well* on his reading test.

   The adverb *well* refers to Calvin's performance. In the following sentences, the adjectives modify Calvin:

   Calvin smelled *bad* after playing in the mud.

   Calvin smelled *good* after his bath.

   Both adjectives *bad* and *good* refer to an attribute of Calvin, his odor.

   But the following adverbs modify the verb:

   Calvin *smelled badly* before taking cold medicine.

   Calvin *smelled well* after taking cold medicine.

   Both adverbs *badly* and *well* refer to Calvin's ability to perceive odors.

Some words can function as both adverbs and adjectives (for example, *little, hard, slow, fast*):

The *child* was a *little* girl. [adjective]

The child was a *little tired.* [adverb]

The function of *little* as an adjective or an adverb depends on the word it modifies, which is a noun in the first sentence and an adjective in the second.

2. Use adverbs to modify verbs, adjectives, and other adverbs.

An extremely athletic Carl Lewis *ran* very *quickly.* [adverb modifying a verb]

An *extremely athletic* Carl Lewis ran very quickly. [adverb modifying an adjective]

An extremely athletic Carl Lewis ran *very quickly.* [adverb modifying an adverb]

3. Use an adjective as a subject complement (see section **21d**):

Betty is *happy* after cutting the lawn.

Happy describes the subject, *Betty.*

4. Use an adjective as an object complement (see section **21c**):

Norm thought the *concert tiresome.*

The adjective *tiresome* modifies the direct object, *concert.*

5. Use comparative and superlative forms of adjectives and adverbs appropriately. The *comparative* form compares *two* items:

Patti's room is *larger* than Lana's. [adjective modifying the noun *room*]

Herman finished *faster* than Roger. [adverb modifying the verb *finished*]

The *superlative* form compares three or more items:

Patti's room is the *largest* in the dorm.

Herman finished *fastest* of any runner on the team.

Most one- and two-syllable *adjectives* add *-er* for the comparative and *-est* for the superlative. Longer adjectives require a modifying adverb like *more* or *less* for the comparative and *most* or *least* for the superlative.

The salesman was *more accommodating* than the manager. [comparative]

The salesman was the *most accommodating* person on the staff. [superlative]

Most one-syllable *adverbs* add *-er* for the comparative and *-est* for the superlative. Two-syllable adverbs require a modifying adverb like *more* or *less* for the comparative and *most* or *least* for the superlative.

Snails move *more slowly* than turtles. [comparative]

The *most evenly* matched teams don't always provide the *most exciting* games. [superlative adverb and adjective]

NOTE:

1. Avoid double comparatives and superlatives, which combine the *-er* or *-est* ending with *more* or *less, most* or *least.* Prefer "The cheetah is the *fastest* land animal" to "The cheetah is the *most fastest* land animal."

2. Avoid making *absolute modifiers* comparative or superlative. Words such as *unique, perfect,* and *square* are absolute; they don't vary in degree: Something is either "unique" or "not unique"; it is *not* "more" or "most unique."

Name ______________________________ Score ____________________

Exercise 33a–33e Adjectives and adverbs

1. Circle and identify the adjectives and adverbs in the following sentences and draw an arrow to the words they modify.

   a. Frank was happy to win a scholarship.

   b. The bus left early for the tournament.

   c. Debbie felt bad when she left for college.

   d. Each snowflake is unique.

   e. The early train leaves at 6:00 a.m.

   f. Although it was long, the class found the lecture enjoyable.

   g. Ellen was better prepared for the test than Marty.

   h. Ellen was happier than Marty.

   i. Wearing heavy gloves, the mechanic felt badly.

   j. Beth very seriously considered going to law school.

2. Correct the errors in adverb and adjective usage, either inappropriate words or uses of the comparative and superlative. Place a check mark before correct sentences.

   a. Buffy did very good on her entrance exam.

   b. Because he arrived in the dorm room before his roommate, Jason chose the largest of the two closets.

   c. The San Diego Chargers are far more better than the record indicates.

   d. The debate team performed real good in the tournament.

   e. Students complained because they thought the food was prepared bad in the cafeteria.

f. Visiting Paris was the most unique vacation Jane could imagine.

g. Larry found biology less challenging of all his classes.

h. The 1990 Iranian earthquake was the worse one to occur there in several years.

i. Ollie was the onliest one to avoid the storm.

j. Even though *The Simpsons* and *Growing Pains* have their fans, *The Cosby Show* still attracts the larger audience.

CHAPTER 34

Editing to Correct Nonstandard English

34a Include all necessary verbs.

Because written English differs from the many dialects of spoken English, writers often must use linking or helping verbs (forms of such verbs as *be, seem, look*) to form complete verbs.

Common Problems

Some spoken dialects omit the linking verbs or helping verbs of standard written English.

Examples

The following sentences require linking or helping verbs to complete the sentences:

Jerome [is] my best friend.

The rooms [are] painted a bright green.

Spenser said he [would] help Paul wash his dog.

If the bracketed words are omitted, the meaning might be clear, but the sentences would not be standard English.

Name ______________________________ Score ______________

Exercise 34a Necessary verbs

Supply linking or helping verbs in the following sentences.

1. Donna said she going to meet Jim at the Student Union.

2. A crowd of people walking down the street.

3. Joshua said that he so hungry he eat anything.

4. Pierre told his mother that he be home before 10:00.

5. Ken been given a fifteen-speed trail bike for his birthday.

6. His teacher said that Bryan the most creative student in class.

7. Betty type much faster than Norm.

8. While she taking attendance, some students doing their homework.

9. Harold hoped he win the raffle for a new car.

10. You need to practice unless you a natural athlete.

34b Add *-s* to form plurals of most nouns.

In standard English, a noun is singular unless it has a plural inflection, usually the ending "-s" or "es."

Common Problems

The plural of most nouns in standard English (the *-s* ending) differs from that of Spanish, French, and some spoken English dialects and can confuse writers.

Examples

The content of the following sentences suggests that the nouns are plural:

NOT: Four young boy were playing basketball.
John stacked the box one on top of the other.

The word *four* denotes plurality in the first sentence, as does the phrase *one on top of the other* in the second.

BUT: Four young *boys* were playing basketball.
John stacked the *boxes* one on top of the other.

NOTE: Some nouns such as *woman, child,* and *goose* form irregular plural endings: *women, children, geese.* Check a dictionary if you are unsure about a noun's plural form.

Name ______________________________ Score ____________________

Exercise 34b Plural nouns

Revise the following sentences to create appropriate plural nouns. Place a check mark before sentences with appropriate nouns.

1. Edgar Allan Poe was one of Saundra's favorite author.

2. Both of his hand had ink all over them.

3. Thousand of people stood in the streets to see their championship team drive past.

4. The thirsty hiker drank three gallon of water after they returned to the campsite.

5. Two statesman with opposing views of government, Ronald Reagan and Mikhail Gorbachev, dominated the late 1980s.

6. Ruth had four teeth pulled before having braces applied.

7. Swimmer swim several mile each day to improve their performances.

8. Congress must decide whether to initiate several Constitutional amendment in the upcoming session.

9. When he looked up, the cowboy saw three mens enter the bar.

10. Killer shark are one of the most dangerous animal in the ocean.

34c Use *-s* or *-es* endings for verbs in the present tense that have a third-person singular subject.

In English, only third-person singular verbs add *-s* or *-es*. While this convention is inconsistent with other forms of person, the endings are essential for standard English.

Common Problems

Writers sometimes use the first- and second-person form of verbs when the subject takes a third-person form. Such verb endings can be an especially troublesome problem when the writer's native language does not follow the conventions of standard English.

Examples

Without the appropriate endings, the following verbs do not use the conventional third person:

NOT: Jason write in his journal every night.
Sam touch his toes fifty times each morning.

BUT: Jason *writes* in his journal every night.
Sam *touches* his toes fifty times each morning.

Name ______________________________ Score ______________

Exercise 34c Plural verbs

Revise the following sentences to create appropriate third-person singular endings. Place a check mark before sentences with appropriate endings.

1. Jeri smoke two packs a day before she quit smoking.

2. Steven bought a van because it hold all his group's musical instruments.

3. The former East Germany hopes its economy will be as strong as its western counterpart in the near future.

4. A typical European speak more than one language.

5. The police officer told the class that anyone who use drugs is trying to avoid life's responsibilities.

6. The Declaration of Independence say that all people have inalienable rights.

7. In the Disney movie, Jimminy Cricket tell Pinocchio what to do whenever he need a conscience.

8. My cousin play chess with me whenever we gets the chance.

9. One never know what the future will bring.

10. Every time she get comfortable with a good book, Wendy's cat howl until she let him out.

34d Use *'s* to form most possessives.

In general, most nouns show possession by ending in an apostrophe and an *s:* cat*'s* paw. If the noun already ends in an *s*, its possessive form adds only the apostrophe: The dog*s'* howls.

Common Problems

Because apostrophes do not affect the way a sentence is read, writers may accidentally omit them.

Examples

The following sentences indicate the possessive:

The dog*'s* tail wagged.

Achilles*'s* heel was his weak point.

The boy*s'* locker room had new showers.

See sections **40a–40d** for a complete discussion of the apostrophe.

Name ______________________________ Score ______________

Exercise 34d Possessives

Apply the conventions of the apostrophe in the following sentences. Place a check mark before the sentences with appropriate conventions.

1. The womens choir performed for the faculty senates luncheon.
2. The Deans Council holds meetings on the first and third Thursdays of the month.
3. A mongoose relies on its speed when fighting snakes.
4. The children movie, *The Little Mermaid,* interests many parents who have read Hans Christian Andersen story.
5. The Coast Guard duty has changed in recent years to include capturing boats smuggling drugs.
6. Jeremy borrow his friend bicycle, and he rode five miles to his cousin house.
7. The earths orbit is not a perfect circle; its shape is more like an eggs.
8. The Tigris and Euphrates rivers enabled great cultures to develop in ancient times.
9. A modern small cars engine provides as much power as larger engines did in the past, so the fuel economy of modern cars has improved.
10. Henry James novels were less popular with his contemporaries than William Dean Howells were, but today the formers novels are taught more than the latters.

34e Use personal and demonstrative pronouns carefully.

When written English uses a personal pronoun (*he, she, they*) as an appositive, the pronoun *precedes* the noun or pronoun to which it is in apposition. Written English also uses the objective case for personal pronouns after a preposition (see section **28b**). Knowing the demonstrative pronouns (*this, that, these,* and *those*) prevents using other pronouns to fulfill their function.

Common Problems

Some dialects and foreign languages use a personal pronoun as an appositive to provide emphasis, the objective case for a personal pronoun after a preposition, and *them* as a demonstrative pronoun. Written English shares *none* of these conventions.

Examples

Omit the personal pronoun as an appositive:

NOT: The vice president, *he* may speak at graduation.

BUT: The vice president may speak at graduation.

Use the objective form of personal pronouns after prepositions:

NOT: How many of *they* were in class today?

BUT: How many of *them* were in class today?

Use *those,* not *them,* as a demonstrative pronoun:

NOT: The new Congress will solve *them* problems.

BUT: The new Congress will solve *those* problems.

Name ______________________________ Score ____________

Exercise 34e Personal pronouns

Revise the following sentences so they use personal and demonstrative pronouns conventionally. Place a check mark before sentences that follow the conventions of standard English.

1. My friend George, he ordered one of them country western albums advertised on TV.
2. Annie gave her dog Brutus two large dog biscuits, and he ate both them bones in two bites.
3. All of we students on the football team, we have to study late at night and early in the morning because of them long practices.
4. Alice invited three friends to her house for pizza, and all of them came.
5. My parents, they took three pictures of I before graduation.
6. The new movies this year, they contain so much violence that most of they are unfit for families.
7. Them hot summer days, they don't seem so bad in December.
8. Not any of we English majors have seen the new version of *Henry V.*
9. Them posters on the wall are of Dolores's favorite group.
10. Sara, she was anxious for me to send her them exercise videos so she could choose which one of they I should give her for her birthday.

34f Avoid double negatives.

Logically, two negatives cancel each other; thus, they should be avoided.

Common Problems

In Elizabethan English, in modern Spanish, and in some spoken American dialects, double negatives are conventional, but they are not in standard English.

Examples

The following sentences should use one of the two negatives, not both:

NOT: Ireland *never* had *no* snakes.

NOR: Washington, D.C., *won't* have *no* voting senators unless it becomes a state.

BUT: Ireland *never* had *any* snakes.

OR: Ireland *never* had snakes.

OR: Washington, D.C., *won't* have voting senators unless it becomes a state.

Name ______________________________ Score ______________

Exercise 34f Double negatives

Revise the following sentences to remove double negatives.

1. The United States had hardly no chance of winning the international soccer match.
2. Mike Royko defines "war wimp" as a political hawk who now favors American forces being involved in military actions, but when they had the opportunity, they did not fight in no battles.
3. A person wanting to buy an American computer can't hardly find none made in this country.
4. The expensive cars do not no longer have a monopoly on airbags since Chrysler has made them available on the Plymouth Sundance and Dodge Shadow.
5. Fred and Ethel never had no vacation until they went to Hollywood with their neighbors.

34g Use the articles *a, an,* and *the* correctly.

The articles *a* and *an* appear before indefinite, or general, nouns. The article *an* appears before nouns that begin with a vowel sound, and *a* appears before nouns that begin with a consonant sound. The article *the* appears before a definite, or specific, noun or an indefinite noun mentioned for the first time, thereby making the indefinite noun definite.

Common Problems

Some dialects do not use *an* at all. Other problems result from confusing the conventions of a foreign language with those of English or from an inadequate understanding of the conventions of English.

Examples

Articles clarify whether the word that follows is indefinite or definite and whether it begins with a vowel or consonant sound:

> He cooked *a* chicken.
>
> He cooked *an old* chicken for *an hour.*
>
> He cooked *the* chicken Donald had raised from a chick.

The first two sentences concern an indefinite chicken; the third deals with a specific one. *An* occurs twice in the second sentence because the words that follow it begin with vowel sounds (*hour* begins with a vowel *sound,* although not with a vowel).

Include articles before the names of buildings, departments, and companies:

> My parents stayed at *a* Hilton hotel, but we stayed at *the* Holiday Inn.

Omit articles before proper nouns such as the names of persons, streets, cities, states, continents, mountains. (The French convention calls for the article in this situation.):

> Fred's parents visited Australia. [not *the* Australia]

Omit articles before general mass nouns or abstractions:

> Farm children help their parents harvest hay. [Not *the* hay, but if *hay* were made definite with a modifier, the article would be necessary: "*the* new hay."]
>
> Most countries want freedom for their citizens. [not *the* freedom]

Omit articles before nouns that have been identified by possessives or pronouns such as *my, any, several:*

> Charice rode in *Susan's* car.
>
> Susan drove *her* car to work every day. [The possessive and the pronoun substitute for articles.]

Name ______________________________ Score ______________

Exercise 34g Articles

Revise the following sentences so the articles conform to the conventions of standard English. Place a check mark before sentences that do not need revision.

1. Often people drink the Coca Cola in the morning in place of the coffee.
2. Taking trip to mountains was lifetime goal of Tony.
3. While driving in Florida, the tourists saw a alligator crossing the road.
4. Dog jumped in front of car, but driver swerved and avoided hitting it.
5. Arkansas is a major source of the rice and the cotton.
6. Bolshoi ballet, one of best dance companies in world, will soon perform in United States.
7. Beth waited a hour for Hedda who was buying an hat.
8. Top of Empire State building provided impressive sight.
9. Superman supposedly travels at speed of the light.
10. Tourist marvelled at the Chicago skyline.

34h Use the correct person, number, and tense for the verb *be.*

Knowing the forms of the irregular verb *be* is necessary because it is so common in English.

Common Problems

The irregularity of the verb *be* makes appropriate usage difficult, and some spoken dialects have different conventions for the forms from standard English.

Examples

The following chart indicates the forms of the verb *be* in the present and past tenses:

Present tense	**Singular**	**Plural**
First person	I am	we are
Second person	you are	you are
Third person	he, she, it is	they are
Past tense	**Singular**	**Plural**
First person	I was	we were
Second person	you were	you were
Third person	he, she, it was	they were

Name ______________________________ Score ______________

Exercise 34h Forms of *be*

Revise the following sentences so the verb *be* conforms to standard English. Place a check mark before sentences not requiring revision.

1. Mike told me that you is his tennis partner.

2. The motorcycle were a total wreck.

3. A Honda Civic be a great graduation gift.

4. Is it true that you isn't going to the football game?

5. I were going to visit my aunt, but she weren't home.

6. Charley, you was my manager and should have made the proper arrangements.

7. The movie weren't over until 12:30.

8. They is planning a Halloween party.

9. I am going with you, aren't I?

10. Jared be Tom's roommate, and they is always together.

34i Use the correct person, number, and tense for the verb *do.*

The irregular verb *do* is one of the most common verbs in English.

Common Problems

The third-person singular *does* causes confusion because all other present tense forms of the verb are *do.* The problem occurs most often in the negative, when writers sometimes use *don't* instead of *doesn't.* Some writers also don't realize that all forms of *do* in the past tense are *did.*

Examples

The following chart indicates the forms of the verb *do* in the present tense:

Present tense	**Singular**	**Plural**
First person	I do	we do
Second person	you do	you do
Third person	he, she, it does	they do

The past tense form is *did* in all cases of person and number.

Name ______________________ Score ______________

Exercise 34i Forms of *do*

Revise the following sentences so the verb *do* conforms to standard English. Place a check mark before sentences not requiring revision.

1. At her party, Carrie had fun, but her mother done all the work.

2. For some tests, it don't matter how much a person studies.

3. The gardener did not know what was to be done, so he did nothing until his employer told him what to do.

4. Jason don't like most food, so his friends don't invite him over for dinner.

5. After she doed her algebra homework, Teresa didn't have anything to do.

6. If Chrysler, GM, and Ford doesn't sell more cars next year, the nation may suffer a depression.

7. Curtis don't think his teacher has a sense of humor, but she do; she just don't show it to him.

8. When she was growing up, Darlene often heard her mother say, "Where do you think you are going?"

9. David looked at the clock and asked himself, "Where do the time go?"

10. Dwayne do like to play basketball games, but he don't like to practice.

34j Use the correct person, number, and tense for the verb *have.*

Like *be* and *do,* the irregular verb *have* is one of the most common verbs in the English language.

Common Problems

Some writers do not realize that the only present-tense form that is not *have* is the third-person singular *has.*

Examples

The following chart indicates the forms of the verb *have* in the present tense:

Present tense	**Singular**	**Plural**
First person	I have	we have
Second person	you have	you have
Third person	he, she, it has	they have

The past tense form is *had* in both person and number.

Name ______________________________ Score ____________________

Exercise 34j Forms of *have*

Revise the following sentences so the verb *have* conforms to standard English. Place a check mark before sentences not requiring revision.

1. I has often walked on this before, but earlier today it has rained and I slipped and fell.

2. Has you ever wanted to skydive?

3. Laura have not been to a movie ever since she started college.

4. When you has finished practicing the piano, you had better do your homework.

5. Jack, who has been elected social chairman, and Jill, who is his date, have the clean-up responsibilities.

6. Collecting comic books from the 1940s have been a profitable hobby for many people.

7. Barry been invited to join a fraternity, but he have very little money, so he have to decline the offer.

8. "Where have all the flour gone?" Bob asked just after he has started to bake his mother a birthday cake.

9. Terry didn't buy the guitar because it have a thin crack on the back.

10. Cheryl Miller have a better college record in basketball than her brother Reggie who have played in an NBA All Star Game.

34k Select the correct form of irregular verbs.

Because irregular verbs have no predictable pattern, writers should verify their forms in a dictionary (see section **29a**).

Common Problems

English verbs are governed by convention more than by logic, and conventions need to be memorized.

Examples

Make certain not to omit helping verbs (*have, has,* or *had*) when using past participles:

Theo *has* just *drunk* three colas in a row.

The two deer *had seen* the hunter approaching.

The girls *have gone* swimming.

Do not force an irregular verb into a regular form:

Roger knew [*not* "knowed"] he would be late for class.

Cindy caught [*not* "catched"] the ball on one bounce.

Do not force a regular verb into an irregular form:

The child dragged [*not* "drug"] the chair across the floor.

Name ______________________________ Score ______________

Exercise 34k Irregular verbs

Revise the following sentences so the verb forms conform to standard English. Place a check mark before sentences not requiring revision.

1. The truck brung the loggers to the forest.

2. The astronomer seen the eclipse through a telescope.

3. The tractor drug the fallen log from the ditch.

4. The batter hitted the ball into the left field stands.

5. The pitcher had threw the ball before he saw the runner begin to steal second.

6. Shawn had went to class before he realized that he had left his paper in his room.

7. Professor Houseman speaked to each student individually about the research project.

8. Arnie had wore his new tie to class to impress Marie.

9. Jeri swum fifteen laps every day for six months.

10. The batter swung the bat and grounded to the first baseman for the final out.

341 Add *-ed* when needed to form the past and past participle of regular verbs.

Although spoken English often omits the *-d* sound at the conclusion of regular verbs, the ending is essential in written English.

Common Problems

Transferring the conventions of spoken English to written English usually reduces the level of formality.

Examples

In speech, verb endings are frequently de-emphasized or omitted:

NOT: Body building *use* to be a sport only for men.

BUT: Body building *used* to be a sport only for men.

To the casual ear, "use to" sounds like "used to." Writers should be alert to these similarities and should know how to correct them.

Name ______________________________ Score ______________

Exercise 341

Revise the following sentences to include the *-d* or *-ed* endings. Place a check mark before sentences not requiring revision.

1. The biology class was suppose to go on a field trip.

2. The machine crush the car into a block of scrap steel.

3. When she walk her Great Dane, Vanasa felt very safe.

4. Arnold Schwarzenegger bench press over five hundred pounds when he compete in body building tournaments.

5. Because no one ask him to help, Carlos watch the men push the car to a gas station.

6. Casey realize too late that he hadn't set his alarm.

7. Rover like to chase squirrels, but he never seem to catch any.

8. In the Old West, cowboys lynch horse thieves who would have been hang for their crime if they had gone to trial.

9. The final exam in Spanish prove to be much harder than Connie had ever dream it would be.

10. Carol laugh as she watch her cat chase its tail.

34m Use prepositions correctly.

Prepositions are idiomatic, meaning their use is agreed upon rather than the result of a grammatical rule.

Common Problems
Regional and other nonstandard dialects often use prepositions differently from standard English.

Example
Some idiomatic uses of prepositions are acceptable in speech or in particular regions of the United States, but they should be avoided in college writing:

> I will wait *for* [not "on"] you at the mall.

Prepositions that cause problems in idiom usually follow the verb. A reliable dictionary will supply the proper idioms.

Name ______________________________ Score ______________

Exercise 34m Prepositions

Revise the nonstandard idioms in the following sentences. Place a check mark before sentences not requiring revision.

1. Aaron wanted to come by my house to pick me up.

2. Many people found the movie *Presumed Innocent* preferable than the book.

3. The actor became so involved in his part he fell off of the stage.

4. Heather became so angry at her roommate that she didn't speak to her for three days.

5. Donna plans on doing her research paper on abortion.

6. Calvin said that he and Hobbes would be sure and come to Suzie's party.

7. Despite being twins, Shelley and Sandra are very different than one another.

8. *Die Hard II* is my type of a movie.

9. Iris disagrees upon Charlotte about majoring in history.

10. According with tradition, the bride takes her husband's name, but for many men and women that idea does not conform with the concept of equality.

Score [illegible]

Exercise [illegible] Prepositions

[illegible] in the following sentences [illegible]

1. [illegible]

2. [illegible] the board.

3. [illegible]

4. [illegible]

5. [illegible]

6. [illegible]

7. [illegible]

8. [illegible]

9. [illegible]

10. [illegible]

34n Check spelling, capitalization, and use of accents.

Many of the conventions of American dialects and foreign languages differ from standard English.

Common Problems

Pronunciation often differs from spelling, and non-native speakers bring conventions from their mother tongues that differ from standard English.

Examples

Some misspellings result because English words are pronounced differently from the way they are spelled:

> Last *February* [not "Febuary"], I lost my *library* [not "libary"] card.

Some misspellings are caused by dialects:

> Mary's aunt *asked* [not "aksed"] her to visit soon.

> The meal was *especially* [not "ecspecially"] good.

Some foreign languages have different conventions for capitalization from English. For example, Spanish does not capitalize the first-person pronoun, the names of months or days of the week, or nationalities; English does:

> When *I* [not "*i*"] saw Juanita last *Monday* [not "monday"], she said that she was leaving for *South America* [not "south america"] in *March* [not "march"].

English does not generally include accent marks, unless they are needed to prevent ambiguity (*to resume, a résumê*).

> The cowboy was trapped in a blind *canyon* [not "cañon"].

Name ______________________________ Score ______________

Exercise 34n Spelling, capitalization, accents

Revise the nonstandard spelling, capitalization, and use of accents in the following sentences. Place a check mark before sentences not requiring revision.

1. Many europeans fear german reunification.

2. People often consider the odd numbers 1, 3, 5, 7, 9, ect., to be lucky.

3. If i take two courses next summer, i will graduate in december.

4. Alot of the summer movies are to violent for young children.

5. John did porely on the test because he spent to much time with his frens.

6. I hope to see the pyramids in méxico in june.

7. Abortion is gonna be one of the major issues of the next elections.

8. Last wensday, Bob aksed his teacher to write him a recommendation, and she still hasent done it.

9. The flag amendment will supposively influence many voters in the next election, but the issue may backfire because voters fear tampering with the constitution.

10. The treaty to return the canal to panamá recebed much praise throughout south america.

PART

7

Punctuation

CHAPTER 35

Periods, Question Marks, and Exclamation Points

35a–35d Use periods, question marks, and exclamation marks appropriately.

The punctuation that closes a sentence affirms and emphasizes the point of the sentence and prepares the reader for the next sentence.

Common Problems

Careless proofreading and failing to understand sentence boundaries causes most errors in using periods. Question marks should not punctuate indirect questions, nor should exclamation marks be used excessively.

Examples

1. Use periods to close statements.

   DECLARATIVE: Aerobic exercise is essential to good health.

   IMPERATIVE (commands): Exercise daily. [The subject, *you,* is understood.]

   INDIRECT INTERROGATIVE (questioning): Richard asked if we had exercised today.

   EXCLAMATORY: Richard stomped and shouted.

   If the exclamation is mild, a period is sufficient; if it is strong, an exclamation point is preferable but never required.

2. Use a period after most abbreviations. A dictionary will indicate which abbreviations require periods.

   Abbreviated titles such as *Ms., Dr.,* and *Prof.* all require a concluding period. Some abbreviations also require internal periods (*a.m., e.g.*).

EXCEPTIONS: Some multiword abbreviations contain no periods (*rpm, mpg*).

Most abbreviations that consist of capital letters do not require periods:

AR, CA, TX (states)
ABC, TNT, ACLU, GOP (organizations)
PhD, MD, BA, BSE, AA (academic degrees)

A sentence that ends in an abbreviation should not contain a second period to conclude the sentence.

Add one tsp.

However, a sentence that ends with a question mark or exclamation point *maintains* the period after the abbreviation:

Should I add a tsp.?

3. End direct questions with a question mark.

Why should I exercise?

Does exercise make me feel good? Strong? Alert?

The second sentence uses question marks to indicate a series of informal questions implied by the main sentence.

4. Use exclamation points to show strong emphasis.

You never exercise! [reveals astonishment]

Stop hounding me! [reveals anger]

NOTE: Avoid exclamation marks in formal writing, as in most college writing. Also, do not use more than one exclamation point for a sentence.

Name ______________________ Score ______________

Exercise 35a–35d Periods, question marks, exclamation points

1. Separate the following paragraph into sentences and insert appropriate end punctuation. (Use each mark of end punctuation at least once. Also add capital letters and commas.)

Until Arnold Schwarzenegger came upon the scene body building attracted little attention from adults most saw it as an activity of narcissistic men who wanted to turn themselves into grotesque imitations of the ideal man an often heard comment was how could he let himself get like that body building wasn't a sport certainly women would never engage in such an activity or would they they most certainly would the change did not result just from Schwarzenegger's impressive string of championships nor from his charisma what was it that he had he had a philosophy that body building was an art form the builder was the artist the medium was the human body balance symmetry and grace were the goals not self-centered apemen fighting off sand-throwing bullies at the beach did Schwarzenegger's approach work indeed it did most people like the idea of being artists women in particular were attracted to the idea of smooth graceful figures in fact women are flocking to gyms and spas in greater numbers than men body building seems to be "in" for the foreseeable future but sometime when I see a body builder either male or female this thought occurs to me are they secretly hoping someone will throw sand in their faces

2. Correct the period, question mark, and exclamation mark errors in the following sentences. Place a check mark before sentences not requiring revision. Use a dictionary when necessary.

a. Sarah asked why she couldn't keep a pet tarantula in her dorm room?

b. Of all the life forms that have been classified, eighty percent are arthropods, and most of those are insects!

c. Argg! The temperature is 101!!! And the air conditioner is broken!!!!

d. Will I ever finish my research paper!

e. Tonya's parents gave her s.c.u.b.a. gear for graduation?

f. Coming back from Pike's Peak, the Tempo got 30 mpg.

g. Bill jogs. He doesn't look athletic!

h. Next spring, Bruce will receive his B.A. in history.

i. Marvin, there is a shark behind you.

j. Does Professor Studymore have an M.F.A or a Ph.D.?

CHAPTER 36

Commas

36a Use a comma before a coordinating conjunction (*and, but, or, nor, for, so, yet*) that connects independent clauses.

The comma and coordinating conjunction function as a unit, a *single* mark of punctuation to separate independent clauses. The comma *always* precedes the conjunction. (See section **8a**.) A coordinating conjunction *alone,* with no comma, separates or joins *parts* of sentences.

Common Problems

When two closely related sentences are joined with a coordinating conjunction, writers often erroneously omit the comma.

Examples

A comma *and* coordinating conjunction are necessary to join the following independent clauses:

Jeri shot the ball**, and** it swished through the hoop.

The mansion was old**, but** the interior was beautiful.

Ted's paper was late**, yet** Ms. Rogers accepted it.

No comma should occur with the coordinating conjunctions in the following sentence because they join only parts of a sentence:

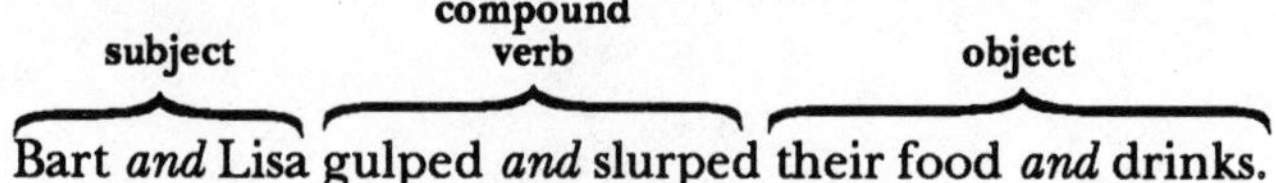

Bart *and* Lisa gulped *and* slurped their food *and* drinks.

Nor are commas used if the compound elements are dependent clauses:

compound subject of two dependent clauses

That you are my friend and *that you are moving* is sad.

NOTE: Two very short, closely related sentences *may* be joined by a coordinating conjunction and *no* comma, but they may also be joined in the conventional way: either "I *ran and* I won" or "I *ran, and* I won" is acceptable.

Name ______________________________ Score ______________

Exercise 36a Comma and coordinating conjunction

In the following sentences, place commas where they are essential and cross them out where they are unnecessary. If a sentence requires no revision, place a check mark before it.

1. Peter visited Roger, and Jessica at their home.
2. Everyone likes Charlie for he's a jolly good fellow.
3. James will not go to the play with us nor will he go to the party afterward.
4. Calvin really liked *Tom Sawyer,* but not *David Copperfield.*
5. Horace wanted pizza three nights straight but that was all right with Mickey.
6. Trudy loaned her copy of *Hamlet* to Claude, and Larry.
7. Vinnie's parents said they would pay his way through college, or he could join the military, or get a job.
8. Open the door and get out of my way.
9. Wendy borrowed Kim's hair dryer, for her own was broken.
10. After Howard finished studying, and after Don returned from football practice, they went to the student union.

36b Use commas between items in a series of three or more words or word groups.

Although the convention is changing, in college-level writing, the comma between the second-to-last and the last elements in a series is required even when they are joined by a coordinating conjunction.

Common Problems

The comma before the coordinating conjunction is conventional rather than logical and is often omitted.

Examples

Use commas between items in a long series whether the items are single words, phrases, or dependent clauses:

> Donald took Huey, Dewey, and Louis to school. [single words]
>
> The lost dog had scratches over his eyes, ticks in his ears, and flea bites over his whole body. [phrases]
>
> The mail is delivered when it snows, when it rains, and when it hails. [dependent clauses]

Although the comma before the *and* is conventional, sometimes it is essential to the meaning, to determining how many elements comprise the series:

> The child had blue, pink, yellow, and red balloons. [*four* groups of balloons]
>
> The child had blue, pink, and yellow and red balloons. [*Three* groups of balloons; each balloon in the last group is red and yellow.]

NOTE: Do not use commas if all elements are connected by coordinating conjunctions:

> Tom and Jerry and Mickey ate the cheese.

Name ______________________________ Score ______________

Exercise 36b Series comma

Place commas in the following sentences to indicate a series. Place a check mark before sentences not needing revision.

1. Heather wanted her future husband to be tall dark and rich.
2. Karen phoned Susan and Maria and Leslie, and they all met at Susan's house for pizza.
3. When he decided to take Spanish, Harry knew that he would have to study several hours daily that he would have to spend hours in the language lab and that he would have to learn to speak before a group.
4. Getting a deep tan playing basketball and talking with friends from high school were Derek's three goals for spring break.
5. After getting caught in a rain storm, Gail had to change her clothes, dry her hair and put on make-up.
6. At the zoo, the monkeys were swinging from one limb to another and howling making faces and other gestures at the crowd and begging for food.
7. Professor DeMand asked if all students had pens paper dictionary and an ink eraser or white-out.
8. Listening to music while studying for a test and eating potato chips and jalapeno dip made Tina enjoy the evening, but the next day she had a stomach ache and failed her history test.
9. The train left the station slowly picked up speed as it left the city and maintained a steady ninety mph until it approached the next metropolitan area.
10. Jason wanted to study French to become an interpreter and to live in Paris—both childhood dreams.

36c Use commas between coordinate adjectives.

Coordinate adjectives each modify the same noun or pronoun. To determine whether the adjectives modify the same noun or pronoun or a compound term, a writer can mentally place the word *and* between the adjectives to see if the sentence makes sense. Or the writer can switch the order of the adjectives to determine if the meaning is still clear.

Common Problems

Writers sometimes erroneously insert a comma between an adjective and the first word of a compound term (these are not coordinate adjectives), or they may not separate coordinate adjectives by commas.

Examples

Coordinate adjectives modify the same noun or adjective and require commas to separate them:

The detective wore a long**,** full-cut**,** yellow coat.

Beth swam in the cool**,** clear**,** calm pond.

In the first sentence, each adjective modifies *coat;* in the second, each modifies *pond,* so the adjectives are coordinate. But in the following example, the adjectives are not coordinate:

For his first jump, Lucky rented an extra tight woven parachute.

Extra modifies *tight, tight* modifies *woven,* and the entire phrase modifies *parachute.*

Name ______________________ Score ______________

Exercise 36c Commas between coordinate adjectives

Revise the following sentences so that coordinate adjectives are separated by commas and so that no commas separate other adjectives. Place a check mark before sentences not needing revision.

1. Barbara wore a baby, blue top and a pair of navy, blue slacks.
2. The poised, self-confident woman waited for an interview.
3. The long sinewy arm of the orangutan reached between the wire mesh fence and the gate and snatched a banana from the feeding tray.
4. The table's heavy plastic coating protected the satin finished oak top.
5. The cool northern breeze broke the summer heat wave.
6. Lee's excellent, mathematical background prepared him for the long, hard entrance exam.
7. The long graceful design of the sailboat was a very attractive sight as it glided over the surface of the water.
8. The confused old Labrador retriever stared blankly as the family cat lay down next to her and meowed.
9. Short succinct answers do not always help students to pass exams.
10. A tall slim masked cowboy rode into town on a regal white stallion, a unique startling sight to many New Yorkers in 1990.

36d Use commas to set off introductory phrases and clauses.

Because a comma can indicate when a phrase or clause ends, a comma after introductory phrases or clauses is often essential, and never incorrect.

Common Problems

Confusion results if the reader cannot determine when an introductory element ends and the main clause begins.

Examples

Even though the reader might understand the meaning of the following sentence without the comma, the courtesy of the comma makes the separation crystal clear:

> When he couldn't make up his mind whether to live in an apartment or a dorm**,** Alan asked his parents' advice.

However, introductory phrases and clauses often require a comma so readers do not read them as part of the main clause:

> CONFUSING: When she saw Jane Ann was going to the bank.
> While the couple was kissing a greased pig howling in fear ran from the young children.

The first sentence seems to be a dependent clause indicating that Jane Ann was going to a bank rather than that one person, Ann, saw another person, Jane. The second sentence requires rereading once the reader recognizes that the couple wasn't kissing a greased pig.

> CLEAR: When she saw Jane**,** Ann was going to the bank.
> While the couple was kissing**,** a greased pig howling in fear ran from the young children.

Short introductory phrases require a comma for separation unless the meaning is perfectly clear, and then a comma is optional. Introductory phrases modifying the subject of the main clause require a separating comma:

> Concluding his workout**,** Patrick took a cold shower.

Name ______________________ Score ______________

Exercise 36d Comma and intro phrases, clauses

Revise the following sentences by moving a phrase or adverb clause to the beginning of the sentence and setting it off with a comma. Place a check mark before sentences in which no movement is possible or the movement would make the sentence sound unnatural.

1. Soccer would become more popular in the United States if our teams did better in international competition.

2. Many Americans thought at the time they heard his famous campaign statement, "Read my lips," that President Bush would have to raise taxes.

3. The crowd wanted to know when it could enter the theater.

4. Tracy knew in a flash that he was not alone in the dark room.

5. Many students prefer to use word processors because they make revision easy.

6. The coach said last week that anyone caught smoking would be kicked off the team.

7. Christy liked to listen to the birds singing early in the morning.

8. Geoff arranged to go home at least once a month because his clothes needed laundering.

9. It was a day when no one went outside.

10. Norm wanted to visit the North Country after he had spent the summer working in Arkansas.

36e Set off nonrestrictive units with commas.

Nonrestrictive means nonessential. If any words, phrases, or clauses are not essential to the meaning of the sentence—not merely that they can be omitted to make the sentence shorter—then the element is nonrestrictive and should be set off by commas. The "essential" (restrictive) word, phrase, or clause requires no commas.

Common Problems

When elements are not essential to meaning, writers often mistakenly omit the commas. Conversely, writers may erroneously enclose prepositional phrases or other grammatical structures in commas because they are not *grammatically* essential to the sentence.

Examples

The omission of the restrictive clause in the following sentence alters its meaning:

> The store owner said he would give every person *who worked more than ten extra hours last week* $100.

But the same clause in the following sentence is *not essential, or nonrestrictive:*

> John, *who worked more than ten extra hours last week,* will soon have enough money to buy a computer.

The second example has the same meaning without the clause, so the clause must be set off in commas.

1. Use commas with nonrestrictive adjective phrases:

> Space probes, *often thought unnecessary,* may provide valuable information for improving our environment, building inexpensive housing, or finding inexpensive energy sources.

The participial phrase provides added information but does not restrict the meaning of the sentence.

> Many Americans have never heard of Belize, *an English-speaking Central American country closer to the United States than parts of Mexico.*

The phrase modifying Belize merely adds information and is set off by a comma at the beginning; the concluding period substitutes for a second comma.

2. Use commas with nonrestrictive *appositives:*

> My best friend, *Joe,* will never let me down.

Because the superlative adjective *best* restricts the meaning, the appositive *Joe* is unnecessary. Commas are therefore essential to set the appositive apart. If the sentence began "My friend Joe," no commas would be necessary.

Name ______________________________ Score ______________

Exercise 36e Commas with nonrestrictive units

Set off the nonrestrictive elements in the following sentences. Place a check mark before sentences not needing revision.

1. Most Americans think Buddhism which originated in India had its origins in Japan or China.
2. Any person who tricks people out of their life savings deserves a long prison sentence.
3. Ken saw the actress Mary Steenbergen in a department store.
4. The tortoise caught in the middle of the highway had little chance of survival.
5. The novel about the problems of baseball players bored Norma to tears.
6. Dinosaurs according to recent theories may have been warm blooded rather than cold blooded like reptiles.
7. John Poindexter who knowingly broke the law was sentenced to a prison term.
8. The Geo Storm which is the sportiest car in the Geo line has found a niche in the new car market.
9. The scandal which poses the greatest threat to incumbent politicians is the savings and loan crisis.
10. Dana is happy because her favorite actor Mel Gibson will be appearing in three movies this year.

36f–361 Use commas to set off or separate units in a sentence.

Commas that define separate grammatical units facilitate understanding.

Common Problems

Omitting necessary commas fails to provide reader guidance.

Examples

1. Use commas with titles, degrees, dates, and places. Traditionally, some elements have been separated from others in a sentence:

   The accused will be represented in court by Jonathan B. Strait, Esq. [sets off the title]

   June Bugg, PhD, and Terry Cloth, MBA, will be the conference consultants. [sets off the degrees]

   Duluth, Minnesota, is the setting for a Gore Vidal novel satirizing middle America. [sets off the parts of a place: city and state]

   The Clampetts won a trip to London, England. [sets off the parts of a place: city and country]

   President Kennedy was assassinated on November, 22, 1963. [sets off the month, day, and year]

NOTE: Do not use commas if the date is written in inverted order (22 November 1963) or if only the month and year are given (November 1963).

2. Use commas to separate units that interrupt the natural flow of the sentence. Transitional words and phrases are nonrestrictive (see section **36e**) and so are enclosed in commas:

   Train travel in the United States is expensive and often inconvenient. Aside from large city routes, for example, few trains are available to most people. And when they are available, they are, in fact, more expensive than planes or buses. In Europe, however, trains are convenient and inexpensive. Consequently, a greater percentage of people travel by train in Europe than they do in the United States.

3. Use commas to set off sentence elements that are out of normal order. Commas clarify the meaning when sentence elements are in an unnatural order:

   The editor admired the completed text, *satisfied.* ["satisfied editor" requires no comma]

   Because *absolute phrases* modify an entire clause or sentence, they have no natural place in a sentence and are always set off by commas regardless of their position in a sentence:

   The stars shining brightly, the deer was visible.

   The deer was visible, the stars shining brightly.

4. Use commas to show contrast or emphasis:

   Abernathy was an associate, not a close friend.

   The running back was slow, but powerful.

5. Use commas to set off interjections, short questions, and the words *yes* and *no*:

   "*Gosh*, that's Tom Cruise, *isn't it?*"

   "*No*, it isn't."

6. Use commas with direct address and interrupted quotations and dialogue:

   "I would like to know, Anita, if you would honor me by attending the prom next year."
   [direct address referring to a name]

   "I would love to," Anita said, "but I have to wash my hair that night."

7. Use commas to mark omissions:

   Japanese cars are reliable; American cars, safe.

   The word *are* is omitted but understood from the context because the second independent clause is parallel to the first.

Name ______________________________ Score ______________

Exercise 36f–36l

Add commas where necessary, and indicate the number (1–7) of the applicable listed item. Place a check mark before sentences not needing additional commas. Sentences may include more than one comma error.

1. "I will receive my BA degree May 19 1993" Paul said.
2. Traffic moved very slowly the road being under repair.
3. New houses cost so much that unfortunately most couples just starting out can't afford them.
4. The accounting text, written by G. S. Peek CPA, made the course enjoyable not the teacher.
5. Even though the carnival was boring, the roller coaster ride however was great wasn't it?
6. Peter Jennings is as a matter of fact the most popular nightly news host: Tom Brokaw second; Dan Rather third.
7. Sad to say young people are less informed on political issues than were earlier generations.
8. A great test short and easy and worth 25 percent.
9. The huskies finished the long race across the Yukon panting and exhausted.
10. "No Ollie you can't do it just because everybody else can" his mother said firmly but not in anger.
11. Hank Williams Jr. has recently released an album including several but not the majority of his father's greatest hits.
12. January 1 2000 will be the first day of the next millennium won't it, or will it be in fact the first day of the last century of the present millennium?
13. Constantinople was the early name of Istanbul Turkey and was named after Constantine I.
14. The concert was great but the long line terrible.
15. "Wow the reruns of *I Love Lucy* are *twice* as old as I am" Beth said. "But" she added "they are funnier than any other show on TV."
16. "Shoot the ball Ervin" the coach screamed, but time ran out.
17. Viewing solar eclipses directly as most know can injure the eyes.
18. No one likes waiting in line do they, but they like having people butt in front of them even less.
19. "May I be excused" Curtis asked. "Yes you may" his father replied.
20. Reno Nevada is further west than San Diego California isn't it?

CHAPTER 37

Unnecessary Commas

37a–37h Do not overuse commas.

Because of many writers' tendencies to overpunctuate, punctuation, particularly commas, should be used only when it can be justified grammatically.

Common Problems

The widely applied procedure of using a comma where a reader would pause if speaking aloud ignores the fact that commas separate grammatical units, not units of speech. Although written English may include commas at points where pauses occur in speech, sometimes no punctuation occurs at these points; sometimes periods, semicolons, dashes, or other marks appear, making the "pause justification" meaningless.

Examples

1. Do not use a comma to separate the subject from the verb or the verb from its object or its complement. The commas in the following sentences are unnecessary:

   Cindy,/ sketched a picture. [between subject and verb]

   Dolores drove,/ the car. [between verb and object]

   Jerome was,/ happy. [between verb and subject complement]

   Kyle thought his essay,/ an "A" paper. [between object and object complement]

   Do not place commas between modified elements or when phrases or clauses are subjects or objects:

   That automobile prices are going down,/ benefits consumers. [a clause as subject]

   The man who ran out of the store,/ is a thief. [subject modified by a restrictive clause]

2. Do not use a comma between compound elements unless they are independent clauses. No comma is necessary when parts of sentences are joined by the coordinating conjunctions *and, but, for, or, nor, so, yet* (see section **36a**).

   Coffee,/ and tea both contain caffeine. [compound subject]

   These beverages *stimulate,/ and enliven* people. [compound verb]

Rushing home from school/ and eating a quick meal/ and then going to work typifies the lives of many college students. [compound subject]

America will market an electric car *when battery technology improves to the point where such cars are affordable/ and when the American public realizes their benefits to the ecology.* [compound dependent clauses]

3. Do not use commas with restrictive modifiers. The modifiers in the following examples are essential to the meaning of a sentence, so they should not be set off by commas:

   Suzanne will give Joe all the money/ that she owes him. [She will give only the money she owes.]

   Edgar Allan Poe's short story/ "The Murders in the Rue Morgue/" introduced readers to the detective, C. August Dupin. [Poe wrote many stories, but only one introduces the character Dupin.]

   Omitting the noun clause in the first sentence and the appositive in the second changes the meaning of the sentences even though the omission does not prevent both from being grammatically correct sentences: restrictive elements restrict the meaning.

4. Do not use a comma before the first word or after the last word in a series.

   Tom, Dick, and Mary/ enrolled in the same classes. The classes were/ math, history, and English.

   A comma after *Mary* separates the compound subject from the verb; a comma after *were* separates the verb and the compound subject complement. (This point is merely a specific application of section **37a**.) If *such as* or *like* introduces a series, a writer may *mistakenly* place a comma after the words:

   Andre loves spicy food, such as/ chili, salsa, and stuffed jalapeño peppers.

   The connecting phrase *such as* introduces the series and should not be separated from it.

5. Do not use a comma before adverbial clauses that end sentences. Adverbial clauses beginning with such words as *after, because, if, since, when,* and *until* introduce the clause, and the comma before these terms is redundant. If the adverbial clause precedes the sentence, no such clue is present and the comma is essential:

   Cheryl drinks Diet Coke/ because she likes its taste.

   Because she likes its taste**,** Cheryl drinks Diet Coke.

6. Do not use a comma between adjectives that cannot be separated with the word *and.*

   The most/ unsatisfying change from *Robocop 1* to *Robocop 2* is that Murphy has given up hope of returning to his wife and child.

   See section **36e** for a more detailed discussion.

7. Do not use a comma before an opening parenthesis. Parenthetical information, which is part of a sentence, refers to the part immediately *preceding* it. Therefore, a comma should not separate the parenthetical information from the section it comments upon:

   Interjections/ (words like *gosh, golly, argg*) should be used sparingly.

   If a comma is necessary when the parenthetical information is omitted, the comma belongs *after* the parentheses.

8. Do not use a comma before or after a period, question mark, exclamation mark, or dash. End punctuation sets off entire sentences, and dashes set off grammatical units more strongly than commas do. Therefore, where end punctuation or dashes would appear at the same place as a comma, they replace the comma:

   "Are you leaving the party now?"/ Joan asked.

   "Certainly!"/ Sam replied.

   He added, "You can come with me, however/."

   "We can have more fun/—as if we were having any fun—making popcorn at my place," she said.

Name ____________________ Score ____________

Exercise 37a–37h Unnecessary commas

Circle the unnecessary commas in the following sentences. Place the number of the listed guideline(s) before each sentence. Place a check mark if the sentence is correctly punctuated.

1. Eddie Murphy, and Nick Nolte have become a successful team, because their film personalities contrast.

2. The man who works at the grocery store, is also a college student.

3. Because he had played so hard, Jim could not sleep, after the softball game.

4. The conclusion of *Robocop 2,* prepared viewers for a sequel, although not nearly as obviously as did *Back to the Future, Part II.*

5. Many people, who would like to wear contact lenses, can't, because they need bifocals, which aren't yet available in contact lenses.

6. Michael Crichton's, *Sphere,* is a spell-binding novel, which has elements of *The Abyss,* and *Forbidden Planet.*

7. "Who knows what evil lurks in the hearts of men?," signaled the beginning of one of the most, popular, weekly radio shows, *The Shadow.*

8. Soap operas, which many people find a waste of time, attract a wide audience, including, students, teachers, politicians, homemakers, and business leaders.

9. Emily Dickinson, whose poetry often seems whimsical, and light, was an innovative stylist and capable of writing dark, foreboding verse.

10. Bicycling may become the "in" exercise of the 1990s, because of the range of activities it offers,—racing, long distance touring, and performing stunts.

11. An FM station, that plays only classical music, can be profitable, but will have a limited audience.

12. When skateboarding first began, few people realized that it would last, much less that it would generate competitive contests, and performance areas.

13. Each year, more viewers are watching college sports, but they are watching them on TV, and not going to the events.

14. Plastic, aluminum, and paper, are all being recycled, which will improve the economy, and the environment.

15. Popular literature, such as, romances, mysteries, and westerns, provide readers an escape from everyday life.

16. Whether students of the 1990s will be like students of the 1970s, or whether they will be like students of the 1980s, will depend more on social, and economic issues than on their parents' political beliefs.

17. "Oh, no!," Bob shouted, "I locked my keys in the car."

18. Professor Hill's light, tan, leather jacket was both functional, and attractive, because it protected her from the wind, and from lacerations from falls, (she drove a motorcycle rather than a car).

19. Wally, who is rather shy, became good friends with Mona, who has an outgoing personality, because they both enjoy golf.

20. Students, who read a great deal, are often good writers.

CHAPTER 38

Semicolons

38a–38e Use semicolons appropriately and effectively.

Semicolons join independent clauses and indicate a *close* relationship between the sentences. Semicolons also separate items in a series that contain internal punctuation.

Common Problems

Writers mistakenly use commas instead of semicolons when sentences are already joined by conjunctive adverbs or transitional adverbs. Writers also sometimes use semicolons to join independent clauses to dependent clauses, resulting in fragments.

Examples

1. Use a semicolon between independent clauses *not* joined by a coordinating conjunction (*and, but, or, for, nor, so, yet*). Like the comma and coordinating conjunction, the semicolon indicates a close relationship between the sentences it joins. Unlike a comma and coordinating conjunction, however, a semicolon doesn't specify the type of relationship (see section **36a**):

    The most common addictive drug is caffeine; nicotine runs a close second.

    The subject of addictive drugs and the prevalence of addiction make the sentences closely related.

2. Use a semicolon between independent clauses joined by a conjunctive adverb (such as *however, moreover, then, nevertheless*) or a transitional phrase. A conjunctive adverb or a transitional phrase can indicate a relationship between sentences to intensify the closeness of the sentences:

    The most common addictive drug is caffeine; nicotine, *however*, runs a close second.

    If the conjunctive adverb begins the sentence, two options are available: making the two independent clauses into separate sentences or joining the two clauses with a semicolon (using a comma would create a comma splice—see section **25c**):

    The most common addictive drug is caffeine. *However*, nicotine runs a close second.

    The most common addictive drug is caffeine; *however*, nicotine runs a close second.

3. Use a semicolon with a coordinating conjunction only if one or both independent clauses contain internal punctuation.

    Because he liked baseball, football, and basketball, Ben tried out for all three teams when he was in high school; but because he had very little ability, he didn't make any of them.

    The semicolon indicates a stronger separation than those indicated by commas in the two sentences.

4. Use a semicolon between items in a series when one or more items contain internal punctuation.

   Monday Courtney wanted to have her hair cut, permed, and tipped; her car washed, polished, and cleaned inside and out; and her room straightened up before her parents arrived for a visit.

5. Do not use a semicolon to connect a subordinate clause with an independent clause.

   Because he liked writing to his friends whenever he got the chance;/ Leron received far more mail than did any of his friends.

   The dependent clause is a fragment if it is joined to a sentence by a semicolon; a comma is the correct punctuation mark in this situation (see section **36d**).

Name ______________________________ Score ______________

Exercise 38a–38e Semicolons

Revise the following sentences to show the appropriate use of semicolons. Place a check mark before sentences not needing revision.

1. Anne was Nora's best friend last semester, however, they hardly see each other this semester.
2. Television meteorologists now use the word *thorm,* which is short for "thunder storm," and *humiditure,* which refers to the heat index; but they don't yet use *worm* as a shortened form of "wind storm."
3. Barbie had borrowed Ken's VCR so she could see the video he had made of her birthday party; but she couldn't watch it until he came over because she didn't know how to turn on the machine.
4. The newest word-processing programs are easy to learn, inexpensive to purchase, and include spell checks and dictionaries, so all college students should think about buying one.
5. If she had only known how important her ACT scores would be; Jennifer would not have gone to a party and stayed out late the night before the exam.
6. Jane caught the measles from her little brother, therefore, she had to miss her mid-term exams.
7. *The National Review,* a conservative magazine, *The Nation,* a liberal magazine, and *The New Republic,* a magazine conservative on some issues and liberal on others, are ideal sources for people who wish to be better informed than those who only watch TV or read *Newsweek* or *Time.*
8. When a hummingbird hovers over a flower siphoning nectar, its wings move so quickly that they are a blur, but slow-motion photography has enabled scientists to understand the complex wing movement.
9. Julie likes to do her homework late at night, her friend Stephanie, in contrast, likes to work early in the morning.
10. George enjoys collecting comic books, it is very profitable.

CHAPTER 39

Colons

39a–39c Use colons appropriately and effectively.

When colons are used with sentences (as opposed to the conventional uses with numbers, dates, and salutations), they *always* must follow an independent clause (a sentence) and the information that follows always must elaborate the first clause.

Common Problems

Writers sometimes erroneously place a colon after a verb instead of at the end of the independent clause when introducing an element. Colons and semicolons are not usually interchangeable.

Examples

1. Use a colon after an *independent clause* to introduce a series, a quotation, an appositive, a definition, or an amplification.
   a. A colon introduces a series of words or phrases.

      Before backpacking in the wilderness, first-time campers should bring the following items: a snake-bite kit, water purification tablets, and bathroom tissue.

   b. A colon introduces a series of sentences.

      The space program offers many advantages to the United States: it is a laboratory for scientific experiments impossible on earth, it develops prototypes of products that will later benefit all citizens, and it carries on the spirit of exploration that has always typified our country.

   c. A colon introduces a series of questions.

      In selecting a college, a prospective student needs to consider the following questions: Am I ready for the work I will encounter? Can I adapt to new situations? Do I enjoy meeting new people? Should I choose a school nearby or far away? Why do I want to attend college?

NOTE: When a declarative or imperative sentence follows a colon, a capital letter at the beginning is optional, but questions normally begin with capital letters.

   d. A colon introduces a quotation.

      It was a wise but cynical person who made the following statement: "Absence makes the heart grow fonder—of somebody else!"

e. A colon introduces an appositive. A period is also correct, but a colon is more formal and emphatic.

> As the Person of the Decade of the 1980s, *Time* magazine made a controversial but defensible choice: Mikhail Gorbachev.

f. A colon introduces an amplification of the preceding sentence.

> Cross country skiing is an excellent exercise: it offers vigorous aerobic exercise of all major muscle groups, yet places little stress on joints.

NOTE: A colon introducing amplification offers a rare opportunity to use punctuation for stylistic purposes: the colon both guides the reader to what follows it and assumes reader awareness of the convention.

2. Use a colon in salutations, in numbers to show time, and in ratios.

a. Formal salutations use colons instead of commas:

> Dear Sir:
>
> To Whom It May Concern:
>
> Dear Ms. Steiner:

b. Colons are conventionally used in particular situations involving numbers:

> 12:18 p.m.   6:23 a.m. [time]
>
> He ran the mile in 3:55:8. [time]
>
> The odds were 15:1 that Mike Tyson would regain the heavyweight title. [ratio]

NOTE: Colons have traditionally been used to separate chapter and verses in the Bible (Matthew 6:5–6). *However,* MLA recommends periods (Matthew 6.5–6).

3. Do not use a colon after a linking verb, preposition, or relative pronoun.

> The primary colors *are*~~:~~ red, green, blue, and yellow.
>
> The primary colors consist *of*~~:~~ red, green, blue, and yellow.
>
> All art students need to know *that*~~:~~ the primary colors are red, green, blue, and yellow.

In each of the above cases the colon does not follow an independent clause: in the first it separates a verb from the subject complement; in the second, it separates a preposition from its object; in the third, it separates the pronoun from the clause it introduces.

Name ______________________________ Score ________________

Exercise 39a–39c Colons

1. Write ten sentences using colons as they are used in the examples above. Show a different use in each sentence.
   a.

   b.

   c.

   d.

   e.

   f.

   g.

   h.

   i.

   j.

2. Circle the colons that are used inappropriately in the following sentences and explain why they are inappropriate. Place a check mark before sentences not needing revision.

   a. Charles was an excellent athlete: he lettered in three sports each of his four years in high school.

   b. When he was feeling depressed, Brett's grandfather told him that: "It is better to have loved and lost than never to have loved at all."

   c. President Bush now regrets that he said: "Read my lips! No new taxes!"

   d. Professor Merrit said that to pass the course Cindy needed to do only one thing: study.

   e. The movie *Total Recall* was about: a man whose memory had been erased, two lovers who finally reunite, and an unethical capitalist's plot to make billions of dollars.

CHAPTER 40

Apostrophes and Quotation Marks

40a–40i Use apostrophes and quotation marks appropriately and effectively.

Apostrophes show possession, indicate omissions in contractions, and form some plurals. *Quotation marks* enclose the *exact* words of another person, the titles of short works, and words or phrases used unconventionally.

Common Problems

Writers sometimes omit apostrophes indicating possession, or they may use apostrophes in a confusing manner. They may use apostrophes to create, erroneously, the plural or possessive of possessive pronouns, which is a redundancy.

Quotation marks enclose *only* exact words, not paraphrases. Their conventional use with other marks of punctuation, including single quotation marks, can be troublesome, as can their difference from italics (underlining) to show emphasis. Writers may also incorrectly enclose special terms with quotation marks.

Examples

1. Use an apostrophe to create possessive nouns. The possessive case shows ownership, but the placement of the apostrophe or whether it appears with an *s* varies: a dog**'s** bone, the students**'** dorm.
   a. For all singular nouns, even if they end with an *s*, use an apostrophe before the *s*: **'s**.

      Donald**'s** duck, the woman**'s** purse, the drinking glass**'s** design, Howells**'s** novels

   b. For plural nouns *not* ending in *s*, use **'s**.

      women**'s** magazines, oxen**'s** yoke, fish**'s** gills

   c. For plural nouns ending in *s* use an apostrophe only.

      the teachers**'** lounge, the deans**'** council [a council of deans], the hogs**'** pen

   d. For compound nouns, use **'s** or **s'** after the last word, as appropriate.

      his sister-in-law**'s** smile, the mother-in-laws**'** reputation *or* mothers-in-law**'s** reputation [the reputation of all members of the group]

   e. For indefinite pronouns (*everybody, nobody, each other,* and so on), use **'s**.

      nobody**'s** fool, everybody**'s** friend, anybody**'s** pen

f. To show *joint* possession, use **'s** after the last noun only.

Nancy and Roy**'s** house, Sam and Janet**'s** evening on the town, the Senate and House**'s** franking privileges

To show *separate* possession, use **'s** after each noun.

George**'s** and Lucia**'s** computers [each has one computer], the men**'s** and women**'s** pay scales [each has a separate pay scale]

2. Use the apostrophe to form contractions or to indicate omissions.

Don couldn't wait for the deer season to begin.

Anne said, "I can wait 'cause I don't want you to kill a deer."

In each case the apostrophe indicates that letters have been omitted (in formal writing, *'cause* for *because* would be unacceptable).

NOTE: Do not create contractions where the meaning might be ambiguous: *I'd* is unacceptable in formal writing because it could be a shortened form of *I had, I would,* or *I could.*

3. To prevent misreading, use the apostrophe to form plurals of lowercase letters used as letters and words used as words. (The letters used as letters and words as words should be italicized or underlined—see section **42c**.)

Wendy received five *i*'s last term because she had the flu and missed her final exams.

Helen's essay has fourteen *there*'s on the first page.

Capital letters usually don't create problems in misreading because they differ from the lowercase *s* used to form the plural: "Wendy received two *B*s and three *C*s." But "Wendy received five *A*'s" requires an apostrophe to prevent misreading the grades as the word *As.*

4. Do not misuse the apostrophe. Do not use an apostrophe with the possessive pronouns *its, whose, ours, yours, theirs, his,* and *hers.*

The tiger bared *its* teeth. [NOT *it's,* a contraction for *it is*]

I know *whose* car is parked outside. [NOT *who's,* a contraction for *who is*]

The Chrysler convertible is *hers.* [NOT *her's;* it is redundant as a form of the possessive and is never used]

Do not use an apostrophe with plural nouns that are *not* possessive.

Three *cars* were parked in front of the house. *[car's* is the possessive of car]

5. Use quotation marks around direct quotations in your text. Quotation marks enclose the *exact* spoken or written words of another person:

In *The Scarlet Letter* Hawthorne writes that Hester Prynne's mark of shame was "surrounded with an elaborate embroidery and fantastic flourishes of gold thread."

If the writer's words interrupt the quotation, each quoted section is enclosed in quotation marks:

"Surrounded with an elaborate embroidery and fantastic flourishes of gold thread," Hawthorne writes in *The Scarlet Letter,* "appeared the letter *A.*"

An *indirect* quotation states the idea, not the exact words, so it does *not* use quotation marks.

Hawthorne describes in *The Scarlet Letter* that Hester's mark of shame was elaborately embroidered with gold thread flourishing fantastically around it.

When one quotation is enclosed within another, use double quotation marks for the outer quotation and single quotation marks for the inner one:

> After reading Hawthorne's description of Hester, Kelly said to her friend, "Don't you find the picture of a young woman with 'dark and abundant hair, so glossy that it threw off the sunshine with a gleam' to be appealing as the heroine of this tale?"

NOTE: Single quotation marks are used only for quotations within quotations; in all other cases, double quotation marks are used.

6. Use quotation marks to show dialogue and unspoken thoughts. Every new speech also begins a new paragraph, even when the same person is speaking:

> "Are you going to take American history at 8:00 next semester?" Jennifer asked.
>
> "No!" Rick said with some intensity. "I can't seem to get going that early.
>
> "Is Hardcase the teacher?" he then asked.
>
> "I sure would hate to face her at 8:00 three days a week," he thought.

When the same speech continues for more than one paragraph, no closing quotation marks appear until the end of the speech, but each paragraph opens with quotation marks.

7. Use quotation marks around the titles of short works.
   a. Articles in magazines, newspapers, and journals:

      "Dewey Defeats Truman!"

   b. Short stories, essays, record titles (*not* albums, which are italicized, or underlined), episodes of a TV series (the series would be italicized):

      "The Tell-Tale Heart" [short story]

      "Billie Jean" [a song from the album *Thriller*]

   c. Short poems:

      "Valediction: Forbidding Mourning"

   d. First line of poem as title:

      "There's a certain slant of light"

   e. Titles of chapters of books:

      "Reconstruction of the Burgess Shale"

   (See section **42a** for the use of italics.)

8. Use quotation marks correctly with other punctuation marks.
   a. Periods and commas always go *inside* both single and double quotation marks:

      "When I was young," Jill's grandfather said with pride, "I used to walk five miles to school every day, even when it snowed."

   b. Semicolons and colons go *outside* the quotation marks:

      "Gosh!" Mike thought, "I'm lucky my parents gave me a word processor for graduation": he had just received an *A* on an essay, and his teacher had praised his neatness.

c. Question marks and exclamation points go inside if they are part of the actual quotation and outside if they are not:

"That's not fair!" Tonya said. [The statement is the exclamation.]

Who said, "College will be the best time of your life"? [The quotation is part of the question, not a question itself.]

d. Dashes go outside quotation marks if they are not part of the quotation:

Did you say you "rode five miles to school every day"?—I meant *walked*, Gramps. I'm sorry.

e. Use a colon, a comma, or no punctuation at all after a word group that introduces a quotation:

Please answer this question: "Why do cats seem to like people who don't like them?"

All quotations must be a part of a sentence; a colon means that the quotation that follows it illustrates or amplifies the sentences which introduces the quotation.

The veterinarian said, "Cats don't necessarily like those who don't like them; it just seems that way because people who don't like them remember the cats' unwanted attention."

The comma introduces the quotation that is a part of the sentence; the introduction to the quotation is not a sentence.

My friend told me that she doesn't like cats because "they're so sneaky."

No punctuation is necessary if, without quoted material, the sentence would not require punctuation at the point of the quotation.

9. When you use words in a special or ironic sense, do not use quotation marks. Recast sentences rather than ask readers to interpret words in quotation marks that imply something other than their literal meaning:

Robin was "overjoyed" when friends "borrowed" her clothes without telling her.

If Robin was "angry" that the friends "stole" the clothes, those words should be used.

Name ______________________________ Score ______________

Exercise 40a–40i Apostrophes and quotation marks

1. Correct the apostrophe errors in the following sentences. Some errors will involve the placement of the apostrophe and the use of *s*'s. Other errors omit necessary apostrophes. Place a check mark before sentences not needing revision.

   a. Fred left his homework at Todds' house.

   b. Nature has a beauty of it's own, and its easy to appreciate; that is one of natures gifts to us.

   c. "Whose goin' to take out the garbage?" Betty asked, hoping her roommates wouldnt remember that it was her's.

   d. The judge quit the mens' club because it's policy didn't allow women or minority's as guests.

   e. Frans' mother always told her to mind her *p*s and *q*s, but Fran didnt know what that meant.

   f. Jeff hoped it was one of his friend's who'd taken his bike.

   g. Karen discovered that three of her' new books's covers were torn.

   h. Huey Lewis's and the News' album, *Picture This*, was near the top of everyones' all-time favorites.

   i. Professor Pickett told Gale to eliminate all the *there is* and *there are* from her essay's.

   j. When she heard that Charles' notification that he had received a Pell Grant had arrived in the mail, Susan wondered if her's would be delivered soon.

2. Revise the following sentences so the quotation marks are used correctly. Some errors will involve adding or moving quotation marks or other punctuation marks. Place a check mark before sentences not needing revision.

   a. One of the most popular songs of the Vietnam era was "Where Have All the Flowers Gone"?

   b. If Ted thought "the exam would be easy", he was mistaken.

   c. "The Simpsons" portrays a "typical" modern family.

   d. "A dog is a man's best friend;" Senator Vest of Missouri repeated that saying in his farewell address.

   e. "To be, or not to be, Hamlet said, that is the question."

   f. Shelley said that Madonna was her, "very most favorite—" her exact words—singer.

   g. Professor Fox said, 'Keats's "To Autumn" is a perfect poem.'

   h. The dying officer's last words in the movie *The Hunt for Red October* were that he wanted to see Montana.

i. "I'll be happy to pick Dad up", Aaron said and thought Mom will certainly let me drive the new BMW.

j. "That was very 'bright!'" Josh said after Jim had accidently erased the disk with his essay on it.

CHAPTER 41

Dashes, Parentheses, Brackets, and Ellipses

41a–41i Use dashes, parentheses, brackets, and ellipses appropriately and effectively.

Dashes, parentheses, and *brackets* enclose written material. *Ellipses* indicate that information has been omitted. Because writers use all of these marks less frequently than others, using them correctly indicates a firm control of conventions.

Common Problems

Some writers mistakenly use dashes, parentheses, and brackets interchangeably. They may also use ellipses unnecessarily at the beginning and end of a quotation. Combining other marks of punctuation with ellipses is also sometimes confusing.

Examples

1. Use dashes to set off a summary, a restatement, an amplification, or an explanation:

   > The extremely exciting Wimbledon men's singles championship match—Becker down early then coming back, then Edberg fighting off Becker to win—will remain one of the most dramatic contests in recent years.

   If a summary, restatement, amplification, or explanation ends a sentence, many would use a colon; in this situation, the dash and colon are interchangeable.

2. Use dashes for an interruption or an abrupt change of thought:

   > Americans have the privilege—no, that's not the word I want—they have the right to a clean environment.

3. Use dashes with a list that contains commas:

   > Muhammed Ali was a great heavyweight—big, agile, and quick—whose brashness and political views cost him popularity early in his career.

4. Use parentheses for additional information or for digressions:

   > Members of the phylum *Arthropoda* (insects, arachnids, and crustaceans) are invertebrate animals with jointed body and limbs.

5. Use double parentheses for numbered or lettered lists within sentences:

 An effective essay usually consists of the following components: (1) an introduction that gains reader attention, introduces the subject in a context, and narrows to a thesis; (2) a body with transitions that guide the reader to the points of the paragraphs and that relate to the thesis and paragraphs that develop the thesis; (3) and a conclusion that extends the implications of the thesis.

6. Use parentheses for in-text citations:

 William Randolph Hearst hired Ambrose Bierce because Bierce's column boosted circulation and was good public relations (Berkove xix).

7. Use parentheses correctly with other punctuation marks.
 a. Do not precede an opening parenthesis with a comma or other mark of internal punctuation, except for in-text lists (see sections **37h, 41e**):

 Roger Maris holds the record for home runs in a single season/ (61, breaking Babe Ruth's of 60).

 b. Use appropriate punctuation following a closing parenthesis:

 When he was assassinated in 1968 (just after winning the California presidential primary), Robert Kennedy had undercut Senator Eugene McCarthy's challenge to Lyndon Johnson.

 A comma is necessary after an introductory dependent clause.

 c. Use parentheses to enclose complete sentences:

 Although written in the last decade of the nineteenth century, Dan De Quille's comic novella *Dives and Lazarus* was first published in 1988 (like his friend Mark Twain, De Quille used a pen name; he was born William Wright).

 Parenthetical sentences that depend on the main clause do not require initial capital letters.

 d. Use normal punctuation within parentheses.

 Although famous as a poet and short story writer, Edgar Allan Poe had a varied career as an author (a literary critic, an author of a textbook on conchology, and a writer of hoaxes and philosophical works).

 The parenthetical information can be written differently as long as it is punctuated correctly:

 (Poe was most famous in his time as a literary critic, but he was also an author of a textbook on conchology. Additionally, he wrote hoaxes and philosophical works.)

8. Use brackets appropriately. Bracketed information explains or clarifies the terms of another, not the writer's own terms.
 a. Use brackets to identify an unnamed person or title:

 The host announced, "I am happy to introduce the poet laureate of Chicago [Gwendolyn Brooks]."

 b. Use brackets to explain complex terms:

 The man looked at the stack of letters he had received from abroad and said, "This is a philatelist's [stamp collector's] dream come true!"

 c. Use brackets to clarify ambiguous pronoun reference.

 His voice teacher said, "Norm, did you see the opera [*Traviata*] on TV last week?"

The convention also allows writers to substitute the bracketed material for the word or words it clarifies.

His voice teacher said, "Norm, did you see [*Traviata*] on TV last week?"

9. Use ellipsis appropriately. Ellipsis (plural: ellipses) consists of three typed periods with one space before and after and one space between each (. . .). It signals the omission of quoted material. Take care that the deleted information does not alter the meaning of the quotation; it is deleted because it is not essential to the point:

ORIGINAL: The Burgess Shale, as many scientists have noted, has provided paleontologists with unique fossils.

QUOTED: "The Burgess Shale . . . has provided paleontologists with unique fossils."

To signal omitted sentences from the quotation, type a period *before* the ellipsis. For example, if *Shale* ended the sample sentence, the quotation would read "Shale. . . . has provided . . .). Ellipsis is unnecessary at the beginning of quotations because readers assume that information has preceded the quotations. Ellipsis is necessary only at the end of a quotation if an omission is made from the last sentence quoted (note the final ellipsis in the preceding sentence).

Name ______________________________ Score ______________

Exercise 41a–41i Dashes, parentheses, brackets, and ellipses

Revise the following sentences to use dashes, parentheses, brackets, and ellipses effectively. Defend your choices by citing the applicable instruction in the list on the preceding pages. Sentences may involve more than one instruction. Place a check mark before sentences not needing revision.

1. Mobile cellular phones, when they first appeared in 1983, they cost over $3,000, are becoming commonplace in the 1990s.

2. Arsenio Hall seems to have equalled Johnnie Carson (in my mind Arsenio has surpassed him) in popularity with late-night viewers.

3. The book stated that "Quetzalcoatl [a god and legendary ruler of Mexico] gave maize to the Mexican people (Lopez 135)."

4. Molly Yard—the president of NOW—explored the feasibility of beginning a new political party.

5. The world's three greatest tenors [José Carreras, Placido Domingo, and Luciano Pavarotti] performed together to raise money for charity.

6. In the 1980s, many of Lyndon Johnson's social programs they were referred to collectively as "The Great Society" were rejected.

7. The nervous student began to recite the passage he had been required to memorize: " . . . Friends, Romans, countrymen. . . ."

8. The Hubble Space Telescope is a major disappointment—at a cost of $1.5 billion, it gives blurred images of the stars.

9. The museum guard shouted, "You! (my friend Angie) Don't touch the exhibits."

10. Sky diving requires several steps performed in a rigid order, 1) check the chute carefully before the flight, 2) make certain to be clear of the plane before pulling the rip-cord, 3) keep feet together and knees slightly bent, 4) have your insurance policy readily available.

PART

8

Mechanics

CHAPTER 42

Underlining for Italics

42a–42f Use italics appropriately and effectively.

Italics is a slanting print conventionally used for certain titles and terms. A continuous underline with no spaces between words replaces italics in handwritten or typed papers.

Common Problems

Writers at times are confused about whether to use italics or quotation marks to show emphasis or to present a title of a work.

Examples

1. Underline (italicize) titles of major publications and other works. Long works or works that contain parts (chapters of books, songs on an album, individual shows of a TV series) are italicized. (Recall from chapter **40** that the titles of short works should be put in quotation marks.)

   American Literature [journal]

   The *Washington Post* [newspaper]

   Paradise Lost [a long poem with several parts]

   In Living Color [TV series]

   Henry V [play, movie]

NOTE: Do not italicize or enclose in quotation marks the following works: your own titles, titles of sacred writings (Bible, Koran, New Testament, Leviticus, Bhagavad-Gita), titles of editions, parts of books other than chapters (introduction, preface, appendix).

2. Underline (italicize) the names of specific ships, aircraft, and other vehicles, not the name of the type of vehicle.

   Enterprise [spacecraft]

   Trump Princess [ship, but not the letters before the name: HMS *Pinafore*]

   Enola Gay [airplane, but not B-52]

   Desire [streetcar]

Bigfoot [truck, but not Dodge Dakota]

City of New Orleans [train, but not Illinois Central]

3. Underline (italicize) words, phrases, letters, and numerals that serve as the subject of discussion.

   What does *patriotism* mean to most people?

4. Underline (italicize) unusual foreign words in English sentences.

   Samuel Langhorne Clemens's *nom de plume* [pen name] was Mark Twain.

   Do not italicize common foreign words that have been assimilated into the language: kung fu, taco, milieu.

5. Underline (italicize) names of genuses and species.

   Technically, human beings are *Homo sapiens.*

6. Underline (italicize) for emphasis sparingly and only for good reason.

   That button will launch a missile. *Don't* push it!

   In academic writing the content of sentences, rather than italics, exclamation marks, or quotation marks, should create emphasis.

Name ______________________________ Score ______________

Exercise 42a–42f Italics

In the following sentences, underline the words that need to be italicized. Place before each sentence the number of the appropriate instruction from the list on the preceding page. Place a check mark before sentences not needing revision.

1. When J.R. was shot in the season-ending cliff hanger, Dallas began a trend that many TV series have continued.
2. The brown recluse spider (Loxosceles reclusa) is as dangerous as the black widow (Lactrodectus mactans), but most people have a greater fear of the black widow.
3. Replays of the classic radio show, The Green Hornet, have made a new generation aware of the breathtaking car chases that the ace crimefighter and his companion Cato made in Black Beauty.
4. Some technical names are difficult to associate with the plant or animal they classify, but not Rattus rattus, the name for the common rat.
5. Mississippi has four i's, four s's, two p's, and an m.
6. When charged with accepting bribes, Spiro Agnew pleaded nolo contendere, which meant he was subject to conviction but could later deny his guilt, which he has done ever since his resignation as vice president of the United States.
7. One of the most often misspelled words is misspell.
8. The Bible, which has been translated into most languages, is now available on cassettes.
9. Gone with the Wind has been popular as both a movie and a book, so popular that books have been written about each.
10. When she sang "On the Good Ship, Lollipop," the child actress, Shirley Temple, introduced a song that she has been identified with for ever since.

CHAPTER 43

Abbreviations and Acronyms

43a–43d Use abbreviations and acronyms appropriately and effectively.

The dictionary lists standard abbreviations and shortened forms of terms. *Abbreviations* may appear in documentation or parenthetical asides but should not appear in the text of academic writing. *Acronyms*, pronounceable words formed from the initial letters of a group of words, may be used in the text of academic writing.

Common Problems

Some abbreviations and acronyms are formed from capital letters; others are not. Some letters are followed by periods; others are not. Many writers become confused about use of abbreviations.

Examples

1. Abbreviate titles before and after full proper names and other words.

First use	**Subsequent use**
Ms. Jennifer L. Pitt	Pitt
Prof. William McLane	McLane or Professor McLane
Sammy Davis, Jr.	Davis
Sen. Edward M. Kennedy	Kennedy or Senator Kennedy

If two people have the same last name, in subsequent references use the first and last names for clarity. In academic writing a person's full name without Mr., Mrs., or Ms. is preferable in first use; in subsequent use, the person, whether male or female, is referred to by the last name only.

When referring to a person by initials only, use the initials with no periods following: *FDR, JFK.* Although usage varies, MLA does not use periods after initials in academic degrees (*MD, PhD, BA, MBA, JD, LLD*).

2. Use acronyms and abbreviations for organizations and corporations as well as for geographic and technical terminology.

NCAA, NFL, NOW, GOP [organizations]

HBJ, TNT, AMOCO, GM [companies]

USA or U.S.A., NY, TX [geographical names]

If the initials or acronym is not familiar, include parenthetically in the first mention the terms that the initials stand for. In later uses, give only the acronym or initials.

Rusty was anxious for the NBA (National Basketball Association) season to begin.

OR

Rusty was anxious for the National Basketball Association (NBA) season to begin.

NOTE: Check the dictionary to determine which initials use periods; when the usage is optional, check style manual for your discipline (MLA for the humanities, APA for psychology and social sciences, etc.)

3. Abbreviate dates and numbers in your text: Use abbreviations such as *a.m., BC, and no.* with specific time, dates, and figures:

   12:18 p.m.

   No. 007

   500 BC

   AD 1066

   (*AD* is the abbreviation for the Latin *Anno Domini,* "in the year of our Lord" and *precedes* the date. *BC* stands for "before Christ" and follows the date)

4. Use abbreviations in parenthetical matter, addresses, and documentation:

   Add one cup (1/2 pt.) [parenthetical information]

   1882 Whistful Vista Blvd. [address]

   Tarzana, CA [address]

   "He who speaks the truth must have one foot in the stirrup" (Arm. prv). [documentation]

   Spell out units of measurement and street, state, and country's names when used occasionally in the text.

Name ______________________ Score ______________

Exercise 43a–43d Abbreviations and acronyms

Revise the following sentences to eliminate errors in abbreviations and acronyms. Place a check mark before sentences not needing revision.

1. Ever since F.D.R., the Democrats have been labeled the party of taxes.
2. The National Organization for Women has fought for the pro-choice position, whereas FLAG has opposed it.
3. Nico Tean's cough became so serious that he went to his Dr. for treatment. Mr. Tean was told to quit smoking.
4. Prof. Cain is a good teacher, but she's always late on exam days.
5. In a campaign speech, Sen. Thornton warned that by 2005 AD the ozone layer will be depleted to such an extent that skin cancer will be as common as the flu.
6. Charlene R. Cart, director of Development at Titanic State University, has asked all students to donate one-tenth of their summer earnings to the university building fund. Ms. Cart's idea has not been met with enthusiasm.
7. Cynthia was happy that her 8:00 am Fri. class had been canceled.
8. A one-way plane ride from Houston, TX, to Little Rock, AR, costs only twenty-nine dollars.
9. The number one killer of African-American women in New York and New Jersey is Acquired Immune Deficiency Syndrome.
10. Dr. Chas. Dean has earned not only his MD but also a Doctor of Philosophy in microbiology.

CHAPTER 44

Numbers

44a–44b Use numbers appropriately and effectively.

Numbers of one or two words are written out. Arabic numerals are used for numbers of more than two words.

Common Problems

Informal prose styles encourage the use of Arabic numerals for one- or two-word numbers.

Examples

1. When numbers appear infrequently, spell out numbers that you can write in one or two words; use figures for other numbers.

    The auditorium held *thirteen thousand* people.

    The auditorium held *13,487* people.

    When a sentence contains a category of numbers, one of which is greater than ten, use Arabic numbers for all:

    The cheerleading team attracted *87* coeds to try out for the *15* positions.

    When one number immediately follows another, spell out the smaller number and use Arabic numbers for the other:

    Dawn's course load next semester will be *two 3-hour* courses.

    Write out any number that begins a sentence; if the number is too long to write out, recast the sentence:

    One thousand one hundred and thirty people attended the wedding.

    The wedding had *1,130* guests.

2. Use numerals for specific places and exact figures.
    a. Addresses: 1600 Pennsylvania Avenue
    b. Ages: The average college freshman is 20 years old.
    c. Exact dates: Susan was born September 2, 1967.
    d. Decimals, percentages, and fractions:

Pi is equal to 3.14159265.

Watson reported that Sherlock Holmes occasionally took a 7% solution of cocaine.

Goldie Locks rejected 13/16 of the porridge available to her. [*But* spell out large fractions when used infrequently: *one-quarter, two-thirds.*]

e. Divisions of books: Act 2 begins on page 41.
f. Identification numbers:

Route 66 [highway]

012-34-5678 [social security number]

Adam-12 [police car]

g. Exact amounts of money:

The scarf cost $45.99.

h. Statistics: Her ACT score was 18.
i. Time of day: Debbie was born at 11:30 a.m.

NOTE: Generally use Arabic numbers. But use Roman numerals for titles (Richard III) or for sections of outlines (capital letters), prefatory pages (lowercase letters), or established terms (Continental Mark IV).

Name ______________________________ Score ______________

Exercise 44a–44b Numbers

Revise the following sentences to eliminate errors in number usage. Place a check mark before sentences not needing revision.

1. 5 two-bedroom apartments are available.
2. The history assignment was to read chapter four and answer the 10 study questions at the end.
3. Chicago is about 300 miles from Detroit.
4. Final exams begin on May eleventh.
5. The two families arrived at the party with seven children, two dogs, and a cat.
6. The game ended at nine twenty and in 16 minutes the parking lot was empty.
7. The average family used to have two and five-tenths children, but now the number is closer to two.
8. Queen Elizabeth II has not granted interviews to the press in over 30 years.
9. The day after Michael Jordan scored sixty-nine points, his teammate Stacy King said, "I'll always remember the night Michael and I scored seventy points."
10. Babysitting for three 2-year-olds deserves combat pay.

CHAPTER 45

Capital Letters

45a–45h Use capitals appropriately and effectively.

Because the conventions for capitalization vary among different languages, memorizing those for English is often the only way to master the practice. A dictionary provides the conventional usage.

Common Problems

When convention rather than logic determines usage, problems always arise, but proper names and people's titles cause the most problems in capitalization.

Examples

1. Capitalize words that begin sentences.

   All the sentences on this page begin with a capital letter.

   Capitalize also a parenthetical sentence if it is not within another sentence.

   Springfield, Illinois, is the capitol of Illinois. (This is the city in which Abraham Lincoln got his start.)

   Capitalize a sentence after a colon if it is a quotation or a question.

2. Capitalize the first word of a direct quotation if it begins a complete sentence or is an exclamation.

   "Shazam!" Andy exclaimed. "Why does Gomer say that?"

3. Capitalize poetry exactly as it appears in the original.

   One's-Self I sing, a simple separate person, Yet utter the word Democratic, the word En-Masse.
   —Walt Whitman, "One's-Self I Sing"

4. Capitalize proper nouns and words derived from them.

   A person who lives in Arkansas is generally called an *Arkansan,* but some historians believe that *Arkansawyer* would have greater historical justification.

Capitalize the names and nicknames of specific persons and the words of family members used as names.

My brother has rusty red hair so our grandfather gave him the nickname Rusty, but Mom always calls him by his given name, Cosgrove.

The adjective *rusty* and the common noun *grandfather* are not capitalized, but the proper nouns *Rusty* and *Mom* are.

Capitalize titles preceding names.

The dean of arts and sciences, Dean Hughes, met with the other deans to determine who would represent them at the Faculty Senate.

Capitalize articles or prepositions that are part of surnames only when they begin a sentence. If in doubt about proper spelling, check a standard biographical dictionary.

De la Vega led the rebels.

Diego de la Vega led the rebels.

Capitalize personifications, which are the names of objects, animals, or ideas given human identity.

As he sat passively in his room, Roderick waited as Fear slowly overcame him, first touching him lightly, then wrapping fingers about his throat, and finally squeezing the life from him.

Unless the personification is developed, don't capitalize: "As he sat in his room, Roderick was overcome by fear."

Capitalize the names of countries, districts, regions, states, counties, cities, lakes, rivers, and so on.

Poland, Zimbabwe, Nicaragua [countries]

Hyde Park, the Bowery [districts]

the Southwest, New England, the Northwest [regions]

Oregon, California, Iowa [states]

Cook, Craighead, Jefferson [counties]

Chicago, Lincoln, Denver [cities]

Erie, Okeechobee [lakes]

Mississippi, Snake [rivers]

Broadway, Main, Stafford, Oak [streets]

Capitalize the names of nations, nationalities, races, tribes, languages, and persons identified by geographic locations.

United States [nation]

Cuban [nationality]

Caucasian [race]

Hopi [tribe]

English [language]

African-American [people identified by geographic location]

Capitalize names of religions and their members, their deities, and sacred books.

Hinduism, Shintoism, Judaism, Christianity, Islam [religions]

Suni Muslim, Baptist [members of a religion]

Allah, God, Jehovah, Zeus [names of deities]

the Koran, the Bible, the Bhagavad-Gita [sacred books]

Capitalize the names of specific organizations, institutions, trademarks, departments, academic degrees, specific academic courses, major political documents, political parties, and fraternal clubs as well as historical periods, major events, and movements.

League of Women Voters, Chicago Bulls [organizations]

Smithsonian, Hoover [institutions]

Coca Cola, Kleenex [trademarks]

Doctor of Philosophy, Bachelor of Science [academic degrees]

Advanced Algebra, Composition 101 [specific academic courses]

the Constitution, the Declaration of Independence [documents]

Republican, Libertarian [political parties]

Sigma Chi, Elks [fraternal clubs]

Renaissance, Neo-Classical [historical periods]

World War II, the Holocaust [events]

Pro-Choice, Right to Life [movements]

Capitalize the months, days of the week, and holidays but not the seasons.

Independence Day, Passover, Easter [holidays]

5. Capitalize the titles of books, articles, and works of art:

The Adventures of Tom Jones, The Politics of Rich and Poor [books]

"'I bring my rose': Emily Dickinson's Gift of Power" [article]

String Quintet in G Major, "Like a Virgin" [Musical compositions]

The Thinker [sculpture]

A Sunday Afternoon on the Island of la Grande Jatte [painting]

Capitalize the first and last words of a work's title and subtitle and all words in between *except* articles, coordinate conjunctions, prepositions, and the *to* of infinitives. If an article includes the title of another work, capitalize the interior title exactly as it is in the full title (note the Dickinson poem included in the sample above).

6. Capitalize the pronoun *I* and the interjection *O.* The pronoun *I* occurs frequently in writing and is always capitalized.

When I saw the car avoid crashing, I was relieved.

While the interjection *O* appears rarely, it can be confused with the letter *o,* so the interjection must be capitalized, but *oh* is not unless it begins a sentence.

7. Capitalize abbreviations and acronyms formed from proper nouns.

TNT (Turner Network Television), TVA (Tennessee Valley Authority)

8. Capitalize the names of genuses (but not species), geological periods, stars, and planets.

The most popular dinosaur is probably *Tyrannosaurus rex,* which inhabited Earth in the Upper Cretaceous period.

Name ______________________________ Score ______________

Exercise 45a–45b Capitals

Revise the following sentences to eliminate errors in capitalization. Place a check mark before sentences not needing revision.

1. When i go to france next summer, i am going to eat french pastry until i run out of money.
2. According to the *illiad,* athena favored the greeks over the trojans because paris failed to choose her as the most beautiful goddess.
3. Two new primate species have been named since the 1960s, *homo habilis* by Louis Leakey in 1964, and *australopithecus afarensis* by Donald Johanson in 1978.
4. Of all of his uncles, buck, whose real name was *Buchanan,* was tommy's favorite.
5. The hurricane season hurts tourism all along the gulf of mexico.
6. Alex liked the movie *navy seals,* but he thought it was not much different from other world war II movies.
7. The greatest mass extinction occurred 225 million years ago and marks the boundary between the paleozoic and mesozoic eras.
8. Although he was a five-star general, president Eisenhower appealed to many americans because he seemed to be like them, while adlai stevenson seemed to be an elitist.
9. Because christmas falls on a thursday next year, dad will have an extra long weekend.
10. When i walked across the Brooklyn bridge, I could see the statue of Liberty in the distance.

CHAPTER 46

Hyphenation

46a–46c Use hyphenation appropriately and effectively.

Hyphens join words or a divided word to make the meaning clear—from a series of words read as a unit to a word divided at the end of a line. The dictionary indicates how words can be divided.

Common Problems

Writers become confused about the inconsistent ways that words can break at the end of a line, depending often on the words' etymologies.

Examples

1. Form compound words effectively. Hyphenate two or more words functioning as one adjective before a noun (but not if the words follow the noun).

   At the Halloween party, everyone was asked to wear costumes representing turn-of-the-century fashions—21st century, that is.

   The exception to the rule occurs when one part of the compound adjective is an adverb ending in *-ly*.

   Show with hyphens that each adjective in a series modifies a noun:

   Amendments to the Education of Children with Handicaps (Public Law 99-457) provides that the public schools will serve three-, four-, and five-year-old children with handicaps.

   Form compound nouns with hyphens.

   The modern woman is often not merely a professional; she is a professional-homemaker.

   Without the hyphen, the sentence would state that a modern woman's profession is being a homemaker.

   Hyphenate written fractions and compound numbers.

   People are supposed to sleep one-third of their lives, or eight hours a day, but college students are lucky to sleep one-fourth of the time.

   Turning twenty-one means more than just becoming an adult—it means debt.

   Use the hyphen to create sound effects and unusual compounds words:

   "'A-womp-bop-a-lu-la-a-womp-bam-boo! Tutti-frutti! All-rooti!' Ah, they don't write lyrics like those anymore," lamented Susan's father.

   It was Allen's ten o'clock class, but he still had that I-just-rolled-out-of-the-sack look.

2. Use hyphens with prefixes and suffixes only in special cases. Generally, prefixes and suffixes don't require hyphens, but do hyphenate those that appear with proper nouns, numbers, abbreviations, or a single capital letter.

   Ivana is relishing a post-Donald life-style.

   The new styles have pre-1960s designs on 1990s fabrics.

   Also hyphenate all words with the prefixes *ex-*, *self-*, and *all-*.

   Because he was an All-American in football and an ex-marine, Pete Dawkins was self-confident.

   Hyphenate all words with the suffix *-elect.*

   The governor-elect has announced a tax increase.

   Hyphenate words that might be misunderstood.

   After he unloaded the firewood, the farmer re-corded it to assure the buyer he was getting his money's worth.

   The farmer again piled the wood in cords. Without the hyphen, the word would be *recorded,* a totally different term.

   Hyphenate words that might be misread.

   The veterinarian wanted to work in a small-animal hospital.

   The vet wants to work with small animals.

3. Follow conventions for end-of-line hyphenation. In academic papers, MLA and APA styles prefer writers *not* to hyphenate words at the end of a line. But if such hyphenation occurs, it must follow convention. Specifically, hyphens always appear at the end of a line, *never* at the beginning. Check a dictionary to see where syllables occur:

   Wednes-day (not Wed-nes-day)

   pneu-mo-nia (not pneu-mon-i-a)

   Never hyphenate one-syllable words. Also, never hyphenate so that a single letter ends or begins a line. Finally, break compound words between full words only:

   suit-case, back-ground, type-writer

Name ______________________ Score ______________

Exercise 46a–46c Hyphenation

Revise the following sentences to eliminate errors in hyphenation. Place a check mark before sentences not needing revision.

1. Xavier McDaniel, "the X man" of the Phoenix Suns, led the nation in scoring and rebounding his senior year in college.
2. During his work out, Arnold did four sets of one and two handed push ups.
3. Pregnant women are warned that during their entire prenatal period they should abstain from smoking and drinking alcohol.
4. An alcoholic might drink more than three fifths of hard liquor a day.
5. Craig grew so much in one summer that he had to buy extra large T shirts instead of medium.
6. Matt was proud of himself because he got a once in a lifetime deal on a brand new CRX.
7. Two thirds of all drivers admitted that they have consciously broken driving laws; the other one third admitted to occasional lying.
8. Because most criminals had low self esteem as children, early education might reduce crime.
9. Woody Allen is one of America's premier actor directors, yet he still lives a modest life.
10. When he met his future father in law, Charles was self confident but was nevertheless extra careful to be on his best behavior.

CHAPTER 47

Spelling

47a–47h Pay close attention to spelling.

The rich heritage of English in drawing words from many other languages creates unique spelling problems for users. Some general rules will improve spelling, but writers should not hesitate to refer to a college dictionary.

Common Problems

Most spelling errors arise from carelessness, unfamiliarity with conventions, and the unpredictable nature of the language. Homophones, words that sound alike, often create spelling errors.

Examples

1. Write word lists and practice speaking troublesome words. Writers can increase their familiarity with words by listing new words they encounter and then reviewing and pronouncing them regularly. Such words as *especially* and *athlete* are sometimes mispronounced as *ecspecially* or *athelete*, or contractions like *could have* are mispronounced ***could of***.

2. Proofread for spelling errors. Effective proofreading requires practice, attention to detail, and a dictionary. To proofread for spelling, read the last sentence of the essay first and, progressively, the first sentence last. This procedure focuses the writer's attention on the proofreading.

3. Distinguish between words that sound alike, and spell them correctly. Pronunciation often differs from spelling. Some of the common problems arise from the following situations.

   a. Possessive pronouns and contractions:

      I know *you're* [contraction] going to turn *your* [pronoun] book in on time.

      They're [contraction] doing *their* [pronoun] best.

      It's [contraction] a shame that the football team lost *its* [pronoun] last nine games of the season.

   b. Two-word phrases and single words:

      Gale is *all ready* for her date, but Bruce is *already* forty-five minutes late.

      Teachers *allot* a great deal of time to discourage their students from using the vague and often misspelled phrase, *a lot*.

      I'm *gonna* fail if I don't write *going to* differently than I pronounce it.

   c. Singular nouns that end in *-nce* and plural nouns that end in *-nts:*

I *sense* that you find the skunks' *scents* very unpleasant—not worth two *cents*.

The medical *assistants* will provide *assistance*.

d. Homophones—words that sound alike and are spelled differently are one of the most common causes of spelling errors:

to [a direction]

too [meaning *also* or *many*]

two [the number]

there [in that place]

they're [a contraction for *they are*]

their [possessive of *them*]

4. Understand and apply the rules for adding prefixes and suffixes to a root word.

a. Prefixes attach to the root without doubling or dropping letters:

*re*move, *in*flame, *mis*spell, *dis*approve

b. Drop the final unpronounced *e* before suffixes ending with vowels, but retain the *e* before suffixes beginning with consonants:

love, loving, lovely

hate, hated, hateful

arrange, arranging, arrangement

c. Double the final consonant before a suffix beginning with a vowel if the final consonant is preceded by a single vowel and if it ends a one-syllable word or a stressed syllable:

hit, hit*ting*

drip, drip*ping*

omit, omit*ting*

occur, occur*ring*, occur*rence*

begin, begin*ning*

NOTE: Many words do not double the consonants before the suffix; consult a dictionary when in doubt.

d. Change *y* to *i* before adding a suffix when the *y* is preceded by a consonant:

plenty, plent*i*ful

pretty, prett*i*er, prett*i*est

tragedy, traged*i*es

Do not change *y* to *i* when *y* is preceded by a vowel:

joy, joyous

valley, valleys

Do not change *y* to *i* when adding *-ing*:

study, studying

fly, flying

Do not change *y* to *i* with any proper name ending in *y*:

Kelly, Kellys

Kennedy, Kennedys

e. When adding *-ly*, do not drop a final *l* from a root word:

Crucial, crucia*l*ly

ideal, idea*l*ly

actual, actua*l*ly

5. Use *ei* and *ie* correctly. The old rhyme generally applies: *i* before *e* except after *c* or when the sound is *a* as in *neighbor*.

f*ie*rce, n*ie*ce, f*ie*nd, bel*ie*ve

rec*ei*ve, perc*ei*ve

*ei*ght, fr*ei*ght, d*ei*gn

Note the common exceptions to the rule:

sc*ie*nce, w*ei*rd, *ei*ther, for*ei*gn, l*ei*sure, s*ei*ze

6. Spell plurals correctly. Add *-s* to form the plural of most singular nouns.

boy*s*, telescope*s*, hotel*s*, 1990*s*, exercise*s*, Smith*s*

a. For words ending in *o*, add *-s* when a vowel precedes the *o*, but add *-es* when a consonant precedes the *o:*

stereo*s*, radio*s*, cameo*s*

avocado*es*, stiletto*es*, hero*es*

EXCEPTIONS: Shortened words—memos, autos, pros
either spelling— stiletto*s*, stiletto*es*
zero*s*, zero*es*
motto*s*, motto*es*

b. Add *-es* to form the plural of nouns ending in *s*, *ch*, *sh*, or *x:*

bus*es*, church*es*, bush*es*, tax*es*

c. For singular nouns ending in *y* preceded by a consonant, change the *y* to *i* and add *-es*:

ninet*ies*, berr*ies*, ferr*ies*, compan*ies*

d. For some singular nouns ending in *f* or *fe*, change the ending to *-ves*:

li*ves*, wi*ves*, shea*ves*

e. Some nouns form plurals irregularly:

women, children, oxen, geese

deer [singular and plural are the same]

f. Some foreign words retain their plural spelling:

Singular	**Plural**
syllabus	syllabi
medium	media
nucleus	nuclei
octopus	octopi
ovum	ova
criterion	criteria
vita	vitae
phenomenon	phenomena

7. Improve your spelling skills by focusing on your troublesome words. Making a list of the words you frequently misspell and then pronouncing them, learning their meanings, and thinking of some associations with the word are useful procedures to overcome spelling difficulties. Some rhymes or phrases help form associations—for example, "there is *a rat* in sep*arate*." "*We* are *we*ird" is another.

8. Misspell only for a purpose. Academic writing discourages intentional misspellings, but sometimes it can be effective:

   I don't think I would like the atmosphere at Titanic State *Un*versity.

   I tried to finish my essay, but my t*ri*pewriter was causing problems.

   If the above examples don't seem particularly effective, they are a demonstration of the reasons to avoid intentional misspellings.

Name ______________________________ Score ______________

Exercise 47a–47h Spelling

Proofread the following paragraphs for spelling errors. Underline the misspelled words, and correctly spell them in the space provided below.

A strange phenomena is takeing place in the ninetys. Every body is liesure conscience and looking for hobbys. Joging is no longer in fashion. Bycycling has replacied it. Men and woman alike are searching for new activitys. But most are just fades; soon people will loose intrest. The reason should be obveous. Few people consceously set out to chose hobbys. They usualy find some activity they enjoy alot and that past time eventualy bares the label *hobby*. That happened to me. For instants, I read an artical about boomeranges in a magazine and thawed I would like to try tossing a "'rang" (that's it's nick name). So I went to a sportstore and brought my first 'rang. It didn't cost to much, but the initial prize was decieving because boomerangs brake easyly (after my forth one broke, I began makeing my own and have been happy ever sense). Of coarse, the only reason your gonna want to thro a boomerang in the first place is that you want it too come back to you. And that's the trick. But alittle guidence is all you need—weather or not your atheletic.

Their are only three things to remeber: the correct gripe, the throw, and the relationship to the wind. If your right handed, hold one arm of the 'rang by the tip, as if you were griping a hammer. The other arm should be faceing in the direction you want to throw the 'rang when you're arm is in the throwing position, elbow bent and the 'rang just behind your right ear. You need to be certian you're holdding the arm so that the flat side of the 'rang is toward your palm. Once you have got the grip right, your ready to throw. But before begining, you have to make sure of your positon. You must throw into the wind if their is any (vary little wind is best). When you throw, swing your arm as if hammerring nailes, snaping you're wrist at the relize, and aim just a bove the horizon. This step is harder than it seams but your patients will reward you.

Its truely an awsome feeling when the 'rang makes its long, swoping ark and floats back to you so that you can catch it. But that probaly won't happen the first time you throw. You have either maid a misstake or omited a nesessary step. So you have to make adjusttments. If the 'rang goes of to the write, you need to turn into the wind. If it goes off to the left, turn a way from the wind. If it just keeps goin a way from you, a frequent occurence at first, you grip is completly wrong, or you our throwng with the wind. If it is hiting behind you, ether aim lower or else the winds two strong, so quite for the day. If you take my advise, you will enjoy a different hobby and recieve alot of prays from freinds and strangers a like.

A 1
B 2
C 3
D 4
E 5
F 6
G 7
H 8
I 9
J 0